WHEN A CHILD GRIEVES

WHEN A CHILD GRIEVES
Psychoanalytic Understanding and Technique

Corinne Masur

PHOENIX
PUBLISHING HOUSE
firing the mind

First published in 2022 by
Phoenix Publishing House Ltd
62 Bucknell Road
Bicester
Oxfordshire OX26 2DS

British Library Cataloguing in Publication Data

A C.I.P. for this book is available from the British Library

ISBN-13: 978-1-912691-93-7

Typeset by Medlar Publishing Solutions Pvt Ltd, India

www.firingthemind.com

Contents

Part II: Clinical consideration

Acknowledgments

I owe a debt of gratitude to many people for helping this book come into being—Salman Akhtar for suggesting years ago that I write a book of my own and believing that I could; T. J. Fallon, my son, for his (gravely needed) technological support; Allyson Killen, for doing the huge job of researching this topic in order to help me update what had originally been my doctoral dissertation (written in 1984), and Kate Pearce, a wonderful editor in normal times and an extraordinary one to have persevered with this and many other projects through an evolving pandemic with all the restrictions, limitations, and deprivations involved.

About the author

Corinne Masur is a clinical psychologist, adult and child psychoanalyst, and an adult supervising psychoanalyst who has worked with children for over forty years. She is on the faculty of the Psychoanalytic Center of Philadelphia and the Institute for Relational Psychoanalysis of Philadelphia. She is a founder of the Philadelphia Center for Psychoanalytic Education, the Philadelphia Declaration of Play, the Parent Child Center of Philadelphia and the blog, www.thoughtfulparenting.org. She treats parents, infants, children, adolescents, and adults. She also teaches, supervises, and plays. She is the editor of two previous books, *Flirting with Death: Psychoanalysts Consider Mortality* and *Finding the Piggle: Reconsidering D. W. Winnicott's Most Famous Child Case*, as well as a number of book chapters and articles.

Author's note

"Death will no longer be denied; we are forced to believe it. People really die; and no longer one by one, but many, often tens of thousands in a single day. And death is no longer a chance event" (Freud, 1915b, p. 289).

Freud wrote these words during the First World War, yet they might as well have been written today. During the Covid-19 pandemic the entire world is either dying or grieving. This terrible shape-shifting virus is causing more people than ever (in recent history) to fear for their lives, to fear loss of loved ones, and to actually experience that loss. One year into the pandemic it is estimated that 37,000–40,000 children have lost one parent to Covid-19 in the US alone (Kidman et al., 2021). Perhaps the book I should be writing would be about that experience—but the pandemic and the losses it has brought are stories with no ending as of now. These are stories we are still living through.

So, in this time of grief, a book about parental loss may be particularly relevant in some ways, insofar as the loss of a parent is an event which some children and many adults are experiencing right now and more will experience as the pandemic continues.

Preface

Aragno (2001) said,

> It is worth noting ... that virtually all major authors of seminal works on mourning have themselves suffered early and profound losses. Freud's writings on death and grieving, and his spearheading paper that differentiated normal mourning from melancholia, appeared after he himself had experienced various family losses. Like all psychobiological, transformative life crisis points, and like the analytic process itself, the progressively shifting course of bereavement has to have been fully experienced and known, for its dynamic permutations and transformative potential to be meaningfully understood. (p. 423)

And so it is that this book has come to be. At the age of fourteen my father died suddenly and without warning. He was in his bedroom, getting up from a nap and I was downstairs having just come home from being with friends. After it was made clear by our next-door neighbor, a doctor, that nothing could be done for my father, I was stunned into paralysis. I sat in a chair for hours. And the next morning when I woke up in my bed, I had to remind myself that my father had died, sleep having temporarily given me a respite from this fact. My denial continued on and off, however, and it was powerful. It superseded reality at various moments—for days and weeks and months to come.

But when the reality of my father's absence *did* register for gradually longer periods of time, I had to reformulate not only what my life was but also who I was. The details of daily life were irrevocably altered but so were the details of my inner life, although I fought to keep this from myself. I became progressively more independent and self-sufficient— perhaps as a way of avoiding the suffering and sadness which would have resulted from the recognition of my very recent dependence on a father who was no longer available. Whatever the dynamic, it worked for me. I went to college far from home, travelled a great deal, spent two semesters in Latin America and rarely returned to see my mother, even after graduating from college.

Then, when I was twenty-five, my mother developed a malignant brain tumor and died within months. This time I was more ready. I had the art of numbing down to a science. But I was also in graduate school in clinical psychology by then and knew that I needed to figure this out. And in the way that many of us do, I decided to write my dissertation on the subject of bereavement in childhood as a way to understand, at least intellectually, what I myself had been feeling—and not feeling—for these eleven years.

This book is an updated version of that dissertation.

Thirty-five years later, I am still trying to understand the meaning of my parents' deaths—and the meaning of death in general, including the effect it has on all of our lives.

Introduction

When a child loses a parent, the course of her[1] life is irrevocably altered and she is forever changed. She is suddenly and violently transported to a place made up of unknowns: Where will I find love now that the person who loved me is no longer alive? How do I love someone who is no longer here to love? Who am I now without my parent compared to who I was when I had her with me?

The death of a parent is a blow like no other. When a parent dies, the child is in a unique situation because of the special nature of her tie to her parent. An adult distributes love among several meaningful relationships—her spouse, children, parents, siblings, friends, colleagues, and others. The child, by contrast, invests almost all of her love in her parents. Only in childhood can death deprive an individual of so much opportunity to love and be loved and face her with so difficult a task of adaptation (E. Furman, 1974).

---

[1] The single feminine pronouns she/her/hers will be used rather than he/him/his or they/them/their, in order to avoid linguistic awkwardness and reader fatigue, but what is said is equally as applicable to boys as girls.

In fact, the relationship between child and parent is the most critical of all formative relationships and the wellspring for all subsequent attachments. The loss of a parent is devastating to the child, to her emerging sense of self, to her personality development, to her feelings about life, and to her future interpersonal relationships and psychological health. The death of a parent interrupts childhood and cannot help but transform the child. Who she might have been is forever altered by loss and its impact.

Most people who lose a parent in childhood remember the moment they found out. This is the moment that their world changed forever. Personal time for the child becomes marked in terms of "before" and "after" (M. Harris, 1995). Moreover, the loss and its impact on the child irrevocably change the child's autobiographical narrative (Coates, 2016).

The unique ways in which children react to parental death will be described in this volume. The impact of such loss will be outlined and the manner in which the child mourns and attempts to cope will be described. This book will also help clinicians learn how to evaluate and treat children who have lost a parent and to understand the theoretical underpinnings of the mourning process from a psychodynamic point of view.

The effects of childhood loss

Children suffer immensely when a parent dies. They experience so many painful feelings—the sadness of missing their parent, the fear of not knowing who will love them and care for them going forward, the emptiness which is left where a much-loved person used to be, the loneliness of being without their parent, the fear of death and all the existential questions that arise from this—and on and on. These are the immediate effects of loss. But it is not just the immediate effects that are of concern. Bereaved children are also vulnerable to experiencing the consequences of early loss throughout their lives.

Many studies have shown both short- and long-term sequelae following childhood bereavement. One study demonstrated that, a year following parental loss, 19% of children show signs of serious problems including social withdrawal, anxiety, lower self-esteem, and lower feelings of self-efficacy than non-bereaved peers, and after two years 21% of children show such problems (Worden & Silverman, 1996). Still other studies have shown evidence that early parental loss may influence physical health in later years, potentially through the development of neurobiological and physiological symptoms associated with stress-related illness (Luecken, 2008). Further studies have demonstrated that children who experience parental loss are more likely than children who have not had this experience to develop depression, anxiety, borderline personality disorder, schizophrenia, and other mental health struggles later in life. However, despite ample evidence of harm caused by the childhood experience of bereavement, there has been far too little empirical investigation of potential factors that may diminish risk for psychopathology following parental death in childhood (Howell et al., 2016). Moreover, scant research has been performed to discover which services—such as community interventions, psychotherapy, or other forms of support—are most helpful.

Within the psychoanalytic literature, however, there is a long history of case reports detailing the treatment of bereaved children. And in the larger body of psychological and psychiatric research, there are studies which look at the effects of bereavement on children. There is a great deal of information which can be gleaned from this literature regarding the specific effects of bereavement on children and the ways in which these children can be understood and helped to grieve. In this volume, the findings of these individual case reports and the results of research in this area will be summarized.

Fulton (Fulton & Bendiksen, 1976) stated that the wise management of grief in children and adults revolves around two major factors: one, the encouragement and facilitation of the normal mourning process, and two, the prevention of delayed or disturbed grief responses. This work is taken on by psychotherapists and psychoanalysts in the treatment of bereaved children, and to a lesser extent these days by clergy, educational institutions such as schools and colleges, and various community organizations.

But what is the normal mourning process, exactly, and at what age can a child begin to undertake mourning? This is a matter which has been hotly debated in the psychoanalytic, psychological, and psychiatric literature. In this volume the position will be taken that from infancy on, children are affected by parental loss and by two to three years of age, children can embark on the mourning process if they possess loving attachment figures and an optimally supportive milieu for the experiencing of grief and for the expression and discussion of their feelings.

Some theorists and clinicians, however, have believed that it is not until adolescence that a child can complete the mourning process. In this volume, the age-old controversy regarding whether children can mourn will be described. The ability to mourn will be discussed in light of the child's developmental stage, preexisting personality factors, external stressors, and/or some combination of these. The discussion will include specific ages at which children can perceive loss, experience grief, begin to mourn, and finally, reattach to new loved ones. Psychotherapy and psychoanalysis will be presented as two of the modes available for the provision of a supportive milieu in which to mourn and for facilitation of mourning.

This work falls into three sections: First, a historical overview of the development of theory regarding the mourning process in adults and children is provided. This is followed by a discussion of the controversy regarding the ability of the young child to mourn. Third, clinical considerations in the evaluation and treatment of young children are presented.

In the study of childhood loss, the work of Erna and Robert Furman and their Bereavement Research Group at Case Western Reserve is particularly noteworthy as this work provided the majority of the psychodynamic clinical articles and books regarding the young child's ability to mourn in the 1960s through the 1980s. From Robert Furman's initial publication in 1964 in which he demonstrated a six-year-old patient's ability to mourn in essentially the same fashion as an adult, to Erna Furman's book *A Child's Parent Dies* (1974), the Furmans unflaggingly promoted the idea that even the young child could embark on the mourning process.

More recently, Susan Coates, Jane Rosenthal, and Daniel Schechter (2003) have contributed seminal insights to the understanding of mourning in childhood, performing extremely important, no doubt lifesaving work, with the children and parents affected by the events of 9/11 at the World Trade Center. They have written extensively about their experiences with these traumatized and traumatically bereaved families. Additionally, clinicians and theorists from the object relations, interpersonal, and relational schools of psychoanalysis have furthered the conceptualization of childhood bereavement, bringing it into the twenty-first century (Hagman, 2001). The approach of this work is to highlight the previously under-discussed notion of the child's ability to mourn, the instances in which the mourning process goes awry, and the ways in which clinicians can attempt to ameliorate the child's difficulty in accomplishing the tasks of mourning. It must be remembered, however, as Erna Furman stated, that even in the case of what can be considered successful mourning, "the experience of a parent's death always remains a very troubling part of a child's life" (1974, p. 26).

It is also important to note that while many researchers have attempted to link later serious psychopathology with early loss, few have discussed the enduring feeling states and non-pathological difficulties in relationships and overall functioning which may result from early loss. This is an area of research which requires much further effort. Moreover, the important research currently gaining in popularity in the area of invulnerability, resilience, and "grit" (Duckworth, 2016; Luecken, 2008; Masten et al., 2009; Rutter, 1993, and others) must be looked to for providing valuable information regarding the mechanisms by which some children manage to withstand trauma including parental loss. The hope is that the strategies of these children may be understood and used by clinicians to help those relatively more vulnerable children to cope with loss and other adverse childhood events.

Parental bereavement was chosen as the specific area of discussion due to the particularly important part the parent plays in a child's life. It was thought that the reactions to the loss of a parent would provide information regarding bereavement in its most extreme manifestation. Moreover, for the sake of clarity and brevity, it is necessary to exclude extensive discussion of loss due to separations of various types from this discussion. However, much of what is discussed here can be applied to other types of loss and separation in childhood.

Statistics

The death of a young parent is not as rare as we would like to believe. In the US, the Childhood Bereavement Estimation Model's 2020 Projected Estimates were that 6.9% of children—nearly five million—have experienced or will experience the death of a parent or sibling by age eighteen. For youth under twenty-five, this estimate more than doubles to almost 12.9 million (Burns et al., 2020). And this statistic does not even cover the number of children who lose parents through divorce, desertion, or chronic mental or physical illness. Moreover, these statistics were compiled before the Covid-19 pandemic started. It is likely that far more children than estimated will become bereaved as a result of this highly contagious illness and that many of these children will come from families and communities with poor access to both health care and mental health care, thus exacerbating their struggles.

How death is handled in Western societies

Despite the fact that parental death, and death in general, is not uncommon, most parents continue to try to protect their children from the knowledge of death. As Yudkin (1967) aptly stated, "Modern children are more likely to be taught about their origins than about their departure from this world" (p. 3). Formerly children were told that they were brought by the stork or found in a cabbage patch but they were admitted to the bedside of dying relatives. Today they are educated in their early years about sex and reproduction, but when they no longer see grandfather, they are often told very little.

Moreover, the loss of a parent by death or desertion in the contemporary nuclear family is possibly even more traumatic than it was for the child in the traditional extended family setting of previous years. The child living with her nuclear family today is often without the familiar supports such as grandparents, aunts, uncles, and multiple siblings which were once provided by the extended family—and as a result may be doubly traumatized, first by the loss of a loved one and second from a lack of care and stability following the death.

Death in general, and the loss of a parent in particular, are problems which cross all boundaries of ethnicity, race, religion, nationality, and political allegiances. Indeed, the experience of parental death in the US is even more prevalent among economically disadvantaged people and minority groups due to poor medical care, the adverse experiences encountered during migrations, and the difficulties inherent in disadvantaged living circumstances. And these same circumstances increase vulnerability when dealing with parental loss (Ellis et al., 2013). These are problems which, despite increasing medical, technological, and research sophistication in Western society, have received too little attention, study, and remediation.

Part I

Theory

CHAPTER 1

The history of the study of bereavement: theoretical underpinnings

Psychoanalysts Sigmund Freud (Freud & Breuer, 1895d) and Karl Abraham (1911) were the first to attempt to conceptualize grief and mourning. Important contributors to follow included Melanie Klein (1940), Erich Lindemann (1944), and Edith Jacobson (1957, 1964, 1965). The work of these luminaries has spawned an explosion of more recent work including case studies and theoretical articles as well as research studies concerned with epidemiology, treatment, and the effects of early bereavement on later functioning. John Bowlby is notable among the post-Freudian psychoanalytic thinkers for having introduced the concept of attachment into the mix and for having integrated the majority of the work in the field into his three-volume series on attachment, separation, and loss (1969, 1973, 1980). And contemporary researcher and theorist George Hagman (2001) is important for having reconceptualized the end point of mourning not as decathexis from the lost loved one but as transformation of the self and incorporation of aspects of the deceased.

In order to shed light on the discussion of childhood bereavement, I shall begin with a review of the theoretical constructs underpinning the theories of adult bereavement.

Adult bereavement: "Mourning and Melancholia" and beyond

While it is Sigmund Freud to whom we look for the early exploration into grief and mourning, it must be noted that these processes were not central to his interest. Only in describing other problems to which they seemed relevant did he mention them (Bowlby, 1961). It was Freud's intent to provide a theoretical model rather than a detailed description of grief. However, Freud did provide seminal insights into the grief process and it is to him that we are indebted for the first understanding of the unconscious mechanisms which occur in bereavement.

In his discussion of the case history of Fraulein Elisabeth von R, which appeared in *Studies on Hysteria* (1895d), Freud described the grief process experienced by his patient after the death of each of three loved ones. He described Fraulein Elisabeth von R as reviewing her impressions of the lost individual one by one in "the work of recollection" (p. 245f.), a phrase that predated his later term, "the work of mourning" (1917e, p. 245f.), which describes the same process. From this time until the publication of "Mourning and Melancholia" in 1917, Freud touched upon the phenomena in a variety of his works; in 1895 in Draft G on Melancholia, Freud related depression and melancholia to mourning and grief; in 1897 in Draft N, he connected mourning with melancholia. In "Five Lectures on Psycho-analysis", Freud (1910a) noted that he told an obsessional patient that a normal period of mourning would take from one to two years.

In *Totem and Taboo*, Freud demonstrated further development of his ideas on mourning by stating that "Mourning has a quite specific psychical task to perform; its function is to detach the survivor's memories and hopes from the dead" (1912–13, p. 65). Moreover, he pointed out that after a death both affection and hostility toward the dead person continue to exist. He stated, however, that the hostility is repressed in order for the mourning to take place (Pollock, 1961). This is a matter about which there has been considerable debate.

In 1917, Freud's work, "Mourning and Melancholia," was published. This paper describes mourning in adults and links melancholia, or what we now refer to as depression, to chronic, unresolved mourning. The model described in this text continues to be one of the accepted formulations for the dynamics of chronic depression within psychoanalysis. Here, Freud described mourning as "the reaction to the loss of a loved person or of some abstraction which has taken the place of one" (1917e, p. 153). The mourning process is said to be the struggle which takes place within the bereaved person between the wish for the beloved to continue to exist and the reality testing that proves that she does not. Each memory or hope which bound the bereaved person to the lost loved one is reviewed, and in so doing, the individual gradually divests herself of her attachment to the lost loved one.

In this paper, Freud listed several distinguishing characteristics of mourning:

- Profoundly painful dejection
- Loss of the capacity to adopt new love objects
- Turning away from activities not concerned with the lost loved one
- Loss of interest in the outside world.

He thus provided a succinct description of the dynamics and characteristics of mourning.

In "Mourning and Melancholia," Freud described identification with the lost loved one as a pathological outcome. However, in later writing in *The Ego and the Id*, Freud (1923b) changed his view, stating that identification can be seen both in melancholia and in normal reactions to loss in which the loved one is set up "inside the ego" (p. 19). He said that identification may be "the sole condition under which the id can give up its objects" (p. 19). This represented a shift in his view of the role of identification in normal personality development—although it is important to note that he was not speaking specifically about bereavement (Baker, 2001).

In the following years, other psychoanalytic thinkers expanded on Freud's original description of mourning and continued to struggle with the distinction between mourning and depression. What occurs in normal mourning, Otto Fenichel (1945) stated, is a gradual working through of feeling which, if released in full strength, would be overwhelming. According to many early theorists, through normal mourning the individual comes to realize that the beloved person no longer exists and the attachment to that person is severed. By the culmination of mourning, the energy of the mourner is freed for reinvestment in other individuals and activities.

In 1924, Karl Abraham published "A Short Study of the Development of the Libido Viewed in the Light of Mental Disorders," adding important concepts to Freud's formula. It was Abraham who first suggested that the mourner introjects the lost objects. He stated, "In the normal process of mourning, too, the person reacts to a real object loss by effecting a temporary introjection of the lost person. Its main purpose is to preserve the person's relation to the lost object: 'My loved one is not gone, for now I carry it within myself and can never lose it'" (p. 435f.).

Slightly in contrast to Freud's conceptualization, Abraham felt that ambivalent feelings may occur consciously in the mourner, although the positive feelings usually far outweigh the negative. The presence of hostility toward the lost loved one in the normal mourning process is a controversial issue and will be referred to in later discussion.

Melanie Klein (1935), in her article, "A Contribution to the Psychogenesis of Manic Depressive States," agreed with Abraham and Freud. She said that in normal and abnormal mourning, there is a reactivation of what she referred to as the infantile depressive state. She felt, however, that what was actually being mourned was the loss of the breast which represented love, security, and gratification to the infant during the infantile depressive phase. Loss through death was, to Klein, a reminder of the original loss of the breast.

Also reactivated, according to Klein, are the feelings that the loss may be due to the individual's own hostile or greedy impulses. Klein theorized that the infant experiences feelings of responsibility for the loss of the breast due to her greedy desire for it. Later, at the time of the loss of a loved one, the individual again feels guilt and believes that this loss was caused by her greed and hostility fueled by infantile feelings of rage toward the lost loved one for having abandoned her. In response to these feelings, the mourner wishes to restore and repair her good image of the lost loved one. In order to do so, Klein said the mourner introjects the lost loved one and in so doing rebuilds her own inner world and enriches her personality with the addition of the representation of the lost loved one. This, according to Klein, was the successful work of mourning (Baker, 2009). The result of this process, according to Klein, is increased trust in and love for these internalized images.

Klein placed less emphasis on detachment from the lost object than did Freud and others. She viewed mourning as a process of reparation during which destructive fantasies unleashed by the loss are contained so that a positive internal relationship with the lost loved one can be reestablished (Baker, 2009).

Edith Jacobson (1957) also offered valuable insight into the grief process. In her article, "On Normal and Pathological Moods, Their Nature and Functions," she elaborated upon Freud's model. She described the circular emotional process in which inner pain triggers the return of happy memories, which in turn stir up longing for lost gratifications, and therefore, cause further emotional pain. Wishful memories and painful anticipation of further sadness become generalized to all persons and situations for a period of time until a sufficient number of painful discharge processes have occurred. In this fashion, the feeling to be discharged diminishes until the point at which the sad mood can lift.

Jacobson stated that sadness and grief appear to develop as a contrast effect induced by the discrepancy between equally overinvested opposing memories and fantasies. Highlighting the contrast to the happy past, the depriving reality of the current loss makes the world appear depriving and empty. As a result, the self feels deprived and poor. In this respect, Jacobson might seem to have diverged from Freud's point of view that in the normal grief process, the world becomes poor and empty, while in melancholia it is the ego itself which feels impoverished. Jacobson, however, agreed that there is no increase of aggression in the relationship to the self (which would lead to either an angry or a depressed mood), although she did feel that sadness and grief affect the self. She maintained that in grief self-esteem and internal relationships remain stable, although subdued.

As already mentioned, Jacobson pointed to the importance of discharge of emotion in successful grief resolution. She stated that strong and persistent confrontation by the bereaved person to the reality of the loss with intense and uninhibited discharge (e.g. crying) is a relieving experience. She also said that while painful, these repetitive, dramatic eruptions lead to equally dramatic relief.

Martha Wolfenstein (1966) basically restated Freud's position when she said that the attachment to the lost loved one is gradually lessened by a process of remembering and reality testing, separating memory from hope. Each one of the memories and wishes that the loved one continue to exist is reviewed and is compared to current reality. This demonstrates the individual's ongoing attachment to the lost loved one. But then the mourner is forced by reality to the conclusion that the loved one no longer exists. That the process occurs gradually serves as a crucial defensive function, as Fenichel (1945) and Wolfenstein (1966) both noted, in protecting the mourner from being overwhelmed by the intrusion of too great a quantity of traumatic material.

Freud, Abraham, Klein, Jacobson, and Wolfenstein are considered to be the thinkers most responsible for the current bases of the psychoanalytic conceptualization of the grief and mourning processes. Others such as Erich Lindemann and John Bowlby looked at grief and mourning using different methodology in order to explore these areas.

Erich Lindemann (1944) was the first to conduct a research study on bereavement using a nonclinical population. His methodology was extremely important as previously most of the literature on bereavement had been based on observations of patients in treatment who were being seen for other pathological conditions.

Lindemann discussed symptomatology and management of bereavement based on his observations of several categories of mourners, some of whom were not part of a clinical population. He studied 101 survivors of and/or relatives of the victims of the Coconut Grove nightclub fire, patients who lost a loved one during the course of treatment, and relatives of members of the armed forces.

Lindemann summarized his major findings as follows:

1. Acute grief is a definite syndrome with psychological and somatic symptomatology.
2. This syndrome may appear immediately after a crisis; it may be delayed, or it may be either exaggerated or apparently absent.
3. In place of the typical syndrome, there may appear distorted presentations, each of which represents one aspect of the grief syndrome.
4. By appropriate technique, these distorted presentations can be successfully transformed into a normal grief reaction and resolution (Lindemann, 1944, p. 141).

Importantly, Lindemann presented grief as a normal, non-pathological process. The syndrome of normal grief which he identified included:

- Sensations of somatic distress occurring in waves lasting for twenty minutes to an hour at a time
- A feeling of tightness in the throat, choking and shortness of breath, the need for sighing
- An empty feeling in the abdomen
- Lack of muscular strength
- Intense subjective distress described as tension or mental pain
- Altered sensorium with a slight sense of unreality
- Feeling of increased emotional distance from others
- Intense preoccupation with the image of the deceased
- Irritability and a wish not to be bothered by other people.

Lindemann also identified five attributes which he considered pathognomonic to normal grief reactions:

1. Somatic distress
2. Preoccupation with the image of the deceased
3. Guilt
4. Hostile reaction
5. Loss of patterns of conduct.

Also important in Lindemann's study was the identification of pathological variants of the grief process. These will be described later in a portion of this work devoted to pathological mourning.

Over four decades, another researcher and theorist, John Bowlby, made a study of the effects of separation and loss. His perspective, while originally psychoanalytic, evolved into one more in keeping with the then modern biological theory. It is important to understand Bowlby's frame of reference while looking at his approach to loss. Having studied the ethological literature on attachment behavior in animal species, Bowlby concluded that a similar process of mother–infant bonding must also occur in humans. Bowlby suggested that there is an attachment between mother and infant independent of oral motivation (feeding having been Sigmund Freud's original explanation for the attachment between mother and infant).

Bowlby discussed attachment behavior as a special class of behavior with its own dynamics. He defined attachment as any form of behavior that results in a person attaining or maintaining proximity to another person better able to cope with the world. The nature of the attachment bond and the effects created as a result of any disruption to it were precisely the areas of Bowlby's interest. Bowlby explained separation anxiety as the reaction to a situation which carries an increased risk of pain or danger. As such, he explained that separation anxiety most often presents itself when there is the threat of a loss of proximity to—or actual separation from—the more competent attachment object.

Bowlby studied separation, loss, and mourning. And unlike Freud and those who immediately followed Freud, he defined mourning simply as the usual response to a loss after it has occurred. He did not specify a particular end point to the process but rather said that it refers to all the psychological processes, conscious and unconscious, that are set in train by the loss. Moreover, unlike thinkers before him, Bowlby stated that normal mourning could include an ongoing sense of the presence of the lost loved one. He did not include detachment from the lost loved one as a sine qua non of the healthy mourning process.

In his study of loss, Bowlby (1980) delineated four specific phases of mourning. These phases were described as follows:

1. Numbing—which usually lasts from a few hours to a week and may be interrupted by outbursts of extremely intense distress or anger
2. Yearning and searching for the lost loved one—lasting from months to years
3. Disorganization and despair
4. Reorganization—which may be achieved to a greater or lesser degree.

Bowlby suggested that individuals may oscillate between any two of these phases at any time in the mourning process, inferring that the phases may not always present sequentially. He also noted that a given phase may be returned to even after it has been experienced. This aspect of his conceptualization is frequently overlooked and he is often accused of having insisted on a phasic model with invariable order.

Bowlby's formulation of the mourning process, while stated differently, shared some similarities with Sigmund Freud's. Bowlby suggested that in healthy mourning there is a gradually decreasing urge to search for and to recover the lost person. He thought that this could be considered to correspond to Freud's description of the wish to regain the lost loved one coming into conflict with the reality testing which demonstrates that the person has ceased to exist. Contrary to Freud, however, Bowlby stated that there may be anger consciously present subsequent to bereavement as the reaction to the individual's inability to locate the loved one. Both anger and sadness were interpreted by Bowlby as attachment behaviors designed to bring the loved one close and which, in the bereaved individual, represent her desire to bring the loved one back.

Phase 3, according to Bowlby, is necessary for mourning to come to a favorable outcome; only if the bereaved can tolerate the pining, the searching, the seemingly endless examination of how and why the loss occurred, and the anger directed at anyone who might be considered responsible can the bereaved individual come to recognize and accept the loss and the necessity for the reorganization of her life.

It is during phases 2 and 3 that the turning away from the environment, as mentioned by Freud and Lindemann, seems most apparent. The bereaved person must first try, become frustrated, and thus recognize the impossibility of completing old patterns of action connected with the lost loved one before she can reinvest in the present and establish new patterns and a new definition of the self. During this stage, the bereaved may actually despair of being able to accomplish these ends. Once the individual does succeed in phase 3, reorganization and redefinition can occur; plans for the future can be made and development can continue.

Several years later, Pollock (1989) made an enormous contribution to the study and theory of mourning, motivated at least in part by his own mother's death. He defined mourning as a phylogenetically evolved, universal, and adaptive process. He stated that bereavement is a subclass of this process, consisting of a sequence of successive stages, each with varied affects or feelings. Furthermore, he said that there are three possible outcomes of mourning:

- Successful completion with creative outcome
- Arrests at various stages of the process
- Pathological or deviated process that may relate to the depressive disorders with a potentially lethal outcome.

He felt that the mourning process has its origins in the separation experiences of early childhood. And he felt that mourning followed a developmental progression with an optimal outcome being defined by increased individuation and creativity (Aragno, 2001).

Distinguishing between clinical depression and mourning

More recently, studies have continued to attempt to distinguish clinical depression from mourning states. Shear (2009) distinguished between the two in the following way: he said that yearning is the sine qua non of grief and is not seen in depression. Yearning is the experience of wanting (a component of the brain reward system thought to be deactivated in depression). By contrast with depression, even during the initial period of acute grief, bereaved people retain the ability to experience positive emotions. For example, positive emotions may be evoked in a bereaved person when recalling pleasant experiences with the deceased or when expressing pride in the lost loved one or telling amusing anecdotes about them. Moreover, sadness is not usually constant during grief; rather, it occurs in waves or pangs of emotion. Most importantly, Shear, like others before him, said that acute grief is associated with preoccupation with thoughts and memories of the deceased, while depression is associated with self-critical or pessimistic rumination.

Reconceptualization of adult mourning

Reconceptualizations of the process of adult mourning and bereavement have evolved out of the object relations, relational, and self psychological schools of psychoanalysis. As Baker (2001) stated, recent clinical data and empirical literature casts doubt on the assumption that the goal of mourning is or should be the detachment of libidinal ties from the deceased loved one as posited by Sigmund Freud and others. He suggested, as had Melanie Klein and John Bowlby before him, that mourning be seen as a process of inner transformation that affects both the images of the self and the other. In the mourner's inner world the tie to the lost loved one need not be broken but rather the attachment can be transformed into a sustaining internal presence which operates as an ongoing component in the individual's internal world. Baker sought to lay to rest the years of debate regarding the question of whether internalization is a component of healthy or pathological mourning, positioning it squarely in the realm of health and normalcy.

Similarly, Hagman (2001) emphasized a shift away from phase-stage models to a task-oriented view of mourning as a highly varied, unique, and personalized transition in which a crisis of meaning and of identity are central to the struggle. Hagman supported a view of mourning as a psychosocial process in which the capacity of the bereaved person to communicate her feelings and to receive adequate response from those surrounding her are crucial to the mourning process. He, like others within the relational and interpersonal schools, sought to redefine mourning not as an isolated effort by the bereaved individual but as a process which is both internal to the mourner and which inevitably involves others. He said, "A model of isolated mourning does not recognize the important role of others in mourning ... the intrapsychic focus of the standard [psychoanalytic] model of mourning does not convey the role [of] other people and the social milieu in facilitating or impeding recovery from bereavement" (Hagman, 2001, p. 21). Further, he viewed the capacity of the mourner to preserve a dialogue with the lost loved one as crucial to the process of transforming what was an external relationship into an internal one—thereby effecting change within both the relationship with the lost loved one and the bereaved individual herself.

Meanwhile, some within the relational and interpersonal schools of psychoanalysis have attempted not to discard the entire intrapsychic model but to draw from the original work on mourning and melancholia and to utilize this model in new ways. Adrienne Harris (2003) discussed the distinction between mourning and melancholia by saying, "In melancholy, remnants of denial and continuing idealization of the lost love remain in a kind of haunting. Mourning is, most agonizingly, the work to accept death's finality and to metabolize the experience of loving and losing a significant person" (p. 145). Moreover, she, along with Coates, Rosenthal, and Schechter (2003) and others have proposed a new conceptualization of mourning, echoing Hagman, which they refer to as "relational mourning" in which the mourning process occurs in the context of ongoing relationships which can mitigate the effects of loss.

Other contemporary theorists have also discussed mourning in ways that have moved theory forward and added complexity to its understanding. Recent focus has been cast on the restitutional, reparative, and creative potentials accompanying loss. In an eloquent and deeply nuanced paper, Aragno (2001) stated,

> Mature mourning is the manifest expression of organismic efforts to absorb, metabolize, and integrate the impact of a profound biopsychosocial, transpersonal, and often spiritual crisis, challenging the deepest strata of intrapsychic and physiological equilibrium. Its analytic study requires an examination of the shifting ratios and concomitant working and reworking—in different ways at different stages—of each of the above dimensions. The multiperspectival-developmental underpinnings of this approach imply that a mature bereavement is predicated on a fully differentiated psychic structure, a capacity for true symbolization, and ego strength sufficient to endure the disintegrative (catabolic) effects of acute and prolonged grief without defensively preempting its full course to personal transformation. Many immature and/or aberrant form-variants of mourning (i.e. avoided, denied, somatoform, obsessional, displaced, incomplete, prolonged, or unending) are determined both by biological age and the nature of the object tie, and by the existing defenses and psychic structure of the bereaved at the time of loss. (p. 431)

Aragno went on to talk about the way in which one loss evokes another. She said that the "labor" of mourning is a fluid, highly multidimensional and multidetermined process which revives all prior losses and separations. She said that this labor calls on the emotional revisiting and reworking of the deepest recesses of intrapsychic organization. And in regard to the concept of decathexis, she said that far from a severance, detachment, or a "decathecting" of the bond with the lost loved one, an important part of its painfully felt yet constructive work consists in redrawing the organization of the self (ego) and of the self-with-other identity. In that way, she said, the self is deepened and strengthened, while transforming the nature of the relationship through a "re-membering" that simultaneously internalizes and preserves the cherished dialogue within (Aragno, 2001).

Research findings

Having covered the theoretical underpinnings of mourning in adult-hood, I will now move on to discuss research findings in both child and adult bereavement.

Research on mourning in adulthood

In the years following the work of Freud, Jacobson, Klein, Lindemann, and Bowlby, there was a great deal of interest in the study of normal grief reactions (Clayton et al., 1968; Clayton et al., 1972; Glick et al., 1974; Gorer, 1973; Hobson, 1964; Maddison, 1968; Maddison & Viola, 1968; Maddison et al., 1969; Maddison & Walker, 1967; Marris, 1958, 1974; Parkes, 1964, 1970, 1972, 1975; Rafael, 1976; Rees & Lutkins, 1967; Shuchter, 1986, Zisook and Shuchter, 1986, and others). In research studies adults who had lost a spouse were the population most often examined. While limited due to methodological factors, including the predominance of widows over widowers, bias toward younger age groups, and the self-selection of the subjects from a larger population, these studies provided a great deal of information regarding normal grief processes.

Zisook and Shuchter (1986) found that widows and widowers continued their connections to their lost loved ones. These connections were made through dreams, memories, possessions, taking on behaviors or traits of the lost loved one and/or by experiencing some kind of continuing contact with the lost loved one (Baker, 2009). Some widows and widowers engaged in internal dialogues with their beloved, others used memories of the lost loved one to help solve problems of the day or to feel a sense of safety and protection (Baker, 2009), thus demonstrating the extreme importance to them of continuing their relationship with the lost loved one.

Research on the link between childhood bereavement and adult psychopathology

Childhood parental loss has also long held a prominent position in the developmental and psychodynamic literature regarding the origins of affective psychopathology. Decades of clinical research have documented links between early parental death and prolonged parental separations with depression, anxiety disorders, schizophrenia and borderline personality disorder (Blum & Rosenzweig, 1944; Brown, 1966; Dennehy, 1966; Granville-Grossman, 1966; Hilgard & Newman, 1961; Hopkinson & Reed, 1966; Pitts ct al., 1965).

Four research stratagems have been used to examine the degree of association between childhood bereavement and later behavior disorders and psychopathology: observations of recently bereaved children, clinical case studies, anterospective or follow-up studies, and retrospective studies. It is important to note that this literature is controversial due to methodological difficulties inherent in some of these research paradigms. One such problem is the fact that relatively few studies of bereaved children used control groups, making it impossible to know what the base rates of particular behaviors or symptoms were in the general population and where controls were used, it often being unclear whether they were matched for age and sex (Osterweis et al., 1984).

Another methodological problem is the fact that much of the psychoanalytic literature on bereavement in childhood has been based on observations of disturbed children who were in treatment. These case reports offer valuable clinical information regarding psychological symptoms and processes as well as providing models for understanding and treating the bereaved child; however, it is impossible to know the degree to which these children in treatment are representative of all bereaved children. On the other hand, random samples of bereaved children that provide more methodologically reliable data do not offer the same depth and sensitivity as do the case reports.

A great deal of the data on early childhood loss from the 1940s through the 1960s is not specific to bereavement but is based on observations of institutionalized children or children who were temporarily separated from parents. For example, Renee Spitz studied institutionalized infants and toddlers in the early 1940s. Some of those he studied were in orphanages in Romania where they were kept in cribs and never handled by staff or stimulated by toys or allowed to play with one another. Undoubtedly these children's responses were based on parental loss as well as on the multiple other losses associated with removal from the home environment, and the unfamiliar, sometimes chaotic, and generally depriving circumstances associated with institutional care. Furthermore, because these children were not followed over a long period of time, it is not known whether their pathologic reactions endured (Osterweis et al., 1984). An excellent review of the older literature is provided by Gregory (1958).

Later, Gregory (1965) performed a study himself which was one of very few anterospective studies of childhood bereavement in the literature at the time. In looking at a sample of 11,329 ninth graders over three years, Gregory found significantly higher rates of delinquency in boys and girls who had lost a parent to death or divorce. Interestingly enough, he also found that same sex bereavement seemed to predispose to delinquency more than opposite sex bereavement.

Brown (1966) noted a significant relationship between parental loss in childhood and adult depression. He found 41% of 216 depressed adults had lost a parent due to death before age fifteen, compared to 12% in the general population. Beck et al. (1963) found that 27% of patients in a "high depressed" group had lost a parent before age sixteen as compared to 12% in a non-depressed group. Bendiksen and Fulton (1975) in summing up these findings stated, "The body of psychological literature dealing with this issue supports the conclusion that, in the main, the emotional development of a child is profoundly impaired by parental loss and that such a loss has serious psychiatric consequences for him through his adult life" (p. 274).

Crawford et al. (2009) looked at a large random community sample in the first prospective study of the developmental factors in borderline personality disorder and found that extended maternal separations before age five were predictive of long-term risk for BPD up to thirty years later. Early separations from mother predicted elevations in BPD symptoms from early adolescence to middle adulthood. Early separations also predicted a slower than normal rate of decline in symptoms with age. They found that long-term effects of early separations were largely independent of childhood temperament, child abuse, maternal problems, and parenting risks. In their discussion they stated, "Separations may be difficult for young children to understand, perhaps leading them to blame themselves for their mother's absence. These cognitions may have a harmful impact on the child's mental representations of self and other" (p. 1025).

Tyrka et al. (2008) looked at childhood parental loss and the development of depressive and anxiety disorders in adulthood and found that participants with separation/desertion and those with parental death were significantly more likely than control subjects to report the subsequent onset of symptoms of a depressive or anxiety disorder. These effects were not fully explained by other factors such as parental relationships or childhood maltreatment.

Using an enormous amount of data, Hoeg et al. (2018) looked at the effect of early parental loss on the development of intimate relationships in adulthood. They found that parental loss was associated with a higher rate of relationship formation for young women, but not young men, and higher rates of marital separation for both men and women. These results were stronger for those who had lost a parent to suicide than to other causes. They also found that people who had experienced the loss of a parent in childhood were more likely to enter common law marriages rather than actually getting married, thus suggesting an effect of early loss on the ability to form later commitment to a relationship. These findings indicate some paradoxical effects of parental loss in childhood. While young women who were bereaved as children may seek out relationships more often than their non-bereaved peers, they may also find it more difficult to maintain intimate relationships, especially when their early loss was caused by the suicide of a parent.

A great deal of study has been devoted to answering the question as to whether the death of the father or the mother has more impact on the development of later difficulties and psychopathology. While some studies have found no difference, Jacobs et al. (2009) found that the death of the father during childhood more than doubles the risk of depressive disorder in adulthood.

Suicide

The death of a parent by suicide carries its own particular ramifications. In a comprehensive review of the literature, Hung and Rabin (2009) reported the following: Cain and Fast (1966) were among the first to call attention to the potential pathological impact of parental suicide. Their results showed that children whose parent committed suicide manifested psychopathology that ranged in severity from mild conditions (e.g. psychosomatic disorders, learning disabilities, obesity) to depression, characterological problems, and psychosis. Moreover, the incidence of psychotic conditions among the suicide-bereaved children was much higher than the incidence within a more general group of disturbed children. Picking up on this theme, Pfeffer (1981) called attention to the finding that both the quality of post-suicide family interactions and therapeutic interventions made as important variables in shaping children's outcomes. In their description of children whose parents had attempted suicide, Pynoos et al. (1981) reported that in the weeks following the event, the children they studied (some of whom had discovered the parent) experienced post-traumatic stress symptoms such as overwhelming affect, intrusive thoughts, and reenactment of the trauma in play and behavior. Guilt and self-blame were additional reactions, which were thought to contribute to depression later in life.

In a contrasting report, Grossman et al. (1995) found that children whose fathers had completed suicide within the three years preceding their study demonstrated relatively low levels of grief and were behaviorally similar to non-clinical children at baseline. Overall reports of post-traumatic stress reactions were low but were higher in children who had been directly exposed to paternal suicide, domestic violence, marital discord, and/or the father's suicidal threats. Their findings also suggested that a stable family environment before and after the suicide served a protective role.

Recent research has shown that children bereaved by parental suicide are at greater risk for a variety of problems, most notably major depressive disorder, post-traumatic stress disorder, high risk behaviors, impaired academic competence, poor social adjustment, and reduced leisure activities as compared to non-bereaved children (Cerel & Roberts, 2005; Pfeffer et al., 1997).

Wilcox et al. (2010) showed that children of parents who died by suicide were at significantly greater risk of suicide themselves compared to children whose parents were still alive. Children of parents who had died by suicide also had a particularly high risk of hospitalization for a suicide attempt and for depressive, psychotic, and personality disorders. In their study the cause of parental death and the age of the child at the time of the parent's suicide were associated with long-term risk of suicide and hospitalization for specific psychiatric disorders in the children.

Another interesting study examined exposure to suicidal behavior and the likelihood of a suicide attempt in a high-risk cohort of children of a depressed parent (Burke et al., 2010). Results showed that children who had been exposed to suicidal behavior were four times more likely to report a suicide attempt at some point in their own lives in comparison to children who had not been exposed to suicide. Suicide attempt history was not associated with the age of the children at the time of the first exposure to suicide, total number or degree (attempt or threat) of exposures, or relationship to the one who was suicidal.

Research on the effect of early parental separation and loss on children during their childhood

A number of studies have looked at the effect of early parental loss on children close to the time of the parent's death. These studies have shown the prevalence of painful feelings and behavioral disturbance, especially in younger children who did not receive adequate support following their bereavement. They also reveal the importance of the child's maintaining a conscious connection with the lost parent and an unconscious internalization of some of the lost parent's characteristics and/or values, the importance of the continuity of familiar routines and social relationships for the child following parental loss, and the importance of the support of other adults in the child's life including coaches, teachers, clergy, and relatives.

In a very good review of the literature, Dowdney (2000) found that the risk of psychiatric disturbance and nonspecific problems in children following parental death appears worst for children with preexisting psychiatric disorders, those whose surviving parent had high levels of psychopathology, males in general, and those whose parent died traumatically including those who died by suicide (Cerel et al., 1999; Pfeffer et al., 2000).

Confirming findings mentioned above, Silverman & Worden (1992) found that most of the bereaved children in their study maintained a connection to their lost parent following the parent's death. This connection was made by having dreams about the parent who died, remembering experiences shared with the lost parent, and keeping possessions which belonged to that parent. A large majority of these children felt that the parent was watching them from heaven and some worried that the parent felt disapproval for them or their actions. More than half of the children engaged in imaginary conversations with the lost parent.

Silverman & Worden felt that maintaining an active connection to the lost parent was adaptive for the children, helping them to endure the loss. A two-year follow-up of these same children (Silverman et al., 1992) described four types of continuing internal bonds with the lost loved one:

1. The deceased parent was conceived of as a ghost whose presence was frightening
2. Memories were perceived as simple reminiscences with no emotional communication with the lost parent
3. An interactive relationship was maintained with the child continuing to talk to the lost parent
4. The child became what they called "a living legacy" through internalization of the lost parent's values, goals, or behaviors as a way of staying connected (Baker, 2009).

Another study, taking a qualitative approach, obtained narratives from thirty-three adults regarding their experiences of having lost a parent in childhood. Ellis et al. (2013) studied the narratives of these adults who ranged from twenty to eighty years of age and who were somewhere between thirteen months and seventeen years old at the time of parental death. They found several common themes in the narratives of those who participated:

• Participants remembered how important it was to them at the time of their loss to maintain continuity in the face of disruption. One woman who lost both of her parents within six months of each other when she was sixteen said: "I didn't want to go to family—I didn't, I think because of the enormity of what had happened … friends [were] the one constant—my school and my friends were the world that didn't change." (p. 60)
• Participants remembered feeling fear and loneliness in relation to the loss of continuity in their lives. These feelings seem to have compounded the difficulties they were already experiencing due to their

loss. Continuity was not only disrupted by changes in physical loca-
tions but also by changes in the surviving parent. One participant
noted that it was not that she had just lost one parent, it was almost
as if she had lost two as her other parent changed so much.

Ellis and colleagues also found that the longer the disruption in the child's
life continued, the greater the effect on the child. When the participants
experienced a series of discontinuous events or continuous events that
did not meet their needs, they were more likely to experience emotional
difficulties and feelings of loneliness and insecurity later in life.

Narratives were also organized around the extent to which social and
institutional affiliations did or did not mediate the impact of parental
death. Several adults remembered the parents of friends or the leaders
of groups they participated in taking on parental roles for them as they
grew up, providing a sense of greater security and guidance.

The degree to which children were communicated with about the
loss was another factor which Ellis et al. found to characterize many
of the narratives. Distress was found to be compounded when children
were not communicated with sensitively and sufficiently—that is, when
they were not given accurate information regarding the death of their
parent and regarding who would care for them after their loss.

To summarize their findings, they said, discontinuity (or continuity
that does not meet the child's needs), a lack of appropriate social support
for both the child and surviving parent, and a failure to provide clear and
honest information at appropriate points relevant to the child's level of
understanding were perceived to have a negative impact in adulthood
with regards to trust, relationships, self-esteem, feeling of self-worth,
loneliness and isolation, and the ability to express feelings.

Kranzler et al. (1990) looked at acute bereavement responses in
preschool children. Parentally bereaved subjects were compared with
matched, non-bereaved children. Bereaved children, particularly
boys, were found to be significantly more symptomatic. Bereaved children reported feeling more scared and less happy than controls. And
bereaved children, especially girls, reported significantly more sadness
when thinking about their parents. Interestingly, the child's ability to
report these grieving emotions correlated significantly with improved
functioning. Children from families experiencing a drop in income after

the death were more symptomatic, and disturbance among subject parents and children was found to be highly correlated.

Howard et al. (2010) examined associations between early mother–child separation and subsequent maternal parenting behaviors and children's outcomes in a huge sample of 2080 families who participated in the Early Head Start Research and Evaluation Project, the vast majority of whom were poor. Their findings revealed that the occurrence of a mother–child separation of a week or longer within the first two years of life was related to higher levels of child negativity at age three and aggression at ages three and five. The effect of separation on child aggression at age five was mediated by aggression at age three, suggesting that the effects of separation on children's aggressive behavior are early and persistent.

Cerel et al. (2006) performed the first large-scale examination of parentally bereaved children and adolescents in which children and their surviving parent were interviewed at regular intervals during the first two years after a parental death and compared with cohorts of clinically depressed and community children to determine the longitudinal course of psychopathology in childhood bereavement. During the first two years after a parental death, bereaved children were found to be more impaired than community controls and less impaired than depressed children. Family socioeconomic status and parental level of depression played important roles in the children's levels of distress. It was found that a parent's death, especially in the context of a family that was struggling financially, typically represented a loss of additional income, which might have been a significant stressor. Financial difficulty was determined to be a hardship which affects the concrete ways in which a family can cope with a death, such as obtaining high-quality child care, health care, and mental health care. Likewise, the loss of a spouse places parents at risk of their own depression, which is another risk factor for childhood depression.

Cerel et al. (2006) also looked at whether anticipating parental death affected children's responses to the death. They found no differences between children who anticipated the death versus those who experienced the sudden death of a parent. This is consistent with previous research about anticipation of parental death but contrary to clinical lore. One explanation for this may be that while a sudden death is shocking, living with a dying parent is also extremely painful for a child and puts stress on the entire family.

Koblenz (2016) also performed a study in which the narratives of children who had lost a parent were collected. This study is particularly illustrative of bereaved children's experience and feelings and, as a result, will be described at length. Koblenz used the participants' own words to demonstrate how they felt about the loss of a parent.

Upon first hearing of their parents' death, many of the participants indicated that they were too young to understand death. They said they were also confused at the funeral. They remarked that they had to learn at a young age that people aren't necessarily permanent. Additionally, many said that they felt that their lives had changed in an instant. They felt that they were treated differently as a result of their loss and they also felt that the process of navigating and understanding death at an early age made them grow up faster.

Reflecting on their childhood, many participants felt that there were things they missed out on, including, especially, missing out on a relationship with the parent who died. Many expressed that they appreciated their surviving parent. It bothered them when other people took their own parents for granted and they envied these people for having both parents. In regard to being treated differently some felt they were spoiled after the parent died, while others felt they were sheltered because of their loss. Many felt that the aftermath of the loss created permanent changes in them. Many wondered how they would have turned out as people if their parent had not died. Others spent their lives dreading Mother's and Father's Days, holidays, and anniversaries because of the painful memories that were evoked on these days and because of the sense of loss they felt at these times.

Some participants were changed in more positive ways, reporting a heightened sense of being alive, a feeling of the importance of not wasting time, and attempting to not have regrets in their life. Others reported being impacted in their interpersonal relationships: They described separation anxiety and explained that saying goodbye was especially hard for them when leaving a friend or family member.

These changes were experienced in romantic relationships as well. Some reported not knowing what to look for in a significant other. They felt this resulted from having lost a parent at a young age. They expressed not having a realistic image of a potential mate due to their idealized perceptions of the parent who died.

Throughout their years of coping, many of the participants in this study said the fact that others did not "get it" about their experience with the loss of a parent made them feel isolated. On the other hand, many felt that support helped them. Participants explained that they felt that there was no good way to bring up their loss to people. This difficulty was attributed to several sources including the feeling that death is a taboo subject. Despite this message, there was still a longing to discuss the person who died. One participant noted that no one talked about it in her family, despite that fact that she had wished that they would. These sentiments gave the overall impression that death is difficult to talk about (in our culture), and this fact added an additional burden.

Continuing this theme, participants reported encountering people who did not know how to act or what to say in reaction to their parent's death. When attempting to open up to others, they found that people often tried to tell them how to feel or how to grieve and they found this less than helpful. They also discovered that sympathy expires before grieving does, indicating that others lost interest or expected them to recover sooner than they could possibly do so.

In response to the difficulty in seeking others for support, participants first assumed that no one else understood. They felt all alone in their grief and felt that they had to handle it on their own. This independence and isolation stemmed from different places. For some this feeling was internal; they felt they had to be strong, that they were different from everybody else and had to grow to be more independent. Many were fearful of being hurt again and as a result did not want to rely on others. Gradually, many of the participants learned to seek help from those who were able to provide it. They reported learning to get support from those they could trust. They also realized that their families were crucial in navigating through the process. They found the surviving parent, their friends, and their pets most helpful. It especially helped to have friends who had lost a parent because they felt they could relate to them.

Participants sought help from other sources as well. Many tried therapeutic interventions, which triggered varying responses. Participants reported that the type of therapy and the connection to the therapist were important in determining whether the therapy felt helpful or not. Therapy appeared to have impacted different individuals differently, but the consensus appeared to be that seeing a therapist right after their bereavement was not helpful while seeing a therapist later was helpful, especially in the cases when the participants chose to go to therapy on their own, as opposed to being forced.

As has been found in other studies cited above, paramount to participants' ability to grieve, aside from support, was keeping a connection to the person who died. Many wished they knew more about the person, including both the good and the bad, to get a realistic image of him or her. Memories of their mothers and fathers helped. Many reported that having a connection to the person who died was important to their identity formation, reflecting that to fully know themselves they had to know the parent who died. In addition to keeping a connection, they did not want their mom or dad to be replaced and said that it was weird when their surviving parent wanted to date again.

Ultimately, participants accepted the death of their parent and realized that losing a parent was part of them. However, they acknowledged needing to find a way of moving on and investing in other things. The first step, many said, was to recognize that there are many different types of coping and grieving, but the best ways were their own. Participants had an array of ways to manage their grief: They used humor, crying, and exercise as coping strategies. Some, whose parents had been ill, found that it was a relief when the parent died and tried to focus on the fact that their parent was no longer in pain. Others found that religious ideas could either help or hinder their ability to cope. They concluded that there is no one right way to grieve, and they embraced that not having a parent was a part of who they were and said they did not want pity.

After the acceptance that death was an inevitable part of life, participants realized that time plays an important factor in bereavement. They found that it gets easier as time goes on, and that it's easier to talk about when you're older. However, they also found that they sometimes thought they were more over it than they were. This led them to conclude that although it becomes easier as you grow older, grieving is a lifelong process.

Traumatic bereavement

Koblenz had child subjects describe their experiences with bereavement and they did so eloquently, demonstrating the pain and potentially traumatic nature of losing a parent whatever the circumstances. Further research has looked at children who experience the loss of a parent in a particularly violent or dramatic way, calling this traumatic bereavement.

Traumatic bereavement refers to the situation in which loss occurs in a way which overwhelms the child's ability to process the event. In such cases, characteristic trauma-related symptoms interfere with children's ability to adequately encode the event in memory, to metabolize the experience, and to mourn the loss of the loved one. Cohen et al. (2002) described the core features of childhood traumatic grief, differentiated it from related conditions, and reviewed the current research in the area. Coates et al. (2003) also studied traumatic bereavement in their work with children affected by the events of 9/11. This work as well as further aspects of trauma will be discussed in separate sections.

Attachment

The attachment literature is also relevant to the subject of childhood bereavement. According to attachment theory, infants, toddlers, and young children need to form and maintain a strong attachment to at least one primary caregiver who can provide the love, nurture, attunement, mirroring, and regulatory functions that allow for optimal development. If the young child experiences the loss of the primary caretaker via separation or death, this can affect the child's capacity for attachment and interpersonal relationships. Following a prolonged separation or loss of the primary caregiver, children who were initially securely attached may become insecurely attached, avoidantly attached, or attached in a disorganized way. The transition from secure to insecure, avoidant, or disorganized attachment is extremely significant as, going forward in development, these attachment styles affect representations of the self and others, and the ability to form and maintain stable relationships. Changes in attachment style during the preschool period are thought to result from, among other factors, changes in the quality of caregiving and life circumstances. In several studies, secure children who became disorganized were more likely to have experienced potentially traumatic family life events, including parental hospitalization and death, than were stable secure children (Dubois-Comtois et al., 2005).

Strong and healthy attachment can help any child who is confronted by a stressful event to self-regulate and yet, ironically, this same strong attachment represents a source of vulnerability to the well-attached child when the person to whom she is securely attached is lost due to death or separation (Fonagy & Target, 2003).

Resilience

The majority of research studies conducted on outcomes of children experiencing parental death has focused on negative psychological and physical effects. However, these alone do not tell the entire story: There is also a subset of children who not only avoid negative outcomes but also grow into healthy competent adults, who actually experience growth from their bereavement experiences (Luecken, 2008). As Leucken said, these children challenge researchers and clinicians to identify factors that promote resilience in the face of early parental death—with resilience being defined as not only the absence of pathology but also by the restoration and advancement of health and well-being during and following stressful events.

Additionally, some children who would not be considered to be in the resilient category per se also experience growth evolving out of their bereavement. Examples of the ways in which children can actually grow from an experience of loss were enumerated by the participants in some of the studies cited above. The positive effects included becoming more independent, growing up "faster," and a heightened sense of the value of life (Koblenz, 2016).

Overlapping with the concept of resilience, Calhoun and Tedeschi (2001) suggested a process which they called post-traumatic growth. While they acknowledged the pain, suffering, and psychological difficulties that can occur as a result of loss, they stated that for anywhere between a significant minority and a large majority of adolescents and adults who experience traumatic loss, growth can also occur. They noted that following bereavement people can experience a change in themselves, a change in relationships, and a changed philosophy of life. And, as the participants in Koblenz's study (cited above) stated, other positive effects can also be experienced.

While people can feel an increased sense of vulnerability following the loss of a loved one, Calhoun and Tedeschi stated that they may also feel stronger and more capable as well as experiencing a sense of life being more precious than they previously realized. Studies of older widows have shown that many of these women report increases in self-efficacy, self-reliance, and a stronger self-image following the loss of their husbands (Calhoun & Tedeschi, 2001).

In an earlier study the same authors reported that survivors of loss often feel increased feelings of connectedness with others, a deepened capacity for empathy, and an increased ability to connect emotionally with others (Tedeschi & Calhoun, 1995).

Moreover, they stated that the struggle to understand loss sometimes leads people to reformulate their world view and in so doing achieve an enhanced sense of the meaning of life. Confrontation with death can lead to grappling with existential issues which, for some, can lead to a growth in spiritual or religious life—or a clarification of beliefs.

Tedeschi and Calhoun found significant evidence of post-traumatic growth in adolescents and young adults—however, it is important to note that they did not research the question of whether post-traumatic growth occurs in children who have suffered loss. Other researchers including Coates et al. (2003) and Koblenz (2016), cited above, have begun to examine the phenomenon of growth emerging from the psychological processes set in train by traumatic experience.

Case example

Regarding the loss of her mother, Natasha Tretheway said, "You get used to it. Most days it is a distant thing, always on the horizon, sailing toward me with its difficult cargo." Tretheway's mother was murdered when Natasha was nineteen. In an interview regarding her recent book, *Memorial Drive*, Tretheway described how writing was one way that she dealt with her mother's murder. In her book she talked about having to approach the subject through poetry and narrative form in order to process and understand her own trauma and loss. She wrote, "When I begin to say out loud that I am going to write about my mother, to tell the story of those years I've tried to forget, I have more dreams about her in a span of weeks than in all the years she's been gone."

Tretheway said that approaching the same dream and the same event via different modes of writing helped her arrive at different insights. "It's like I need more than one form to address it." Subsequent to her mother's violent death, Tretheway finished college, became a writer, and eventually a poet laureate of the United States and a Pulitzer Prize winner. An example of someone who used her creative process to metabolize her trauma, Tretheway could be said to be a person who was truly resilient in the face of horrendous and traumatic loss.

Research regarding the parenting of children who experience parental bereavement

Research findings of the effect of parenting on outcomes in childhood bereavement are unanimous in indicating that a lack of attunement, support, and availability in the surviving parent is predictive of poorer outcomes for bereaved children while parental availability and empathic attunement is predictive of better outcomes. Hung and Rabin (2009) summarized: "Positive parenting, which includes parental warmth as well as consistent discipline, has been implicated as a protective factor that fosters resilience and adaptive outcomes in bereaved children, independent of negative life events (Haine et al., 2006; Lin et al., 2004), and as a predictor of reduced psychopathology in bereaved children (Kwok et al., 2005)." Conversely, as Silverman et al. (1992) found, surviving parents who coped with the death by feeling helpless or ignoring or dismissing its harmful effects on themselves or their children compounded the negative legacies for their children.

Intervention

Research suggests that intervention programs targeting children and their families who experience extremely stressful life events are of vital importance in preventing the deterioration of attachment relationships. Such programs should focus on caregiver sensitivity (Bakermans-Kranenburg et al., 2003) as well as on the wider family context.

Interventions range from individual psychoanalysis and psychotherapy for the child to parental guidance, parental therapy, family therapy, group therapy for any of the various family members, manualized, "evidence based" therapies such as cognitive behavioral therapy, as well as programs in the wider community such as self-help groups, bereavement centers, and religiously affiliated programs.

CHAPTER 2

Childhood bereavement: Can children mourn?

Jana was four years old when her father died after a long illness. On the day of the funeral the extended family gathered at the church and many watched as Jana ran around and sniffed the various flower displays. She laughed as she pulled a flower from one particularly beautiful arrangement and ran to give it to her mother. Was she mourning for her father?

* * *

Amanda was six when her mother died of a heroin overdose and six months later her father left her at her grandparents, and did not return as he said he would. Amanda stayed with her grandparents, attended school, and played happily with her best friend every day after school in the months following her mother's death. Was Amanda mourning?

* * *

Jason was seventeen when his mother died in a car accident. He had not seemed to be particularly close to his mother and yet he retreated to his room, played video games instead of socializing, and he did not fill out his applications for college. He continued this way through senior year and, in fact, missed all the deadlines for the colleges he had previously been interested in. Was Jason mourning?

Theoretical underpinnings

One of the most fundamental questions in the study of childhood bereavement is whether and to what extent children can mourn. A debate has raged in the literature since the early 1960s regarding this question. Previously, it was well accepted that the child's ego was too weak to successfully undertake the work of mourning. That is, cognitive processes and ego capacities, such as reality testing and affect tolerance, were considered to be insufficiently developed prior to adolescence to provide the necessary substrate for mourning. More recently, however, researchers such as John Bowlby (1980), Robert Furman (1964a, 1964b, 1968, 1969, 1973), Erna Furman (1974), Lopez and Kliman (1979), and others have agreed that even very young children are capable of mourning.

In order to evaluate the question of childhood mourning, there are three important variables which must be examined: The first is the definition assigned to the term mourning; the second is the mode of inquiry of the researcher; and the third is the researcher's theoretical predilection.

While the definition of mourning employed by the individual researcher is an important variable in the position which the researcher takes on whether and to what extent children can mourn, this will be discussed later in the sections on "Loss and Mourning" and in the later chapter, "Children Can Mourn."

Starting with the early literature and continuing to the recent past, information regarding the processes of mourning in childhood has often been gathered from the reports of adult patients (who lost a parent during childhood) engaged in psychoanalysis (Altschul, 1968; Cerel et al., 2006; Deutsch, 1937; Fleming & Altschul, 1963; R. Furman, 1968; Howard et al., 2010; Koblenz, 2016; Kranzler et al., 1990). Conclusions, thus, have been based on retrospective data from the analyses of these patients. The deficiencies of this type of data have often been enumerated, and result largely from the fact that they derive from small sample sizes, from clinical populations, and rely on the memories of the participants. Later studies (Becker & Margolin, 1967; Bedell, 1973; Black, 1997; R. Furman, 1973; Wolfenstein, 1966) have been based on actual data from the observations and treatment of bereaved children. With the acquisition of information from direct observation of children experiencing either brief separations or permanent loss, more specific information has been gained regarding the child's reaction to loss.

Prior to more recent studies on children's reactions to loss, psychoanalytic thought had been unified in the belief that children could not mourn, but since the early 1960s divisions have arisen. Some investigators and clinicians continue to believe that children cannot mourn, while others (E. Furman, 1974; R. Furman, 1964a, 1964b; Lopez and Kliman, 1979; Masur, 1984) have shifted their thinking toward the belief that children can begin to mourn at very early ages. Unfortunately, more empirical data regarding how large samples of individuals of any age respond to loss are needed to study this question. Those studies which are available will be discussed below.

Separation

In order to lay the groundwork for later discussion of the most useful definition of mourning and the extent to which children are able to mourn, it is first necessary to examine the literature describing the effects of both separation and actual object loss from infancy onward as well as the literature which examines mourning itself.

The reactions of children of different ages to separation from the parents under a variety of conditions have been studied and documented by investigators including Anna Freud and Dorothy Burlingham (1944), Arsenian (1943), Spitz (1945, 1965), Spitz and Wolf (1946), Bowlby et al. (1952), Prugh et al. (1953), Robertson (1953), Vaughan (1957), Schaffer and Callender (1959), Bowlby (1960, 1961, 1963, 1980), Mahler (1961), Micia (1962), Heinicke and Westheimer (1965), Cox and Campbell (1968), Rheingold (1969), Ainsworth and Bell (1970), Robertson and Robertson (1971), Macoby and Feldman (1972), Marvin (1972), and others.

Rene Spitz (1945) pioneered the early work on object loss using an institutionalized population of infants who were deprived not only of their actual mothers, but also of adequate caretaking of any kind.

In 1946, Spitz (Spitz & Wolf) described "anaclitic depression" as the reaction of the infant to object loss occurring in the second half of the first year of life, with object loss being defined as the loss of the primary caretaker. Spitz described anaclitic depression as appearing when the infant experienced the loss or separation between the sixth and eighth months of life and when the separation lasted for a period longer than three to five months. Anaclitic depression as described by Spitz is characterized by crying and clinging in the first month, wailing and weight loss in the second month, and a refusal of contact with others in the third month accompanied by facial rigidity, whimpering, lethargy, and a decreasing developmental quotient. Spitz found that after three months of separation end stage symptoms became progressively predominant. However, if prior to the end of the three months the mother returned, symptoms disappeared. Spitz suggested that sequelae in later life may occur in those individuals who suffered anaclitic depression although at the time of his initial investigation, he had little evidence to substantiate this hypothesis.

Given a separation from the mother of longer than five months, the symptomatology of anaclitic depression merges with the syndrome which Spitz (1945) called "hospitalism." In this syndrome, increasingly serious and irreversible deterioration occurs in the infant. In these infants, Spitz observed a marked lowering of the developmental potential to the extent that, at the end of the second year, the average developmental quotient of these children was assessed at 45% of normal. Motoric development was seen as being severely delayed and, if allowed to deteriorate (i.e. to remain without adequate nurturing), these infants developed marasmus and died.

Spitz understood the development of these syndromes in the context of object relations. He suggested that the infant's relationship with the primary caretaker or loved one provides an outlet for her aggressive drive. Therefore, in the absence of the parent, both aggressive and libidinal (loving) drives (which are not yet discriminated by the second half of the first year according to Spitz) are deprived of their target. Aggression is thus turned back against the self with resulting self-mutilation and anorexia. Spitz understood the infant's initial weepiness as the attempt to regain the lost loved one with the help of the aggressive drive. In the face of the defeat of this aim, according to Spitz, visible manifestations of aggression decrease and somatic symptoms appear instead (Spitz, 1965).

It is important to note that Spitz's observations took place in orphanages where the infants were not only separated from their mothers but also deprived of contact with all family members and given little to no stimulation or care of any kind other than the most basic feeding and diapering. The development of anaclytic depression and marasmus can now be considered to have resulted not only from separation but also from the lack of any kind of adequate substitute caretaking or stimulation.

Around the same time, Margaret Mahler (1961), a pioneering infant researcher, was devising a developmental scheme which she named the "separation–individuation process." She supported Spitz's conclusions regarding the etiology of anaclitic depression. During the second half of the first year, Mahler saw the infant as symbiotically involved with the mother (or primary parent). According to Mahler, a need-satisfying relationship, which provides the environment in which this symbiosis can occur, is a prerequisite for normal growth. And without the need-satisfying object, she felt that the infant cannot successfully develop.

While Spitz was making his observations of institutionalized children, and Mahler was formulating her theories around separation–individuation, the study of infants and young children in very brief separation was beginning in England and the U.S. From the work of Arsenian in 1943 to the present, researchers have amassed a great deal of information regarding children's reactions to separation. The data seems to indicate that in a benign but somewhat strange situation, young children between the ages of eleven and thirty-six months who are brought up in families are quick to note mother's absence and commonly show some measure of concern. The degree of concern varies considerably, but usually anxiety and distress are demonstrated. Play activity decreases and may cease in the absence of the mother. When alone or in the presence of a stranger, infants tend to search for their mother immediately upon realizing her absence. In research which looked at the infants' reactions to their mothers' departure from a room in which they were together, infants and toddlers began searching for their mothers in the chair in which she had been sitting, looking at the door through which she had departed, and crying. After the mother's return some of the infants then demonstrated ambivalent behavior toward her.

The behavior described here was called attachment behavior by John Bowlby and Mary Ainsworth, and it was seen as following a developmental sequence from birth through maturity. For example, in the one-year-old infant, attachment behavior was seen as requiring physical contact, while in the two year old, just being able to see the mother was sufficient to make the toddler feel secure (Lee & Hankin, 2009). Macoby and Feldman (1972) noted that by age three, children have an increased ability to communicate with the mother verbally and thus to make the attachment with her that way as well as to understand that when she leaves she will return.

John Bowlby went on to conduct further research with Joyce and James Robertson, by examining children's response to separation with particular regard to those variables not accounted for by Spitz (e.g. the effect of illness, hospitalization, the type of caretakers substituted for the parents, the quality of relationship enjoyed with the parents before and after the separation, and the like). Bowlby, the Robertsons, and others looked at the effects of separation on young children through observation of how young children behave during periods of absence from the home and upon their return. These researchers also made observations of how children and adults behave during and after separations from loved ones, observations of how children respond after the loss of a parent, and observations of differences found in clinical work with children and adults who, during childhood or adolescence either experienced a long separation or a loss or had grounds to fear one.

Bowlby et al. (1952) presented a model of attachment and separation in which they described a sequence of:

- protest
- despair
- detachment

when the infant (from twelve months to three years) was separated from the mother (or primary parent). That is, whenever a young child who had the opportunity to develop an attachment to a mother figure was separated from her unwillingly, she demonstrated distress by protesting, experiencing despair, and then detaching from the parent. When placed in a strange environment and cared for by a succession of strange people, the distress was observed to be intense. At first, the infant protested and tried by all means available to recover the mother. Later, she seemed to despair of the mother's recovery but continued to be preoccupied with the mother and vigilant as to her return. Finally, the infant seemed to lose interest in her mother and become detached from the mother (Bowlby, 1980, p. 26). Bowlby saw these phases as indicative of the underlying processes of separation anxiety, grief and mourning in the protest and despair phases, and the initiation of defensive functioning in the detachment phase.

In 1952, Bowlby et al. first showed their now well-known film, *A Two Year Old Goes to the Hospital*, which demonstrated the reactions of Laura, a healthy two-and-a-half-year-old girl to an eight day hospital stay during which she was rarely able to see her parents. Her reactions were intended to be illustrative of those typical of eighteen to thirty-six-month-old children who are separated from home and loved ones.

In the film, Laura demonstrated protest, yearning, and searching. She expressed her longing for her mother and actively searched for her. The despair described by Bowlby, Robertson, and Rosenbluth (1952), however, was not demonstrated in full force; Laura's protests were muted. Bowlby explained that the full emotionality of her desire for her mother seemed to be more subtle in general and became more so as her stay lengthened.

Most striking in this film, according to Bowlby, was the transformation in Laura's ability to respond to her mother upon her visits; during the first two, Laura burst into tears when she saw her mother. On one of these occasions, she also turned away from her mother. During the second two visits, Laura met her mother with a blank expression and made no attempt to get in contact with her.

Crying after short separation and a blank expression after longer periods were thought by Bowlby and colleagues to be typical of young children. Similarly, Laura's clinging to a particular blanket and teddy bear, her anger toward another doll on the fourth day of her stay, and her comforting of other children were also thought to be typical responses.

These include the use of transitional objects for comfort, displacing the need for the mother onto the transitional object, displacement of angry feelings toward the mother (onto the teddy bear), and projective identification through giving the comfort to others which the child so desperately wants herself. Bowlby et al. described these behaviors as defensive.

Following the original studies performed by Bowlby, Robertson, and Rosenbluth in 1952, further work was conducted by their colleagues at the Tavistock Child Development Centre as part of the centre's research on the effects on personality development of separation from the mother in early childhood.

Heinicke and Westheimer (1965), for example, performed a study in which children who were separated from their parents and placed in residential nurseries were observed. It was found that crying was the most predominant response upon separation, and then again at bedtime for the first three days. Sporadic crying was typical of most of the children for at least the first nine days. Often the children in the study initially refused to be dressed, fed, or toileted by their nurses. However, as time went by, the children gradually began seeking reassurance or affection from these same nurses. All but one of the ten children observed brought favorite items from home. It was noted that for the first three days the children clung to these and became upset if a nurse accidentally took hold of the object while trying to help the child do something. After the first three days, however, treatment of the transitional object became mixed, with clinging alternating with throwing away the object. Furthermore, as the two weeks progressed, hostile behavior increased in the children and, in most of them, there was a breakdown in sphincter control, with occasional toileting accidents. Moreover, four children became more active, while two children became less so. Some rocked, others seemed frequently to be on the verge of tears, often rubbing their eyes. It is important to note, however, that in those children who entered the nursery with a sibling, these responses to separation were appreciably diminished.

While at one time it was thought that distress occurring in children at the time of separation from their parents followed by ambivalence and anxiety upon return to the parents was indicative of a preexisting difficulty in the mother–child relationship, Heinicke and Westheimer concluded that even healthy children from satisfactory homes behave and feel this way. They observed that healthy, well-nurtured children experience protest, despair, and detachment with marked ambivalence toward the mother displayed upon reunion after they have been separated from their mother and placed in a strange environment. According to Heinicke and Westheimer, the only children who do not experience this sequence are children who have never had a figure to whom they could become attached or those who have experienced repeated separations and have become permanently detached.

Because studies up until this time dealt with children separated from their mothers under less than optimal conditions, in 1971 James and Joyce Robertson designed the first study to compare children under optimal foster care conditions to those children placed in residential nurseries. The Robertsons took four children into their own home, one at a time, during brief separations from their parents due to the birth of a second child. Joyce Robertson gave each child her full-time care, attempting to adopt the child's own mother's methods of caretaking. From their observations, the Robertsons concluded that under optimal separation conditions, the reaction of protest, despair, and detachment did not necessarily occur. They stated that the children's reactions under such conditions differed qualitatively from those of children who experienced more traumatic or less well managed separations.

Bowlby, in his work *Separation: Anxiety and Anger* (1973), questioned the Robertsons' interpretation of their findings, suggesting that while the sequence of protest, despair, and detachment may be greatly curtailed under optimal circumstances of separation, it cannot be considered absent. Regardless of the differences in the interpretation of their findings, both Bowlby and the Robertsons agreed that "separation is dangerous and wherever possible, should be avoided" (Bowlby, 1973, p. 22).

Bowlby mentioned in his work on loss (1980) that it was formerly accepted that children who are separated from their mothers forget them and get over their misery. He said pithily that such a conclusion is derived only from a combination of wishful thinking and inadequate observation, and is not borne out by careful observation.

Bowlby's ultimate conclusions highlighted the importance of continuity of care for all children. He said that whether a child is in a state of security, anxiety, or distress is determined in a large part by the accessibility and responsiveness of her principal attachment figure.

Loss and mourning

The literature on childhood bereavement is as vast as it is controversial. Integral to this literature is the debate as to whether children can mourn. A brief summary of the debate will be provided here with further discussion of the question to be presented in the following chapter.

That preadolescent children cannot bear the work of mourning is a view which was advanced by many early psychoanalytic writers including Deutsch (1937), Mahler (1961), Fleming and Altschul (1963), and Wolfenstein (1966). Deutsch stated that the ego of the child is not sufficiently developed to bear the strain of the work of mourning and that the child therefore utilizes some mechanisms of narcissistic self-protection to circumvent the mourning process. She postulated two possible reactions of the child to the impact of loss: (1) infantile regression expressed through anxiety, and (2) mobilization of the defenses intended to protect the child from anxiety or other psychic dangers. She said that in the most extreme manifestation of defensive self-protection, the absence of feeling may be seen and that this is often the rule in young children, by virtue of their stage of development. And to prove her point, she presented the cases of four adults whom she treated in psychoanalysis whose treatment demonstrated that they had experienced incomplete mourning processes following the early loss of a parent.

To illustrate, she said: "As long as the early libidinal or aggressive attachments persist, the painful affect [feeling] continues to flourish and vice-versa, the attachments are unresolved as long as the affective process of mourning has not been accomplished" (Deutsch, 1937, p. 21).

In other words, Deutsch felt that until the feelings associated with loss are felt and processed, mourning cannot be accomplished. In order to remedy the situation, Deutsch felt that the neglected feelings must be brought to the fore, even if later in life, mastered, and directed toward the mourning process.

Similarly, Altschul (1968), in analyzing adult patients who had suffered the loss of a parent between the ages of four and eighteen, stated that patients may adapt to the death of the parent by a denial of the actual loss or by a denial of the painfulness of the loss. As a result, he said, these children and teens may experience an arrest in ego development at the level achieved at the time of the loss.

Altschul concluded that, at least for some individuals who were bereaved in childhood, the task of mourning appears to be too great for them to manage at the time of the loss and that further development is also hampered by the loss (Altschul, 1968). However, he did take a more moderate position than Deutsch in that he pointed out that some individuals adapt successfully to loss, but they are not those who are likely to be seen in treatment. He made the distinction, therefore, between the clinical populations of patients who experience early loss and suffer pathological consequences and those individuals who experience such loss but do not come into treatment, perhaps because of having achieved an adequate level of adaptation following the loss. The criticism often made of psychoanalytic studies is thus supported by Altschul who intelligently pointed out the limitations of his findings due to his lack of contact with a nonclinical population.

Altschul did find that young children can experience the beginning feelings of sadness and anger when they experience the loss of a parent. And he postulated that children (who later suffer from depression or other symptomatology as adults) may recognize the actuality of the loss but under the pressure of these beginning feelings then deny the meaningfulness of the loss and continue to act as if the parent were still alive as protection against further painful feelings.

All of the above may be true of individuals who present with a history of early loss and the development of depression or other psychopathology in childhood, adolescence, or adulthood. By definition, these would be the people for whom mourning went awry. However, the important questions remain: Were Deutsch and Fleming correct or not? Can the majority of children suffering the loss of a parent acknowledge the loss and the feelings associated with loss, and in so doing accomplish the tasks of mourning, or are they unable to do so because of their age and stage of development?

John Bowlby (1960, 1961, 1963, 1969, 1980) was one of the principal dissenters from the early consensus opinion on the nature of children's responses to the loss of a parent. He derived his data from observing children's responses to separation from a parent by studying children as young as a few months old through later childhood.

Bowlby, as mentioned, based his work on the ethological perspective, emphasizing the importance of attachment behavior between the infant and the mother. He believed that once the child has formed an attach-ment to the mother figure, which has ordinarily occurred by the middle of the first year of life, its rupture leads to separation anxiety and grief and sets in train the processes of mourning (1980). Moreover, he felt that the very young child's response to the loss of the mother figure differs in no material respect from the response observed in adults.

When, in 1960, he first drew attention to the similarities between the responses of young children following the loss of the mother and the response of bereaved adults, he stated that these similarities had not been observed before. He received a great deal of criticism for this view, and in an article published in 1963, he appeared to renege somewhat on this position. He stated instead that mourning responses seen in infancy and childhood do indeed share many of the features of pathological mourning in adults. This statement was used by the proponents of the school of thought which considered children unable to mourn as proof that Bowlby agreed that children could not mourn.

On the contrary, however, upon closer reading one may see that Bowlby continued to discuss the child's ability to mourn. What he did state is that the form of the child's mourning may take on the appear-ance of what is considered pathological mourning in adulthood. It was in his 1963 article that he began to recognize that mourning in child-hood is often not completed. In his own defense, Bowlby later refuted the terminological rigidity that demanded that mourning be defined in such a way that unless the process is completed, it cannot be considered true mourning. He said, "Were we to accept the injunction to restrict the term mourning in the way proposed, we should have to limit it to psychological processes with an outcome that is not only predetermined as an optimum but which Freud himself rightly suspected is never com-pletely attained" (1980, p. 17). By 1980 Bowlby instead defined mourning as denoting a fairly wide array of psychological processes set in motion by the loss of a loved person, irrespective of their outcome.

In redefining mourning, one of the major difficulties in the study of childhood bereavement was pointed up. As mentioned, for years this study was dominated by the question concerning whether children can or do mourn. The definitional or terminological issues confounded observers. If mourning could only be the process which culminates in complete decathexis from the lost loved one, then it was necessary to infer that children who deeply miss their parent or who maintain a connection to the lost parent have not fully mourned. Furthermore, if the signs of mourning seen in adulthood were looked for in children it would be inevitable that children would be said not to mourn as they do so differently from adults. This part of the argument was pointedly reminiscent of the debate which raged in the 1960s concerning childhood depression. That is, only until observers were willing to look for depression in children in forms distinct from its manifestations in adults were they actually able to find this diagnostic entity in children and to admit to its existence.

Wolfenstein (1966), for example, found in her observations of forty-two bereaved children that mourning as described by Freud did not occur; sad feelings were curtailed and there was little weeping. Immersion in the activities of everyday life continued. There was no withdrawal into preoccupation with thoughts of the lost parent. She stated that the fact gradually emerged that the child was denying the finality of the loss. The painful process of decathexis (removal of energy from the lost parent) was put off with a more or less conscious expectation of that parent's return. Wolfenstein hypothesized a developmental unreadiness to mourn in the children she observed.

Wolfenstein went on to suggest certain developmental preconditions for mourning. She said that the following are necessary for mourning to take place:

1. The ability of the child to modulate affects and thus to gradually decathect from the lost object. She said that children deny and ward off feelings in order to protect themselves from the potentially overwhelming and traumatic experience of having these feelings due to the fact that children operate on an all or none basis. A tentative trial of what it would mean to let go of a lost parent evokes the threat of being overwhelmed (experiencing all of the feelings at once) and the child thus reverts to defensive denial (experiencing none of the feelings at all).
2. The ability of the child to tolerate regression. Depression and mourning have regressive components (e.g. crying). Particularly in latency and early adolescence, the developmental push toward maturity is so strong that the child is loath to involve herself in any activity which

might be considered babyish. Thus, crying, for instance, may be inhibited.

3. The ability of children to tolerate affects. Wolfenstein stated that children make desperate efforts to recapture pleasurable feelings in whatever circumstances. As a result, she said, children can only tolerate small amounts of sadness at a time. She said that children thus have what she called a "short sadness span."

4. Understanding the irreversibility of time. Because young children do not understand that time is irreversible, upon the death of a loved one they maintain the belief that the loved one can return.

Wolfenstein held that it is not until adolescence that the child has all of these capacities and therefore meets the developmental preconditions for mourning. She saw adolescence as a time in which a natural process of separation occurs and said that adolescence is the prototype for later successful mourning. Regarding the bereaved child she said, "Until he has undergone what may be called the trial mourning of adolescence, he is unable to mourn. Once he has lived through the painful, protracted decathexis of the first love objects, he can repeat the process when circumstances of external loss require a similar renunciation" (1966, p. 117).

In 1960, however, Anna Freud responded to Bowlby's previously published article on childhood mourning and began to help clarify the controversy. She presented mourning as a twofold task:

1. The acceptance of the loss in the external world
2. The effecting of a corresponding change in the inner world.

In doing so, she outlined some of the ego capacities necessary for the completion of these two. Most importantly, Anna Freud considered object constancy "a prerequisite for even so much as the perception of loss" (A. Freud, 1960).

Similarly, Zetzel (1965) emphasized that before object loss can be recognized and tolerated, self-object differentiation and some ego identification must have occurred.

Following Anna Freud's example, Robert Furman (1964b) considered more specifically how the child comes to accept death. Taking a developmental approach, Furman delineated five abilities necessary for the child to master the concept of death:

1. Sufficiently stable and differentiated self and object representations so that the integrity of the self-representations can withstand the threat implied in the death of someone else
2. Sufficient ego mastery over the id so that the concept of death can be relatively more integrated within the ego's expanding pool of knowledge rather than utilized for the arousal of instinctual derivatives
3. The ability to distinguish animate from inanimate
4. The ability to understand time in terms of past, present, and future
5. Sufficient secondary processes allowing the child to understand the reality of death, for example understanding that because something is dead it cannot do certain things.

Robert Furman held the position that the mourning process is initially dependent upon the ability to have a concept of death and to have achieved a phallic level of object relations (usually attained by age two to four).

While a primitive concept of death is considered by Anna Freud to have been acquired by the age of three, Robert Furman (1964a) maintained that a sufficient level of object relations to support mourning requires further development and stability of inner world representations. He stated, however, that a two- to three-year-old is capable of mastering the concept of death with the help of external ego support (e.g. an adult who can frequently remind the child of the realities of death) and that by three to four the child can mourn.

Robert Furman (1964a) presented the case of a six-year-old boy whose mourning occurred with the help of psychoanalytic treatment. Similarly, McDonald (1964) presented clinical material regarding the reactions of two girls aged two and a half and four, as well as the reactions of their classmates to the loss of their mother. These case reports support the views of Erna and Robert Furman and, to a lesser extent, Bowlby, by demonstrating that these children did indeed experience the affects associated with grief and mourning including anger, sadness, as well as, on a level appropriate to their development, some understanding of death.

Nagera (1970) presented a developmental approach to childhood mourning which was helpful in advancing the discussion. He understood children's reactions to loss by first understanding the role that important relationships play in a child's life at each successive developmental stage and then by observing the reactions to the loss of such relationships at various ages and stages.

He distinguished between overt manifestations of loss and the "true mourning reactions to that loss," categories which he stated were often combined and which needed to be distinguished.

Nagera accepted the protest, despair, denial model proposed by Bowlby but he asserted, as did Anna Freud, that the mechanisms of this response are far different in infants than in adults. Nagera, like Wolfenstein, felt that mourning, as described by Freud (1917e) and as observed in the adult is not possible until the detachment of the parental figure has occurred in adolescence. He stated, however, that following the development of object constancy (another hotly debated subject but often considered to be around age three) some aspects of the mourning process do occur in childhood as a reaction to the loss of important figures in the child's life. Later discussion will include a look at the development of object constancy and to what extent the acquisition of this ability affects the mourning process.

Nagera suggested that the death of a parent causes complications in the resolution of the typical developmental conflicts and, as such, may be considered to constitute a developmental interference. He stated that whatever mourning is possible takes place simultaneously and in subordination to such developmental needs as are appropriate to the age of the child. Nagera pointed up the difference between mourning reactions in children versus those of adults. He said that children frequently react with abnormal manifestations such as neurotic conflict, anxiety, regression, and abnormal behavior. Nagera stated that rather than sustaining mourning over a prolonged period, the child may instead develop symptoms demonstrating the developmental stress which mourning places on her. Nagera cited Bonnard (1961) who gave examples of children who reacted to a parent's death with truancy and stealing. It was interpreted that these children were seeking punishment out of their own sense of guilt for the parent's death. Nagera noted that in normal adult mourning such reactions are not usually observed.

Erna Furman (1974), taking the position favoring the young child's ability to mourn, stated that normal children are capable of mourning after they have reached the beginning of object constancy in the last part of the first year of life. This idea will be discussed at length in the following chapter.

Coates et al. (2003) further redefined mourning by putting it into the relational framework. In an important contribution to the study of childhood mourning, Coates and colleagues proposed the term "relational mourning" and suggested that human bonds mitigate the effect of loss and in particular, traumatic loss in childhood. Coates et al., like Anna Freud and Dorothy Burlingham before them, suggested that the more the child is able to access her connection to others in times of danger and/or loss, the less likely it is that the child will be severely traumatized. And this may be the key: Previous theorists and researchers felt that until the child had achieved certain developmental prerequisites, mourning could not be accomplished. But this was based on an assumption that the child undertakes mourning alone, an assumption consistent with the one person model of psychoanalytic thought at the time. Starting with Robert and Erna Furman and culminating with Coates, Harris, Hagman, and others, the idea that mourning can be undertaken within the relational context of an emotionally available surviving parent or other supportive adult (including a therapist or analyst) has been put forward. This idea opens up the possibility that the immature ego of the child can be helped to tolerate feelings and sustain the remembering process through the use of the mature ego capacities of the adult. The previous ideas of Deutsch, Altschul, Wolfenstein, and others regarding the likelihood of a pathological outcome in young children were well taken—but would seem to apply more to cases in which the child is unable to tolerate the feelings associated with loss due to pre-existing psychopathology or a lack of relational support, rather than to the majority of children. This hypothesis is in keeping with the fact that this early work on mourning was done within the context of a clinical population.

Adrienne Harris also emphasized the need of the bereaved child for external support. In her beautiful paper, entitled "Relational Mourning," Harris (2003), like Hagman (2001), discussed mourning in an interpersonal framework. She said that the outcome of children's mourning depends on the surviving parent, in particular, the parent's ability to contain intense and terrifying affect. Harris described her term, relational mourning, as the process which occurs in a family when a loved one is lost and it is necessary for the surviving adult(s) to protect the children in two ways. She said that first the children must be helped to "titrate" their feelings, thus protecting them from emotional flooding due to the loss; and second, the children must be helped to see that the remaining parent can tolerate her own feelings and her own mourning. This is important in order to prevent the children from suffering the anxiety which results from the perception of the parent as anxious as well as the prospect of losing the remaining parent to her own mourning process. Harris stated that the surviving parent must be able to manage the "triple consciousness of processing" in which she must process what has been lost in the family, within the self, and for the children. In so doing, according to Fonagy and Target (1997), the parent must be able to focus on her loss as well as keeping the child's perception of loss in mind. It was their opinion that the ability of the parent to do this will enable the children to develop their own capacity for reflective functioning or, as they call it, mentalization, and will also facilitate their mourning process.

CHAPTER 3

Children can and do mourn

Janie was three when her father died in a car accident. Each morning for several weeks thereafter when she got out of bed she went to her parents' bedroom to look for her father. And when she did not find him, she looked all over the house, calling out, "Daddy, Daddy, where are you?" When she did not find him she would sit silently by herself for a few minutes, tears streaming down her face. It was during this time that Janie recognized her father's absence and felt extreme yearning and sadness.

✳ ✳ ✳

Stella was eleven when her mother died from cervical cancer. Stella did not want to go to the funeral. She did not want to talk about her mother. She stayed in her room for days, communicating with her friends on her phone, talking about everything other than her mother. However, a few months later when her father wanted to repaint the living room, Stella said no. And a month after that when her father wanted to go to their mountain cabin for a weekend, Stella also said no. Repainting the living room would have changed it from the way it had been when her mother was alive and Stella could not allow that. And going to the mountain house without her mother just did not seem fair.

* * *

Jacob was fourteen when his father died in an industrial accident. Jacob was an avid woodworker and while he did not talk much about his father, he spent hours each day in his father's workshop in the basement, working on projects. It was there that he could review his memories of time spent with his dad creating furniture and fixing odds and ends that had broken around the house.

Theoretical underpinnings

Simple observation proves that children experience the feelings associated with grief. But it is also obvious that they often show their feelings (such as sadness, anger, yearning, and searching) in a manner that is quite different from the way that adults show grief. Children will sometimes talk about their feelings but more often they use action rather than words to express themselves. Moreover, children do not mourn alone. They mourn in the context of their relationships with family, friends, relatives, school, and community.

With external support, children of all ages are capable of doing the work of remembering and comparing their memory of the parent to the current reality of the parent being gone. Children as young as two years of age will see a photo or a possession of the parent who has died and remember them. At this tender age they may also ask for the parent, look for them, and want them. Older children can and do remember the lost parent and many interactions with them, time shared together, and events where the parent was present.

In her recent memoir, the poet and writer Natasha Tretheway, who was nineteen when her mother was murdered, meditated on the personal power of coming back to images and memories. "I think that's one of the places I find the *most* meaning—in repetition and the way that something not only repeats but also is transformed through repetition …

I think that's why I have revisited … scenes from my childhood the older I get, because I see something that I might not have seen earlier by looking again and again at it."

As reviewed in the previous chapter, many theorists and clinicians have felt that children do not mourn and cannot mourn. It has been stated over and over that children do not or cannot do the work of remembering and comparing the memory of the parent being alive to the current reality that they are not, and they do not do the emotional work of feeling sad and angry over a prolonged period. As was illustrated, the history of the study of childhood bereavement is notable for the number of issues which have been debated. And in fact, the controversy around the question of whether children can mourn has severely delayed the very study of the specific mechanisms by which children *do* react to loss.

Among the questions which have been volleyed back and forth are: whether childhood mourning is like adult mourning, whether childhood mourning is like pathological mourning in adults, or indeed, whether mourning occurs in childhood at all.

As discussed previously, critical to the position taken on the question of whether children can mourn is the definition of mourning and how it is employed. For those who adhere to the particular portion of Sigmund Freud's definition oriented toward the outcome of mourning, the issue is simple: children, especially young children, cannot mourn. If one holds to the statement, "The task of mourning is to detach the survivor's memories and hopes from the dead" (Freud, 1912–13, p. 65), then the term mourning comes to assume a specific outcome which is decathexis. As Anna Freud stated, "Mourning, taken in the analytic sense, is the individual's effort to accept a fact in the external world (the loss of the cathected object) and to effect corresponding changes in the inner world (withdrawal from the lost object)" (A. Freud, 1960, p. 58). The accomplishment of this specific outcome requires sophisticated intrapsychic and ego capacities which, as Deutsch (1937) and others have stated, exist only after the completion of adolescence. While Sigmund Freud actually did not limit mourning to the accomplishment of decathexis, some analytic adherents have.

Current theory

It is debatable, however, as Freud himself stated, whether complete deca-thexis (detachment) from the lost loved one is a possible or desirable accomplishment by anyone of any age. As Erna Furman (1974) stated, "Knowing and understanding that [the] loved one is dead is not the same as accepting it. Clinical examples [have shown] that people of all ages grapple for varying periods of time and for different reasons with the task of integrating reality" (p. 51).

If an expanded, process oriented definition of mourning is utilized, then it is more possible to accept that even the youngest children can experience mourning.

John Bowlby (1960), for example, suggested simply that mourning is made up of the psychological processes set in motion by the loss of the loved object. Erna Furman (1974) defined mourning as the mental work following the loss of the loved object through death. Furman included in her understanding of this mental work an effort at sufficient deca-thexis to allow the development of other significant relationships. These definitions highlight the importance of psychological processes and the mental work following bereavement as important in and of themselves.

While both Furman and Bowlby spoke about the effort at decathexis, they both indicated that this no longer needed to be understood as the sine qua non of a successful mourning process. As stated, some theorists including Bowlby chose to simplify this argument by defining mourning as referring to the feelings associated with loss as grief. And it is known that children do experience grief. Period.

The feelings associated with grief such as sadness, yearning, and anger will be discussed here as part of the process of mourning and not distin-guished from it. It is the use of an expanded understanding of mourn-ing which provides the most heuristic framework for the exploration of the processes involved in children's reactions to loss. Rather than per-petuating a tired debate which has waged long and provided little in the way of meaningful data, the newer definitions and the understanding of mourning which they illustrate set the stage for specific inquiry into the nature of the mental processes experienced by the child following loss, and the determinants of these.

So what then *is* mourning? At this point, following all the years of debate, research, theory building, and opinion, it can be said that mourning is comprised of the intense feelings set in train by the loss of a loved one and the processes, both internal and external, which must be accomplished to accept that the loved one is gone and to adapt to this reality.

The questions of controversy in regard to childhood mourning therefore become:

1. At what age can the infant perceive loss?
2. At what age does loss begin to affect the infant or child?
3. At what age does the infant or toddler begin to understand death?
4. At what age does the toddler or child begin to mourn?
5. What ego capacities are necessary to experience grief and mourning?

These questions will be examined here in the context of the view that even young children can begin a mourning process and that there is a developmental progression in the capacity to carry out the tasks of mourning.

The developmental progression of mourning

One of the major difficulties in the discussion of children's mourning and in the history of research into this area has been the tendency of psychoanalytic writers to group bereaved children of various ages together and to make generalizations about their capacity for mourning, rather than looking at mourning as a process which follows a developmental sequence similar to the general developmental lines proposed by Anna Freud (1965).

Moreover, many variables affect the individual child's reaction to loss. The ability to process loss must be seen in the context of the bereaved child's development, the quality of her relationships, her preexisting character, defensive functioning, temperament, ego strength, the environmental circumstances in which she finds herself, and the amount and quality of ongoing adult support to which she has access.

Helene Deutsch (1937) stated that children resort to narcissistic self-protection in the face of overwhelming affect by regression, by the mobilization of defenses, or by the absence of feelings. And this may very well be the case in children at certain levels of development, those who are unsupported in their mourning or who are at the mercy of environmental stressors. However, it is not equally true of all bereaved children. It is important to continue the early work of Deutsch and others by discriminating between the variables which affect the mourning process. In doing so, it may be seen under what conditions and at what stage of development children can begin to work through the feelings associated with loss.

Historically, there has been a notable lack of attention paid to the environmental stressors which impinge upon the child at the time of the loss and which affect her capacity for mourning. These and other factors affecting the child's capacity to mourn will be discussed below.

At what age does loss begin to affect the child?

The newborn: birth to four months of age

Since the 1970s it has been known that a bonding process occurs between the mother and the newborn within the first forty-eight hours of life (Klaus & Kennel, 1976). It has also been understood since this time that the neonate is aware of visual, olfactory, auditory, and kinesthetic phenomena which she associates with her mother (Brazelton et al., 1974). Moreover, in the past twenty-five years the field of developmental cognitive science has arisen and shown that infants as young as two months of age have the capacity to imitate facial expressions, hand gestures, and head turning. What's more, contrary to previous opinion, evidence has been found that even the youngest of infants possess the capacity for episodic memory (Coates, 2016). This information suggests that the newborn who has sustained contact with her parent during the first forty-eight hours of life establishes a special and unique relationship with her parent. Moreover, it indicates that the newborn is immediately aware of the difference between mother and non-mother. From this it can be hypothesized that being cared for by the mother in the first days and weeks of life will include a sense of familiarity and perhaps even comfort which can be remembered in a primitive fashion and which is different from the experience of being cared for by an unfamiliar person.

Prior to the 1960s it was thought that the main function of the mother was to provide milk for her infant and that the process of feeding formed the bond between mother and infant. However, in drawing on the ethological literature, John Bowlby made the observation that the newborn human infant is reliant on the parent not only for feeding but also for comfort and nurture and the establishment of physiological and emotional regulation. From this, Spitz (1965), Harlow and Harlow (1965), Bowlby (1969), Erna Furman (1974), and others proposed that in the early months of life care by someone other than the mother (or primary caretaker with whom the infant is familiar) constitutes a disruption in the infant's experience. They asserted that such a disruption may result in regression and difficulty in maintaining physiological and emotional regulation, that is, if cared for by an unfamiliar adult, the infant may develop digestive difficulties, changes in elimination habits, difficulty sleeping, fussiness, and difficulty being comforted.

However, it is the more recent work of Myron Hofer detailed in his chapter in Coates and colleagues' volume on September 11 (2003) which further informs the discussion of the effect of separation on young infants. Using an animal model, Hofer and his team found that newborn mammals experience physiological dysregulation in sympathetic, parasympathetic systems, sleep-wake cycles, activity level, and sucking pattern when they experience the loss of closeness, feeding, and warmth provided by the mother. He described the mother as providing crucial physiological regulatory functions (which he called "hidden regulators") for the infant. And he made the important distinction between the affect regulation as proposed by Schore (1994) and the physiological regulation which occurs between mother and infant which he demonstrated in his work. Both are crucial to the well-being of the infant and the loss of either is an obstacle to the ongoing development of the infant.

The importance of Hofer's work includes the revelation that specific maternal behaviors elicit specific critical physiological responses in young mammals including humans. This indicates that it is not just an "enduring social bond" (as Bowlby put it) that makes the mother important to the infant—just as it was not only the feeding capability of the mother that made the mother important as previously thought. What is equally important to the feeding and bonding opportunities is the physiological regulation promoted by continuous contact with the mother throughout early infancy.

Another factor which makes the loss of the mother in infancy detrimental is the fact that from an emotional and cognitive standpoint, the infant is unable to discriminate her own bodily sensations from the parent's ministrations. Sensory stimuli associated with the parent are indistinguishable from the infant's sense of self. Loss of the primary care-taker at this stage may therefore result not only in a subjective sense of discomfort, disequilibrium, and physiological dysregulation but, also as Erna Furman (1974) stated, in serious narcissistic depletion and in later psychopathology related to defects in narcissistic investment of the self.

The effect of loss at this stage of development may be affected by the infant's innate predisposition as well as external factors such as the adequacy of fit of any substitute caretaker (for instance, the substitute parent's ability to simulate the original parent's caretaking style and tolerance for the infant's unique characteristics such as activity level and temperament). During this stage of development, the baby's reaction to loss of the primary caretaker is based on a primitive memory of mother/primary caretaker and her ministrations and on the somatic experience of change in the quality of sensory experience and comfort level when a substitute caretaker is provided.

An important factor in understanding the dearth of literature on the effect of loss in infancy is the fact that it was not widely recog-nized that young infants experience physiological and emotional pain until the 1980s. In the years previous to this, infants were routinely sub-jected to medical procedures including surgery without the benefit of anesthesia. It was thought that young infants and toddlers would not remember the pain they felt during medical procedures and would not be affected by this pain following the procedure. However, in a study published in 1992, Anand and Hickey found that survival rates in young infants undergoing surgery were vastly improved by the use of deep anesthesia. Of those studied, nearly one third of infants who did not receive deep anesthesia died as compared to the infants receiving deep anesthesia, none of whom succumbed. Moreover, these researchers found that infants who had only light anesthesia experienced massive hormonal stress responses and that of those infants who died, all of them had the highest level of hormonal stress response (Coates, 2016).

Similar to the denial of infant physiological pain has been the denial of psychic pain in infancy. Up until the 1970s infants and children who were hospitalized were denied visitation by their parents. The need for parental love and care were considered unimportant in the physical recovery process and the attachment needs of the young child went completely unrecognized in medical circles.

Even now, the question remains as to whether trauma and/or loss occurring in the earliest weeks of life can be remembered. If the infant is separated from the parent or primary caretaker in the first weeks of life will this be encoded in memory?

As mentioned above, for many years it was accepted that infants did not remember what happened to them before approximately eighteen months of age, that is, prior to the beginning of language acquisition. It was believed that procedural memory (involved in learning new skills) was available from the earliest weeks of life but that episodic memory and the ability to encode events in memory was not. As Coates (2016) says, it now appears that a "kernel" of episodic memory, or rather of the capacity to form episodic memories, may be available from the beginning of life and may develop simultaneously with procedural memory.

For the purposes of this discussion the important question is whether there is any evidence of memory for painful or stressful events occurring in the first weeks of life. If indeed neonates have a kernel of episodic memory of neutral content even from the first days of life, we might expect that aversive stimuli would have even more of a chance of being remembered, and of serving as the basis for an emotional memory. In fact Coates (2016) suggested that traumatic events would be expected to have greater salience for very young infants than would neutral stimuli and this has since been demonstrated. One researcher cited by Coates attempted to assess the effect of painful minor medical interventions such as circumcision on newborn boys followed by vaccinations at four and six months. He found that infants who had been circumcised as neonates without pain medications cried more and had more contorted faces when receiving their vaccinations. He suggested that this indicated some residual effect of the earlier experience with pain.

And in one of many such observations made by experienced clinicians, Coates (2016) reported the case of a young man who felt pain in his heels whenever he was stressed as an adult. His early history revealed that the young man had repeated heel sticks as a newborn. The experience of pain in his heels as an adult seemed to be a somatic memory or reexperiencing of the early pain he suffered in infancy. Thus, there is some evidence that even the earliest trauma can be represented at the time of the trauma and can be reexperienced later in life through painful affects, somatic experience, and behavioral enactments.

Four to eight months of age

During the fourth to the eighth month of life, the infant begins to perceive the caretaker as separate from herself during times of need (Mahler et al., 1975). The loss of the primary caretaker at this time was, in the early years of psychoanalysis through the 1950s, often associated simply with the loss of need gratification (A. Freud, 1952; Hartman, 1952). More recently, as stated above, it has been recognized that the bond between infant and parent goes far beyond one made meaningful by the provision of food. The baby of several months experiences attachment to the parent and the parent fulfills a huge number of functions beyond just the providing nutrition—including her role as mirroring partner, helper in physiological regulation and the processing of affect, and provider of reciprocal feedback, affective communication, social referencing, and most importantly, love. Thus the loss of a primary caretaker, even in the first few months of life, represents the loss of both a critical relationship and a large number of necessary interactive regulatory patterns and functions.

Spitz, Bowlby, Erna Furman, and others suggested that from the earliest weeks of life, loss of or separation from the primary caretaker may affect both the infant's current and later functioning in terms of narcissistic investment in the self, attachment style, sense of physiological and emotional safety, and many other areas of functioning.

As a rule, it seems obvious that functions which are dependent upon the narcissistic investment of the primary caretaker are those which will be detrimentally affected by the loss of the caretaker. These may include the positive perception of and investment in the body and its functions, a sense of the self as valuable and loveable and the capacity to experience trust and comfort in the presence of another.

At what age does true mourning begin?

The age at which one can consider the child truly capable of grief and mourning, not just some of the feelings associated with loss, is an entirely different question than the one previously entertained regarding at what age loss can affect an infant. The point at which true mourning begins depends entirely upon which ego capacities one believes necessary to understand that a loss has been sustained. According to Erna Furman (1974), those skills include perception, memory, and object constancy. First, the infant must be able to perceive the caretaker as separate from herself and to do so, the infant must have reached the phase of what Margaret Mahler and colleagues (1975) called "differentiation." Second, the infant must be able to hold the image of the caretaker in her mind even when the caretaker is not present (object constancy), a capacity which the very young infant does not possess. From this point of view, the achievement of object constancy can be considered to be the crucial variable which allows the true experiencing of grief and mourning to take place.

As Nagera (1970) stated, "It is only at the point at which object constancy has been reached that the nature and quality of the energy directed at the caretaker can at least in rudimentary form be compared to the level, nature and quality of energy directed by the adult to her closest loved ones. It is this special type of attachment that determines the intense suffering observed when the loved one is lost" (p. 370).

However, there is considerable disagreement as to the understanding of the term, "object constancy." While some believe that object constancy is the capacity to maintain the representation of the caretaker in his or her absence (E. Furman, 1974), others consider this ability only one part of object constancy. Selma Fraiberg (1969) described the capacity to maintain the image of the mother as "evocative recall" which is possible starting in the second half of the first year of life. Evocative recall refers to the ability of the infant to bring a picture of the caretaker to mind in his or her absence. In the second half of the first year of life—at six to twelve months of age—evocative recall is ephemeral, lasting perhaps minutes. Later, as the toddler matures, the capacity to bring the caretaker to mind in her absence lengthens.

Erna Furman dated the acquisition of object constancy at the same time as the acquisition of evocative recall, that is, in the latter half of the first year, around the time that stranger anxiety occurs (Spitz, 1965). Margaret Mahler (Mahler et al., 1975), however, placed object constancy at around thirty-six months of age. Anna Freud, who had originally stated that the object constancy necessary for mourning occurred in the latter half of the first year, later agreed with Mahler and began to talk about an "object centered phasic level of relationships" (1960, unpublished lectures, quoted by R. Furman, 1968), as being necessary for mourning.

According to A. Freud, the object centered phallic level of relationships also occurs around the beginning of the third year. As a result of the differences in opinion between various theorists, it is not clear whether the object constancy necessary for mourning refers to the point in development at which the child can hold a mental representation of the caretaker in her mind when the caretaker is briefly absent, when the caretaker has been absent for a period of hours or days or weeks, or whether it refers to a later stage of development when the child can hold a fused image of her previously split good and bad mother in mind, that is, the stage of true, fully developed object constancy. The former notion suggests that by the second half of the first year of life the child has achieved object constancy sufficient for mourning, while the latter assumes that this cannot occur until two and a half to three years of age.

Because so many authors date the ability to mourn with the acquisition of object constancy, the question as to when object constancy is achieved is pivotal to the discussion of the development of mourning. Otto Kernberg dated the inception of the stage which encompasses the coalescence of the good and bad images of the mother and of the self and the differentiation of the affects (that is, true object constancy) at some point between the end of the first postnatal year and the second half of the second year, and considered that it continues to evolve through childhood (Kernberg, 1972). This is consistent with the previously stated idea that evocative recall expands as the infant matures. According to Kernberg, this stage overlaps the Practicing, Rapprochement, and Object Constancy phases of Margaret Mahler (Mahler et al., 1975), that is, from around six months to three and a half years of age.

It is perhaps most useful to integrate Kernberg's sense of object constancy as a developmental course of progressively more integrated self and object representation into the discussion of the child's capacity to mourn. Just as it has been postulated that the child's internal image of the primary caretaker begins to develop and is solidified between the end of the first year and the end of the second, so does the child's ability to more fully mourn develop. The literature reflects the difficulty inherent in attempting to pinpoint a specific age at which object constancy can be said to have developed. Instead, it can be proposed that there is development of a progressively greater sense of object constancy and thus, since object constancy is a prerequisite for mourning, a developmental progression in the ability to mourn.

As the infant develops so does her sense of herself-with-other. As the infant differentiates herself from her primary caretaker, she develops a sense of herself within the context of this relationship. When the loss of a parent occurs, this sense of self-with-other is supplanted by a self that is without the other, which is a devastating and developmentally deviant identity (Aragno, 2001).

Starting at approximately eight to twelve months of age, the infant can certainly feel sad and dysregulated when the primary caretaker is not present for a prolonged period. She can experience sadness, anger/protest, and yearning and searching as described previously. However, the capacity to bring detailed memories of interactions with the caretaker to mind and to process the fact that the caretaker is no longer present and will not return is not possible.

To illustrate, in observing young children from twelve to twenty months of age who were placed at a reception center (children's placement home), Aubrey (1955) described their affective response to separation:

> Tears are often continuous, interrupted by paroxysms and short moments of respite during which the child lies exhausted in his bed. It can last for several days; some children cried almost without interruption for six or seven days. Most often the crying expresses despair [but] sometimes despair gives way to anger. Sam, 17 months, stood in his bed, shrieking at the top of his voice without any respite and looked hostile; when he saw the observer in the distance, he went into paroxysms of rage, shook the bars of the cot and stamped his feet. His cries became even stronger and raucous and he thrust the observer away violently. Despair is sometimes accompanied by fear and anguish. Most of the children who do not speak show by their attitude that they are waiting and looking for their mothers. Their eyes watch the door and when it opens they start [to] come out of their apathy to examine

the person who comes in. If the child is walking, he wanders sorrowfully about the room looking in the corners. (Aubrey, 1955, quoted by Heinicke & Westheimer, 1965, p. 278)

How does loss affect children at each age and stage of development?

At any age or stage of development, the most recently acquired functions will be those most impinged upon by the experience of loss, and the normal developmental conflicts and challenges will be those most influenced by the loss and the subsequent mourning process.

Birth to one year

The newborn infant requires intensive attention, nurturance, stability, and love in order to begin the process of physiological regulation and the development of a healthy capacity for attachment and affect regulation. If, during this process, the primary caretaker is lost, the infant will experience a subjective and bodily sense of discomfort and dysregulation. Normal developmental processes will be disrupted, and the implications for future development may be severe. The infant requires immediate substitute caretaking by a loving, attentive person who can replicate the familiar routines and methods of interacting and soothing as closely as possible.

Depending on the age of the infant, she will experience anything from a sense of bodily discomfort and a disruption in familiar and comforting sensory input (for a newborn) to a more consciously experienced sense of disruption and loss which will be noticed and reacted to with feelings of real sadness, yearning, and searching (for example by around eleven months of age).

One to two

At the age of one to two years, the toddler is more fully differentiated from the primary caretaker, becoming progressively more aware of the existence of mother, father, and the self as separate entities. The processes of separation and individuation are central to this accomplishment.

A hallmark of this age is the toddler's new ability to say "NO!" as a way to differentiate herself and her own mind from that of the parent. Defiance and the desire for control are typical of this age and represent the toddler's recognition that she has desires separate from those of the parents. The toddler of this age is acquiring many new abilities including motor and language skills and bladder and bowel control. The desire to master these skills is intense. If, during this time, a parent is lost, the toddler will suffer terribly. The child of this age *needs* the parent in order to have someone to rebel against, and from whom to differentiate herself. The young toddler also needs the parent to help her with affect regulation and the internalization of this capacity. She needs to be soothed and reassured when she is overwhelmed by her own emotions and exploits. If a parent is lost, the toddler will yearn for the return of the parent in a prolonged and intense way and her development will be negatively impacted.

Research on separations during the toddler years was performed by Bowlby, Robertson, and Rosenbluth. They described the young child's reactions to loss by delineating several phases of reaction (referred to earlier). They specified that these stages need not be experienced in order and each stage may be returned to:

1. Protest
In this initial phase, which may last from a few hours to seven or eight days, the child has a strong conscious desire for the lost mother and the expectation—based on previous experience— that the mother will respond to her cries. The toddler is acutely anxious, is confused and frightened, and seeks to recapture the parent by the full exercise of her limited resources. She has no comprehension of the situation (when a parent has died or left her) and she is filled with fright and urgent desire for satisfactions which only her parent can give. She will cry loudly, shake her cot, throw herself about, and look eagerly toward any sight or sound which may prove to be her missing parent. She may seek to cling to whatever adult is available even if only slightly familiar.
2. Despair
This phase gradually follows Protest and is characterized by a continuing conscious desire for the parent coupled with increasing hopelessness. The active physical movements have diminished or

come to an end, and the crying is now monotonous and intermittent. The child is withdrawn and apathetic, makes no demands on the environment, and is in a stage of deep mourning. This is the quiet stage known to nurses and pediatricians as the successor to Protest, and erroneously presumed to indicate a diminution of distress.

3. Detachment

This is the phase which gradually follows Despair, and because the child shows more interest in her surroundings, it is welcomed by those caring for the child as a sign of recovery. It is, however, a defensive device for coping with distress. (Bowlby et al., 1952)

Thus, from the work of Aubrey and Bowlby et al., it can be seen that children from twelve months on may experience longing, sadness, anger, anxiety, and despair when separated from their parents. The length of the separation in part determines the response of the child with longer separations leading to more pronounced despair and detachment. In Bowlby's (1953) study of children separated from their parents, he found that children between twelve and forty-eight months of age experience a "tumultuous mixture of desire and anger" (p. 135) when reunited with the parents after two to three weeks. He said, "Although the feeling they had for their parents was confused and compounded by extremes of love, demand and hostility, a strong relationship remained" (Robertson & Bowlby, 1952 quoted by Heinicke & Westheimer, 1965, p. 274).

It is important to note that a very different outcome was observed in children whose separations began at about the same age but continued for much longer periods of time. Bowlby stated that the period of Detachment continued to the point that desire for the primary caretaker or any kind of intimate maternal care seemed to disappear. The implication here for children who suffer the permanent loss of their primary caretaker through death and who do not receive an adequate substitute caretaker is extremely serious, indicating the possibility for more permanent detachment. It must be noted that Bowlby's sample was comprised of forty-nine children, all of whom were either hospitalized or placed in residential nurseries. Thus, the extreme reaction to separation which he described may have occurred not only due to the length of the separation as Bowlby initially postulated, but also because of the deprivation of nurturance by one consistent caretaker. This speculation is supported by the work of the Robertsons in 1974 (referred to earlier) in which it was found that children placed in optimal foster care situations suffered far less from the devastating effects of separation.

From the age of approximately one year, then, young children can experience feelings associated with loss. This reaction is made up of longing for the lost loved one (E. Furman, 1974), protesting the loss of the loved one (Bowlby et al., 1952), despair (Aubrey, 1955; Bowlby et al., 1952), and, depending on the child's adaptation to the loss and the provision of adequate substitute parenting, either detachment and deterioration in functioning or reorganization and reattachment.

Obviously, as development progresses, the child's inner resources increase; the young child can experience loss in an increasingly sophisticated fashion the closer she is to adult-like object constancy. Perhaps one of the primary differences in the response to loss in early childhood versus later childhood, adolescence, and adulthood is the ability to independently reorganize. Toddlers and young children do not have this capacity as they cannot mediate their response to loss with cognition or sophisticated defensive functioning. Difficulties in reorganization at this age arise from the child's relative inability to understand the permanence of loss due to her lack of the cognitive capacity to understand the irreversibility of death (Piaget, 1960). Additionally, as a result of the concrete and egocentric nature of the child's cognitive processes in the early years, and as a result of the child's fantasies and associations with death (which are linked to age appropriate developmental or instinctual concerns), difficulties in reorganization following loss may occur. Moreover, as stated previously, the availability (or the lack) of sensitive and supportive substitute caretaking will either ameliorate or exacerbate the effects of loss at this age.

According to Sigmund Freud and traditional psychoanalytic theory, the concerns of the one and a half to two and a half year old are organized around the anal zone. That is to say that the child of this age is concerned with sphincter control, elimination, power, autonomy, and control in general. At this time, the child's favorite word is "NO!" and the parents may find themselves also having to use this word quite frequently! Difficulties arise between the parent and the child as a result of the child's normal developmental conflicts. While the child of this age continues to require the parent's investment and protection, she is endeavoring to separate herself from the parent, to become her own person, and to assume some control over herself. Of particular concern at this time is the parent's desire to toilet train the child and the child's desire not to be toilet trained, but rather to wet and soil when and where she pleases. At this time, the child is caught between the desire to do as the parent wishes in order to maintain his/her love, and to do as she herself wants.

The loss of the primary caretaker at this point in development creates particular difficulties for the child. Given her angry and destructive wishes toward the parent for all the limitations and dictates she feels are being imposed on her (don't touch this, don't go there, etc.) and due to her egocentrism (the world revolves around me and what I need!) and feelings of powerfulness, she may actually feel responsible if her parent dies. Alternatively she may see herself as having been "bad" at times and feel that because she disobeyed her parent, the parent *wanted* to leave her.

Lopez and Kliman (1979) reported on the analysis of Diane, a four-year-old girl whose mother committed suicide when Diane was nineteen months of age. They stated that her analytic material demonstrated a "prominence of magical ideas that somehow she herself had been the cause of her mother's disappearance, and grandiose wishful ideas that she could somehow cause her mother to return" (p. 264).

A variety of other fantasies may also arise at this stage of development related to anal phase concerns. Children of this age commonly believe their parents to be all seeing and all powerful. Following the death of a parent a child of this age may believe in the parent's continued existence (in heaven or elsewhere) and/or they may believe that the parent who has died can continue to observe or watch over them.

If interactions with the parent have been predominantly good up until this time, some theorists believe that the child's internal representation of the parent will also be primarily good, while if the interactions have been predominantly negative there will be more unintegrated, bad internal representations of the parent (Rinsley, 1976). The child's ability to recall an image of the mother as good represents progression in development and defensive functioning and, according to Rinsley (1976), indicates the child's use of repression of the previously envisioned bad mother.

If, during this phase of development, the child experiences the loss of the mother, the implications for the development of later psychopathology are of serious concern. Regression to the use of the split good and bad maternal object representations may occur and indicates a failure of the newly acquired capacity for repression and, according to the large body of recent literature on the subject, may indicate the potential for later development of borderline personality disorder if further ego development does not occur. Extrapsychic factors such as the provision of immediate and satisfactory substitute parenting or the lack thereof may determine whether such a regression occurs. Further research on this question is necessary to validate such a hypothesis.

Case example

In a Modern Love Column in *The New York Times* (July 26, 2020) Kacey Vu Shap recounted the story of his mother's death. He wrote that his mother died when he was two years old while she was giving birth to a brother who also died. At the age of five Kasey could not remember his mother but he talked frequently with his grandmother about her. His grandmother told him stories about his mother and reminded him that his mother wanted him to be like her. He wrote, "I peppered my grandmother with questions about my mother. 'Grandma, you have my eyes, my nose and my cheeks. Do you think my mother also looked like me?'" He could not bring an image of his mother to mind three years after her death—but he hungered to reconstruct her image from the memories his grandmother provided.

Three years of age

Following what has been described as the anal phase and rapprochement subphase of the separation–individuation process are the phases of development which have been called pre-phallic, phallic, and "on the road to object constancy." At this time, during the end of the second and the beginning of the third years of life, the young child is far more differentiated from the parent. The child can do many things independently and can understand quite a bit about the world around her. Mobility is well established and speech is becoming increasingly more sophisticated. The effect of loss of the parent on the two and a half or three year old is thus somewhat more like that on the older child, although still influenced by her relatively egocentric view of the world and her continued dependence on the parent for practical help, guidance, nurturing, love, mirroring, social referencing, reciprocal communication, the regulation of impulses and feelings, and the acquisition of language and information.

Barnes (1964) reported on the analysis of Winnie, a little girl who lost her mother at the age of two and a half. It was noted that this well-developed, highly verbal little girl required a substantial increase in the amount of physical mothering (which she received from her grandmother and housekeeper) following the loss of her mother in order for her to maintain her previous good level of functioning. Due to all the responsibilities heaped upon her, Winnie's grandmother was not able to fully mourn her daughter for several months. And, interestingly, it was also not until about six months after her mother's death that Winnie was able to discuss her feelings about the loss of her mother. Barnes speculated that it was not until her grandmother was able to openly grieve the loss of her daughter that Winnie was able to grieve and discuss her own loss.

This example suggests the need of the child of this age for modeling of appropriate grief as well as open support and encouragement of the grief process. Barnes also noted that Winnie was extremely worried about the possibility of other losses or abandonments in the year following her mother's death. In unsupported mourning at this age, yearning for the lost object may continue indefinitely, and anxiety about the loss of other beloved adults may be intense and ongoing. As reported in the case of Patrick, a three year old child placed at the residential Hampstead Nurseries where Anna Freud presided, it was observed that he would stand by himself repeating a litany of the details of his mother's return as he imagined it—how she would put his coat on him, zip it up, and put on his pixie hat. As the weeks progressed, Patrick's longing for his mother began to undergo repression. He was not as sad as he had been previously. However, Patrick was observed to continue to stand by himself and to move his lips unintelligibly in a ritual whose meaning was lost both to Patrick himself and to new observers (Bowlby, 1961).

Four years of age

At four years old, the child can hold a mental representation of the parent when the parent is not present regardless of his feeling state about them. Object constancy is well established by this time and the child has moved from the dyadic relationship between herself and her mother to a triadic constellation where the father assumes increased importance as a person in and of himself and as competition for the mother's love and attention (in boys) or as the object to be won away from mother (in girls). Similarly, siblings, peers, other close relatives, and adult role models are assuming increasing importance for the child. She is no longer as dependent upon the parent for help in personal care and in navigating the world. The capacities for mobility, self-control, speech, and cognition are important to the child in and of themselves and not only because the parent is invested in them, as previously. It is for these and other reasons that Robert Furman (1964a), Erna Furman (1974), Bowlby (1980), and others believed that at this point the child can begin to mourn in ways very similar to the adult and she can be helped to master loss. As Robert Furman (1968) said, this does not mean that the child will spontaneously mourn after she has suffered a severe loss, but it does mean that she *can* mourn if she is given the proper support and a milieu in which she will be realistically assured of the fulfillment of age appropriate needs.

The five- and six-year-old

At ages five and six, the child is a lively participant in the world. She has relationships outside of the home, attends school, is actively learning and acquiring new skills and capacities. However, she is still reliant on the parent for love, nurturance, support, reassurance, guidance, and role modeling. If the parent is lost at this age, the child experiences intense sadness, longing, anger, and a multiplicity of other feelings. She is affected in a profound way which reverberates throughout her inner world for months and years following the loss. At this age, the child has generally had some experience of death and is capable of understanding, to some extent, what it means for a parent to die. Although her understanding of death is incomplete, with helpful explanations from adults, the five and six year old can understand that mommy or daddy is not coming back.

The intense feelings which occur at this age have to do with missing the parents themselves, missing their love, and missing all the many functions the parent provided in terms of caretaking including helping to manage emotions, helping to understand the world and the people in it, and making the child feel important and safe.

Case example

In the same *New York Times* column referred to above, Kacey Vu Shap wrote about losing his grandmother after he had already lost his mother. For reasons that were not clear to him, his grandmother left him at an orphanage when he was five years old. He said, "I tried to follow [her] but strong hands gripped me. I screamed for my grandmother, begging her to take me home. After she left, I waited for days at the entrance [of the orphanage], hoping for her return."

Kasey went on to say, "A quarter century has passed since my grandmother left me that day. I still carry her handkerchief safely tucked away with me wherever I go but her scent has since faded. There are so many things that I have wanted to share with her of my American life: my loving parents, friends, dog, and freshly minted PhD. There are also so many questions I have wanted to ask her."

At ages five and six and continuing through middle childhood and adolescence, the investment of the parents, grandparents, and other loving adults is of critical importance to the child's development and sense of self. If a parent dies or leaves when a child is of this age, substitute caretakers and other adults will be needed to provide the child with a sense of being safe, being taken care of, and of being important for who she is. As the example of Kasey illustrated, the child will miss being able to share who she is and what she has accomplished with the lost loved one, and the ability to know, relate to, and receive the love from the lost loved one on an ongoing basis will be grievously missed. At this age, the child will try in various ways to maintain a connection to the lost parent—for example, by valuing a possession of the parent's and by keeping it with her.

Middle childhood

The child of seven through eleven is able to experience grief in all of its manifestations and with appropriate support will be able both to mourn and to understand the full meaning of her loss. Like the younger child, she will miss her parent intensely. But she will have a greater capacity than the younger child to understand the significance and permanence of the loss, to review her memories of the parent and to experience the pain of realizing that the parent no longer exists. The child of this age will also, of course, still need the nurturance and support that the parent provided in order to continue forward development and to maintain a stable sense of self, and she will need careful help and support in the mourning process.

Children of ten and eleven may or may not show their sadness as openly as the younger child, however. They may keep some of their feelings so private that adults close to them may wonder if they are indeed sad. They may attempt to keep up a good face and to proceed with life as if nothing has happened. At this age, children do not want to be different from their friends (who still have both parents) and they often do not want to talk about their difficult feelings. Crying may be hard for them as it can be associated with being a baby, something the ten to eleven year old does *not* want to be.

Normally, the child of this age is actively engaged with school and peers. She has become very interested in life beyond the family. Outside interests such as friends, sports or clubs, musical instrument practice, video games, social media or activities on the computer or cell phone will often consume much of her time. However, this does not mean that she does not need the love and presence of the parents to help her to feel safe, secure, and motivated to achieve. The loss of a parent at this age is devastating to the child and any diminution of demonstrated feeling can not be taken as indicating that she is any less sad or any less affected than the younger child.

Adolescence

The adolescent has the intrapsychic capacity to mourn much as an adult does. However, there is a crucial distinction between the teenager who loses a parent and an adult who loses a close loved one: the adolescent still has a developmental need for the parent.

The adolescent may experience all of the feelings associated with loss and mourning and she may also be able to accept that the parent is gone to the same extent that an adult is able to—that is, variably. However, the adolescent is still in the process of developing and continues to need the love, care, guidance, and identificatory models of both parents in order to move into young adulthood in the healthiest way possible.

For the teen who loses a parent, certain dilemmas will arise. The adolescent will want to know who will care for her in the ways that the lost parent did. She will ask these questions, whether out loud or in her own mind: Who will love me? Who will do the things my parent did for me? Is there anyone who can or do I need to do these things for myself? Who will provide a model for what it is to be an adult?

The teenager will never say so, but she may want to know who will help her to learn about her own body, to learn about navigating relationships with friends and/or potential partners, and who will reassure her when she is unsure of herself, when her confidence dips, and when she questions the meaning and purpose of life.

The adolescent who loses a parent or who has lost a parent earlier in development has an absence where there ought to be a presence. And this absence will generally have an indelible effect on the teen and her future development. She may attempt to fill that void herself through a sort of pseudo-independence, she may seek others to depend on, or she may suffer the pain of loss more directly.

And despite the maturational capacity for mourning, there will be specific difficulties involved in coping with the loss of a parent based on the normal developmental challenges faced in adolescence. The adolescent is in the process of building her identity, answering the existential questions of "Who am I?" and "What is the meaning of my life?" Following the loss of a parent the answers to these questions may change; the discussion will have been enlarged.

Teenagers who lose a parent are faced with the need to redefine themselves and this may become a crisis of personal identity. Who I was before is no longer who I am now. Who I was when I had my parent has changed. I am now a person without a parent who has experienced a terrible loss. And who does that make me?

Bereavement for teenagers must be understood in this context. If the loss is experienced as a major source of vulnerability and insecurity the teen, who may have previously felt powerful and secure, may feel quite differently—less sure of herself, more in need of help. And a teen who was previously quite dependent and who reacts to the loss by stepping up to take on new responsibilities following the loss may suddenly feel more powerful and more competent. The teen's identity may shift and change. Susillo (2005) quoted a seventeen year old who said of her mother, "We were so close; she loved me unconditionally. I felt like I lost half of myself when my mother died." This young woman had to rebuild and transform her sense of self without the external presence of her mother. She had to find a way to deal internally with the loss of someone who she saw as being a part of herself and someone who was also an important source of love, care, emotional attunement, daily interaction, stability, role modeling, and reassurance. She had to find ways to obtain these resources—whether through internalization of these functions, precocious development of the self, acquisition of new relationships, or through redoubled reliance on previous relationships.

One strategy for survival following the loss of the parent sometimes employed by teenagers is finding a love interest. This may be adaptive or it may be a defensive activity used to ward off the affects of sadness and grief—or it may be both. It is not uncommon for young women who lose a father to develop a precocious interest in dating or a pronounced interest in boys where there was little prior to the father's death. Similarly, in young teenaged men who lose their mothers, it is not unusual to see an interest in finding a teenaged partner to serve as nurturer and provider of love, attention, and affirmation.

Experiencing the death of a parent in adolescence can come as a particular shock given that this phase of development is often characterized by a felt sense of invulnerability. The adolescent typically struggles with deep feelings of insecurity—the feelings of being incompetent and unimportant—which then lead to self-conscious feelings, embarrassment, and the fear of rejection. As a reaction, the adolescent may reverse these feelings and develop a defensive stance of invincibility. Risky behaviors such as smoking, drinking alcohol, trying psychoactive substances, and experimenting with fast driving, sexual activities, or perilous physical feats are common. The adolescent plays with her vulnerability and invulnerability and she finds it hard to believe that she herself could ever die.

When a loved one dies, however, death suddenly becomes real to the teenager. And it can be an extremely violent realization. The defensive bubble of invulnerability is burst and this can prove challenging for the adolescent and her existing sense of self. Not only does she need to come to terms with the reality of death but she is also face to face with the knowledge that she too will someday die—something that she previously knew intellectually but kept at bay through the attitudes of invulnerability and invincibility.

Unfortunately this process stands at odds with the normal separation-individuation process of adolescence (Blos, 1966). The teenager is developmentally at the stage where she must begin to separate her identity from that of her parents and to become more of her own self. She is experimenting with independence and autonomy. In order to do this, the presence of a stable relationship with both parents is optimal. In other words, the parents have to be there in order to be left. And they have to be there so that the teen can also return to them after leaving—whether the leave taking is actual or metaphorical—whether it is through physical or emotional distancing. With the death of a parent comes the risk that the teen will be tempted to regress into a position of greater dependence on the surviving parent and/or on friends, teachers, etc. or will attempt to become precociously independent. With the death of a parent, smooth negotiation of the normal separation–individuation process of adolescence can be challenged.

Additionally, some adolescents' individuation process is harder than others. For some there can be a more embattled pushing away of the parents. When a parent dies during this process, the adolescent is deprived of an opportunity to finish the stormy aspect of the process and then to reconcile with that parent. In such cases, the teen may remain angry with the parent without resolution or she may feel angry with herself for the way in which she treated or felt about the parent and she may blame and punish herself as a result. Future conflicts around self assertion and separation may result and these may complicate both the mourning process and the course of future development (Susillo, 2005, pp. 144–145).

In fact, all the processes which were in train at the point at which the parent died may be interrupted. Whether the teenager was in the middle of an identificatory process with the parent, whether she was learning to negotiate opposite sex relationships via the relationship with the parent, etc., the abrupt loss of the opportunity to fully work through these processes will have consequences for the teenager's development.

Additionally, the loss of a parent can represent a way that the teenager feels different from her peers. This can be a source of feelings of shame, inferiority, or deprivation. She may compare her friends' experiences and life situations with her own and feel envious of those friends who still have two parents (Susillo, 2005).

Moreover, the teenager's relationship with reality must change once she is confronted with death. The reality of permanent separation and the possibility of loss may become part of her expectation in each and every current and future relationship.

Case example

Caroline was a twenty-eight-year-old student of social work who embarked on an analysis as part of her training. She spoke at length in her treatment about her father's death. He had been a successful and charismatic businessman when he died suddenly. Caroline, who was sixteen at the time, was shocked by her father's death but continued to function well socially at school and at home. She remembered having felt intensely alone and unprotected after his death. Just after her father's death she was unable to talk about him, but over the weeks and months following his loss she began to talk to a selected few friends about him and about his death and to write some poetry about her loss. She helped her mother to manage and, in a way, became her mother's "partner." Her older siblings had moved out of the house but she and her mother enjoyed a companionable relationship through the end of high school. Caroline, unlike her two brothers and sister who had not dated at all in high school, began dating a few months after her father's death. During high school she had several boyfriends, all older than her and all bright, responsible guys. She had sex with these boyfriends and became the "expert" among her friends regarding relationships, birth control, etc. During her analysis Caroline began to understand the deep loss she felt after her father had died and the ways that she tried to find boyfriends to fill in for him by providing her with a sense of being less alone and more protected in her life. She realized that she had circumvented some of her sadness by engaging in an exciting series of relationships. At the same time she also realized that she had gained a new identity as the "one who knows about boys" among her friends, an identity which made her feel competent and strong which was preferable to her than feeling weak and bereaved.

Determinants of the child's reactions to and difficulties with mourning

What is required of a person to adapt to the loss of a loved one?

As Adrienne Harris said, mourning "is deep psychic work, entailing a thought process utterly dependent on [the] emotional capacities [of the individual] and on [the] surrounding community and family" (p. 145). Those children with greater emotional resources will find it easier to embark on the mourning process and those children with fewer internal resources and less external support will find it more difficult to adapt to loss. In other words, the child's reactions to and difficulties with accomplishing the tasks of mourning will result either from intrapsychic or extrapsychic determinants or some combination of each.

Among the intrapsychic factors which affect the way in which the child deals with loss are: the child's character structure and defensive functioning, preexisting feelings about the deceased parent, preexisting constitutional factors, the interaction between developmental conflicts and the loss, and the stage of development at which the loss occurs.

Defensive functioning

While the development of defensive functioning has not been clearly delineated in the literature, I will attempt to present a description of the progression of the use of defenses by the bereaved child.

The purpose of defensive functioning, in general, is to ward off feelings perceived by the individual as being overwhelming. And the loss of the primary caretaker at any point in life and especially in childhood is, by its nature, indeed an overwhelming event. In order to protect the self from the full brunt of this trauma, defenses are employed when possible. The manner in which each bereaved child responds to the loss of her parent will depend upon the strength of her ego, the relative development of her defensive functioning at the time of the loss, and her characteristic way of operating intrapsychically.

Birth to one

In the young infants who developed anaclitic depression, hospitalism, and marasmus as described by Spitz (1965) and referred to earlier, it can be understood that defensive functioning was so primitive as to be insufficient to provide any sort of adequate protection from loss. For these infants, the feelings of discomfort and dysregulation, and in slightly older infants, sadness, desperation, and rage associated with loss and abandonment were experienced directly and devastatingly. Without external support, that is, nurturing and loving care, to ameliorate their severity, the destructive influence of these powerful feelings was felt in full force by these infants and, as a result, the outcome was dire. The effect on any infant whose primary caretaker is lost and who is not provided with an adequate substitute, or any infant placed in institutional or foster care which is neglectful and understimulating, can be expected to be similar.

For those infants who experience the loss of a parent but who are provided with adequate substitute parenting and good environmental stimulation, the outcome is likely to be less dire. While defensive functioning is negligible at this age (as stated above) the caretaker who steps in for the lost parent can provide the necessary soothing and nurturing functions to protect the infant from the worst of her suffering.

One to two

By the end of the first year of life, the infant can begin to consciously experience the feelings associated with loss as well as the bodily manifestations of dysregulation. Sadness, yearning, bodily discomfort, irritability, difficulties with homeostatic regulation including sleep and eating can all be experienced following the loss of a parent, particularly if the parent was the primary caretaker. Certainly by a year to a year and a half, the child will search for the absent parent, yearn for them and feel sad when their absence is recognized. At this age, it may be assumed that increased ego development including the progression of cognition and memory may account for the child's increased ability to experience various well-distinguished feelings. At this point, the modulation of these feelings continues to be mostly dependent upon external controls (e.g. adult soothing), although primitive defensive measures are in the process of development. At this age a child can be distracted from her pain or sadness and she can also purposely avoid reminders of the lost parent. Children of this age can be seen to turn their head away when shown a picture or a video of someone they prefer not to think about or with whom they are angry.

According to Altschul (1968), avoidance is the earliest and the primary mechanism for dealing with unpleasant feelings or ideas in the first two years of life. For example, the young child of two may attempt to avoid the subject of mommy in her absence. She may throw a picture of mommy when it is presented to her or to say "No" when someone tries to talk to her about mommy. She may attempt to cling to the parent or caretaker who is available rather than thinking about the one who is not. Other early defenses to protect against the overwhelming sadness or the recognition that a beloved parent is gone include altering one-self, activity, and flight. An example of the use of such defenses can be seen in very young children who become overactive following the loss of a parent, attempting to interest themselves in other things and other activities at a mad pace in order to distract themselves from their own primitive thoughts, memories, sadness, and recognition of the absence of the parent.

In young children, especially those under three, avoidance and denial may not be sufficient to circumvent the breakthrough of anxiety regarding the parent's absence following the death of a parent. Without the previous level of care and stability and without sufficient narcissistic investment in the child by two loving parents, the young child may demonstrate her distress at these losses through regression, which in such cases is being used defensively. The most recently attained functions such as toilet training, new vocabulary, or new motor skills may be temporarily lost.

Three to four

As the child enters the third year of life, the defensive repertoire continues to be limited. The defenses available at this point include avoidance, withdrawal, activity, denial, regression, and repression, and these are the mechanisms available for dealing with the painful feelings associated with loss.

In younger children, the use of avoidance and denial may be seen in the rapidity with which they seek to find another adult to call "mommy" or "daddy." Frequently grandmother or other female substitute caretakers will be called "mommy" shortly after the loss of the mother. The father may even be called "mommy" on occasion. Even in older children, who would not normally call the new caretaker by this name, slips are often made, indicating the wish for the reinstatement of the mother and the attempt at a denial of her loss.

Melanie Klein (1940) noted that in situations of loss the ego develops methods of defense which are directed against pining for the lost love object. It has been shown repeatedly that young children (i.e. those who are able to consciously perceive the absence of the parent) will initially avoid or, in a primitive sense, deny the loss. The degree to which this denial of the parent's death is utilized will determine the progression of the mourning process. However, the use of defensive mechanisms is neither healthy nor unhealthy—it is merely the way in which the person attempts to protect herself from experiencing too many painful or anxiety provoking feelings at once. As Klein (1940) stated, it is the extent to which such defenses are utilized that determine whether they are components of either a healthy or a pathological mourning process.

It is only with adult support and guidance that the very young child can begin to verbalize and discuss her concerns about her loss and about death in general without retreating into overuse of defensive activity. And it is only through an empathic and understanding observation of bereaved children's activities following loss that the status of the child's reaction to her loss can be correctly understood.

Four to eleven

Later in childhood the defenses of repression, denial, projection, and in some cases, intellectualization become predominant. For example, a nine-year-old boy named Lee was seen in treatment because he did not show overt signs of sadness following his father's death. He spent his sessions in a whirlwind of activity, challenging the therapist to endless games of basketball and soccer. Lee was in a state of unconscious denial. He was engaging in all the active games he could, both in and out of his therapist's office, in an attempt to protect himself from his sad and lonely feelings—although he did so without consciously realizing his own motivation. As far as he was concerned, he just wanted to play as much and as often as he could. It could be said that he was using activity as a defense, and this would be true, but at this age it is likely that some degree of repression and denial were also at work. And it can also be said that this degree of repression and denial were necessary for Lee. He did not feel capable of recognizing his terrible loss and dealing with all the feelings that would erupt if he did. However, when the therapist recognized that soccer and basketball were two of the games that he had played with his father, and with gentle interpretations of these activities—and with help from his understanding mother—in between games of soccer and basketball he gradually became more able to talk about his sadness and his missing feelings.

Counter dependence or a pseudo independence may also be adopted by children from around eight and up following the loss of a parent. In her study Koblenz (2016) noted that some of the children said that they felt they could no longer depend on others after the death of their parent and instead began to depend on themselves. The children in the study were quoted as saying that they were "strong" and "could handle it alone" but Koblenz felt that this demonstrated the children's difficulty conveying their vulnerability. In the event that there was no one available to help them, the children felt that it was best to try to go it alone, the risks of feeling or showing vulnerability or need being worse than attempting to take on a new task or responsibility themselves. In this way, these children repressed and denied their real feelings of helplessness in order to protect themselves from the possibility of further disappointment should they express the feeling and be met with no offers of help. Their defensive strategy was one of changing themselves into people who did not feel the need for help from others.

In these older children and in brighter children, the higher order defense of intellectualization may also be seen. These children will use their good intellects to try to understand what happened to their parent as a way of coping with their loss. This defense can be adaptive as in the case described below or it can be maladaptive if used to avoid feelings.

Kaufman and Kaufman (2005) cited the case of a young boy who experienced the illness and death of his grandfather. Initially the grandfather had a stroke and was hospitalized. Subsequently he had a dissected thoracic aortic aneurysm and was intubated. At this juncture, the grandson desired to learn what had occurred medically and the parents utilized the mayoclinic.com website to review aneurysms with the child. The boy appeared relieved to understand the illness process and it made it possible for him to understand that his grandfather would die soon. After the grandfather died, the grandson asked to speak at the funeral. When giving the eulogy, the grandson spoke eloquently. At the graveside, he requested and shoveled earth onto the coffin of his grandfather. Clearly intellectualization helped this boy to understand his grandfather's illness and to prepare for and respond to his death.

In children at the top of this age bracket, the loss of the parent may also be experienced as overwhelming. Even at this age children may suffer regression following the death of a parent with difficulties being seen in the areas of sleep, eating, night-time bladder control, investment in cognition and learning, and peer relationships. School performance may deteriorate, as may friendships.

Individual defenses explained

Denial

Denial of the actual loss and denial of certain feelings related to loss is a normal part of mourning for people of all ages, especially just following the loss. In fact, Bowlby (1980) named the first phase of his model of mourning, "Denial" as mentioned previously. Generally the shock of death is so great that the ego of the child or the adult launches a quick retreat into denial in order to protect itself. Denying that the loss has occurred protects the mourner from the devastating feelings which may arise.

Total denial of the loss generally lasts for just the first few hours or days following the loss. And individuals who continue in total denial of a loss or who deny the significance of the loss beyond the initial days and weeks may be considered to be experiencing a disordered variant of the mourning process. In this case, denial subsumes the progression of mourning.

However, it is normal for children under four or five years of age, and often for children of this age and older, to have difficulty tolerating the fact that a parent has died and tolerating the feelings associated with this loss. In fact, it has been reported in individuals of all ages that the sadness, anger, and other feelings associated with the loss may be so painful as to make the acknowledgment of the loss difficult or impossible without further defensive measures or additional support and guidance. Freud (1900a) described the mechanisms by which the ego makes a split between reality recognition of the loss and defensive denial of the loss. He quoted a bright ten-year-old boy who said, "I know father's dead, but what I can't understand is why he doesn't come for supper" (p. 254).

Traditionally, this split has been seen as being characteristic of both the first phase of mourning in adults and the difficulty which children have with mourning in general. As Krueger (1983) said, "Without the cognitive development to comprehend the abstract concept of death as final and irreversible, it is conceptualized by the child as a reversible departure ... It is a common fantasy of the child who loses a parent to expect a return; waiting for the reunion is at first consciously and later unconsciously experienced" (p. 584). Similarly, Parkes (1970) made mention in his study of adult women who were widows the prevalence of the fantasy that the husband continued to live. Despite cognitive realization of the death, many widows maintained an unconscious or preconscious fantasy regarding their husbands.

In one case, a policeman mistakenly came to the door of a woman who had been widowed six months previously to tell her that her husband had been in a car accident and had been hospitalized. In the moment before realizing that the policeman was at the wrong house, this woman reported having thought that she was right all along and that her husband had not died after all. This makes clear that magical thinking (or the continuation of denial) occurs not only in young children, but in older children and adults including those who would not be considered to be experiencing a pathological course of mourning. While this idea is not in agreement with much of the psychoanalytic literature on grief, recent research has indicated that continuing denial under the mechanism originally described by Freud is not only characteristic of young children, but of individuals of *all* ages.

Such denial can also occur at moments of vulnerability in a person's life. For example, a normally well functioning woman in her late fifties who was diagnosed with an invasive abdominal tumor asked what her husband thought of this diagnosis. In fact, he had died a decade earlier, but in her moment of need the woman lapsed into a wishful fantasy that her husband was still alive and could advise her on her situation—and she wondered aloud to her daughter about what he thought.

Again, it is the extent to which denial occurs and the degree to which the further course of mourning and adaptation is affected which determine whether the use of this defense is adaptive or pathological.

Regression

At all ages, regression may be seen via the use of more primitive defenses than the child had previously utilized. The narcissistic injury suffered by the child at the loss of the parent may be so overwhelming as to provoke a regression in defensive functioning and behavior. The use of denial, idealization, identification, and/or narcissistic rage directed toward the self may occur to the exclusion of higher order defenses (Palumbo, 1981).

For example, Winnie, the child reported on by Barnes (1964), became withdrawn and regressed following the death of her mother until the grandmother and housekeeper were advised to increase their physical "mothering" of her and to attempt to keep to the mother's routines in so far as possible. When they did so, Winnie brightened noticeably and regained the lost functions.

Regression may be understood to occur as a result of the narcissistic injury suffered by the child or as the child's attempt to return to a time when the much longed-for loved one was still there. Regression may also represent the child's inability to maintain a newly acquired function without the parent's encouragement and investment. It may also be a manifestation of the anxiety being experienced by the child while having to continue to live and to function without the parent.

Idealization

In regard to idealization, children may remember the parent as having been perfect and may devalue their own worth. They may also feel incapable of or uninterested in doing the activities of daily life without the parent, they may blame themselves for the parent's death and/or they may think of themselves as bad, stupid, helpless, or incompetent.

Identification

In children of three and older, it is not unusual to see evidence of the use of defenses such as identification and introjection. By four or five years of age, these defenses assume an importance in the accomplishment of mourning not unlike the importance which they hold for adults. Freud (1917e) hypothesized that withdrawal of energy from the lost loved one is commonly accomplished by identification with the loved one. In *The Ego and the Id* he stated, "It may be that identification is the sole condition under which the id can give up its object" (1923b, p. 11). In other words, the person, in this case, the child, may take on characteristics or behaviors of the lost parent as a way of becoming like them and therefore keeping the lost parent with her forever. Instead of missing the lost parent, she *becomes* the lost parent or takes within herself a part of the lost parent. For example, the child may suddenly decide that she likes the same foods that mommy or daddy ate or she may adopt a similar style of talking or word use. Sometimes the child takes up a hobby or an interest that the parent enjoyed. The adolescent girl mentioned in the case example described previously adopted some of the roles her father had played in the household, mowing the lawn, for example. She also went around locking the doors at night as he had. In these instances, a particular role or talent of the parent's can be used in the service of progression and growth (E. Furman, 1974).

It appears, according to Erna Furman (1974), that in children the use of identification is largely dependent upon the child's general pattern of ego functioning and mental health. As she said of the children in her study, "It appeared that the bereaved person's capacity for integration and adaptation helped him to a certain extent to 'choose' to maintain those identifications which fitted smoothly into his functioning and to give up those which were ego alien" (p. 262).

On the other hand, there are times when identification with the dead parent can take on a pathological aspect and represent an arrest in development and/or in the mourning process itself. Frequently children are observed to identify with an element of the parent's last illness and to develop related somatic symptoms themselves. One adolescent girl developed headaches after her mother's death from a malignant brain tumor and went so far as to have a complete neurological workup identical to the one her mother had prior to her diagnosis. This somatization and medical help seeking was a substitute for actively feeling the sadness and yearning for her mother which the girl might have felt had she been capable of experiencing these feelings directly.

Children may also identify with a particular aspect of the parent's personality after the parent's death. For example, a child who was previously even-tempered might take on the irritability shown by the parent during his or her illness. Or, as another example, one adolescent girl enjoyed spending her money on cosmetics and clothes prior to her very frugal father's death. Following his death, this teenager began to save her money; she looked for bargains and complained when her mother asked her to use her own money to buy clothing and other expensive items. She identified with the frugal habits of her father and took them in—perhaps in a trial identification—or perhaps in an identification that would be long-standing.

One determinant of the type of identification chosen, according to Erna Furman, is the degree of ambivalence which the child had toward the parent previous to death. She stated, "Ambivalence in some cases led to identification based on idealization and in others to self-punitive or self-damaging identification" (1974, p. 65). For example, one child might identify with her parent's work ethic and become a more hard-working student than she was previous to the parent's death, while another might identify with a lost parent's critical nature and never feel that she is working hard enough. In all cases of childhood bereavement, Furman believed that identification is present in some form and as such comprises a necessary part of the mourning process, irrespective of its use or outcome.

Themes of loss and mourning in play

A great deal has been written about children's tendency to ward off painful feelings, that is, to defend against the experiencing of loss and its attendant sadness, or to experience such feelings only in short bursts (as in Wolfenstein's "short sadness span"). More often than not, however, as was previously mentioned, children do indeed demonstrate their feelings or the derivatives of these feelings and concerns through play or other activities. As was mentioned, games act as vehicles for mastering loss, other activities may be chosen in identification with the lost parent, and acting out may serve as a means for bringing on punishment in children who feel guilty regarding the part they feel that they may have played in causing the parent's death.

At least one motivator in the historical insistence regarding children's inability to maintain painful affects is the adult's desire for the child not to do so. Often, when a child goes out to play following news of the death of her parent (or other significant person in her life), or when she does not speak of the loss, this is interpreted by the adults present as denial, avoidance, or adaptation to the loss. In many cases, the adults make this sort of interpretation for their *own* protection. As Kliman (1968) noted, children are often used as proxies for adults' denial, that is, the adults' wish to deny their own painful feelings and the adults' wish to deny that a child they love is in pain. Often, surviving relatives truncate their own mourning, ostensibly for the children's sake. It must be supposed that it is actually quite difficult for the adults involved to experience the loss themselves and that they may welcome a rationale for not doing so. As Becker and Margolin (1967) observed, "The insulation of the young child is a displacement of components of the surviving parent's own conflicts about issues of mourning" (p. 756).

As Jean Piaget said, play is the work of childhood. As a result, it is to play that we must look for the child's attempt to understand and master loss. And we can look at the specific play activities of the child to understand whether they are defensive, expressive of concerns about the loss, or means of mastering the loss. Terr (1988) reported that children as young as three enact trauma in play through motoric behavior, somatic responses, and symbolic representation. She said that when a child has been traumatized (as is often the case for young children in the event of parental death), the traumatic nature of the play is easily recognized. She stated that such play is distinguishable from normal play in that it is compulsively driven and presents reenactments of the trauma. However, evidence exists that traumatic play can be seen in children even younger than three. Barnes (1964) described Winnie, a two-and-a-half-year-old girl, playing activities such as "London Bridge Is Falling Down." Barnes described this as a reenactment of Winnie's mother's death and as an attempt to master an understanding of death. Through falling down and lying still as the song and the game dictated, Winnie was attempting to actively experience and understand her dead mother's situation. By getting up and continuing to play, she was experiencing herself as a still-living person.

Robert Furman (1968) stated that "There is nothing in [the] dynamic concept of mourning that says how the unfolding of the internal mental process should appear externally to any observer of the mourner's behavior" (p. 55). What is often identified as denial, that is, the child's rapid return to so-called normal activities such as play, cannot necessarily be considered as such. While Wolfenstein (1966) wrote that the child's desire to return to her regular routine was an indication of a "short sadness span" (p. 101) there is clear evidence that many if not most grieving children over the age of two and a half to three can tolerate their sad and missing feelings long enough to express them and begin to process them through play and other activities. As Barnes (1964), Robert Furman (1964b), Erna Furman (1974), and others have beautifully illustrated in their case reports of bereaved children, play activities, dreams, and disturbances in previously conflict-free areas actually demonstrate the child's ongoing concern about the loss of the parent. Play may include themes of disappearance and reappearance (such as in the games of hide-and-seek or peek-a-boo); it may take the form of medical play (playing doctor to sick or dying animals or people), super-hero play (saving those in danger), search and rescue play, or any of a myriad of other imaginative scenarios. And while the child may look happy and carefree to the casual observer, play in these cases is often being used as a way to master difficult events and feelings and to show what is on the child's mind.

Constitutional and interpersonal contributions to mourning: invulnerability and resilience

Other factors that affect the way in which a child responds to the loss of her parent are those that are internal to the child. For example, the child's constitutional makeup will be an important determinant of her adaptation to loss. The child who is constitutionally strong, less reactive in general, or, using E. J. Anthony's (1973) term, "invulnerable," is more likely to withstand even significantly negative events without develop-ing serious psychopathology, especially when provided with adequate environmental support.

The concepts of invulnerability, resilience, or "grit" constitute a rel-atively new area of investigation which bear further exploration. One way that the invulnerable child has been described is as follows: the child is robust, has a good health record and better than average energy resources, smooth vegetative functioning, a trusting and confident rela-tionship with a parent preoccupied with her needs, has adapted flexibly to change, and has developed mastery and coping skills which put her on the offensive with life. This sort of child feels genuinely competent (Anthony, 1973).

Anthony (1973) said, "The 'invulnerable syndrome' is associated with the coexistence of high risk with low vulnerability. One is surprised at the absence of disorder in the presence of appalling living condi-tions, horrifying experience, chronic physical ailments and disruptive development. In the presence of all this emerges an individual who is energetic, well balanced and normally active and reactive" (p. 539). The child who copes well following a loss or, as aforementioned, uses the loss as a progressive force in development may be able to do so at least in part due to possessing the constitutional factors discussed by Anthony.

In cases such as that of Hank described by Erna Furman (1974) below, it can be seen that an "invulnerable" or constitutionally sound child may use defensive processes such as identification in the service of forward development and a productive mourning process:

> Hank was four and a half years old at the time of his father's sudden death. The father had been a keen amateur actor and singer. By the time Hank was six, he had developed a persistent interest in the theater. He organized many shows successfully within the family and with friends. Singing became a favorite activity for him as it had been for his father. Hank maintained these hobbies in later years. They brought him personal enjoyment and appreciation from adults and peers. (p. 66)

As Anthony noted, exposure to stressful events is not the whole story; vulnerability and mastery also play integral roles in the response to stress. The child who is more vulnerable due to constitutional makeup, temperament, sensitivity, character, illness, learning differences, or disability of any sort may be more vulnerable to being overwhelmed by the loss of a parent and more at risk for the consequent development of a pathological mourning process or other difficulties in adaptation following the loss.

Extrapsychic factors affecting the child's response to loss

It is only recently that researchers and theorists have taken a serious look at the importance of the child's external environment at the time of the loss of a parent. When it was assumed that the child's ego was too weak to undertake the work of mourning, stressors attendant to the loss were not taken into consideration as contributing factors in the child's inability to engage in the mourning process as the child was already considered unable to mourn. We now realize that various factors occurring simultaneously with the death of a parent are often almost as important as the death itself.

Many changes often coincide with the loss of a parent. As a result of the surviving parent's financial and/or emotional circumstances, there may be either fewer or more plentiful changes in the home situation. Not infrequently the surviving parent has to change living circumstances including moving to a less expensive home or apartment or taking on a job due to financial hardship. In so doing, the child loses her home and familiar surroundings, compounding the loss of her parent.

In addition to changes in financial and/or living circumstances, the surviving parent may also be suffering emotionally due to the loss of the spouse and this may cause disruptions in the routines of the family. The surviving parent may be sad, lonely, lack energy, become depressed, and may be relatively less attentive to the child. They may start a new romantic relationship or marry precipitously because they cannot bear to continue to feel helpless or alone. Children respond to such changes as further traumatic losses. In many cases what is perceived by the adult as less stressful is experienced by the child as more so. As Erna Furman (1974) noted, while objectively avoidable, these difficulties result from the conflict between the children's and the adult's emotional needs following the death.

Furman also noted that of the children she observed who experienced the loss of their mother, those who were best able to experience the feelings of loss and to undertake the task of mourning were those who felt personally safe and able to rely on remaining relationships. Minimal changes in daily routine and care by the surviving parent or a regular substitute caretaker such as a grandparent and/or a familiar housekeeper, nanny, or babysitter help bereaved children feel secure.

Case example

Kelsey was eleven when her mother died as a result of a cerebral aneurism. A day after her mother's death, Kelsey's father fired their long-time housekeeper and babysitter. Kelsey's grief exploded when she saw the housekeeper leave the house and Kelsey chased her down the street crying and begging her not to go.

The importance of the prior relationship with the parent who died and with the surviving parent

The child's previous relationship with the parent who died is also important to her adaptation to the loss. Hilgard and Newman (1959), in their research on parent loss, found that the degree of trauma in parentally bereaved children was partially dependent upon the relationships within the home prior to the death. Children who did not experience a good relationships with the parent who died, who are ambivalent or anxiously attached, insecure or extremely self-sufficient may experience difficulties in the mourning process. It may also be hypothesized that reattachment to a subsequent caretaker is also more difficult under these conditions. To the extent that the child was already angry with the parent, the adaptation to the parent's loss will be more problematic due to the unresolved nature of the anger and the consequent guilt which may be suffered by the child. As Erna Furman said, "While ambivalence is a part of all relationships, those children who had particularly conflictual relationships with their mothers prior to death, suffered interferences in the mourning process" (1974, p. 112). Bowlby (1980) concurred with this formulation when he stated that conditions favorable to healthy mourning include a secure relationship with the parents prior to the loss. In those children who trust and are close to the surviving parent and other adults such as aunts, uncles, grandparents, coaches, and teachers, adaptation is facilitated. Those children who do not have such positive relationships will be more at risk.

But even the most loving and well-connected surviving parent is in a particularly difficult position, having to cope with her own devastating loss while simultaneously trying to care for a grieving child. As Furman (1974) said, "It is a paradox that the very person who is deeply afflicted himself, namely, the surviving parent, is, from the child's point of view, best suited to help him grasp and handle the traumatic event" (p. 17).

Circumstances of the death

The circumstances of the death of the parent are also extremely important in influencing the child's reaction. Both prolonged illness and sudden death present particular difficulties for the child.

The terminally ill parent

When a parent is terminally ill, a variety of factors will affect the child's response to the illness and the eventual death of the parent. The age of the child during the illness, the way in which the parent viewed their own illness, the way in which the child was told about the illness, the frequency with which the child had contact with the parent, and the amount of physical deterioration and suffering which the child witnessed all affect her response to the death.

Generally, young children (eleven and below) idealize their parents; they are proud of their parents' skills and knowledge, they look up to their parents, and they often imagine that the parents know how to do everything. Such a view of the parents allows the child to feel safe and protected. Should a parent become ill and debilitated, the natural idealization of the parent is interfered with. This is very troubling to the child and gets in the way of her developmentally appropriate wish to see the parent as capable and powerful.

At the same time, even the youngest of children will often be quite empathic with the parent's illness and suffering. Children have all experienced what it is like to be sick and when they see the parent in bed or on the couch feeling unwell, they will also suffer, attuned as they are to the parent's feelings. Children may try to care for the parent or to do various things to help the parent feel better. As the parent becomes more ill the child may feel quite frustrated, helpless, and guilty that she cannot relieve the parent's suffering.

The experience of having a gravely ill parent at home also presents an enormous challenge for children. Their home is transformed from a familiar, comforting place to a quasi hospital with strangers such as nurses and social workers coming and going. Often the ill parent looks more and more ill and becomes increasingly helpless while the well parent is increasingly preoccupied with the ill parent's care. For these children the experience of being able to stay close to the parent during their final illness may be comforting or it may be frightening or it may evoke a combination of these powerful feelings. In this situation children need a well parent or other adult to explain to them what is happening at every step of the way and to guide them as to how best to interact with the ill parent.

Older children including teenagers will also be disturbed by a parent's illness and deterioration—but in a different way than the younger child. Teens are in the process of separating from their parents. They are often at odds with the parents as they explore and discover their own opinions and values. When a parent is ill, it is more difficult for the teen to freely disagree or to disidentify with the parent. The teen may feel guilty for feeling angry with the parent and obliged, instead, to be kind and caring. At the same time, the teenager may wish to escape the sick room, to be out with friends, and to have a life outside the one at home where illness is center stage.

Children and teens whose parents are hospitalized and who visit the hospital as their parent receives treatment may experience the hospital itself as frightening, the medical equipment as scary, and the look of their parent in bed as unfamiliar and disturbing. These children and teens desperately need an adult to help them to understand what is happening. They need adults to talk with about their impressions and feelings—even when they deny this need.

Sudden death

Children who lose a parent suddenly will also suffer in specific ways. As M. Harris (1995) said, the sudden death of a parent is jarring and terrifying; it shatters the child's sense of safety and security. If life was previously seen as being predictable by the child, it is no longer so. Sadly, as Harris notes, an event of such significant magnitude can change a child's core beliefs about life.

Moreover, children whose parents die suddenly may have a particularly hard time keeping denial at bay. They may ask themselves, "Is this really real?" They may want to see the parent's body or to be reminded of the events which led up to the parent's death. Often they will remember for the rest of their lives the exact moment they found out that their parent died, how they felt, and what exactly happened.

The way in which the death occurred, whether or not the child was witness to the death or was involved in the situation in which the death occurred (e.g. automobile accident, fire, natural disaster, etc.), and the degree to which the child felt responsible either for causing the event or failing to rescue the parent will strongly affect the child's reaction to sudden loss.

Suicide

The suicide of a parent is a devastating and life altering event for a child. The idea that a parent could kill him- or herself on purpose is just too horrifying. Particularly for children who witness the suicide or who find the parent after the suicide, the shock can be enormous and paralyzing. In such cases, the implications for the child are particularly serious.

Death by suicide is a special case in which the death is felt by the survivors to have been unnecessary and the tendency to apportion blame is enormously increased (Bowlby, 1980). The child whose parent committed suicide will wonder why the parent did so and may develop the fantasy that she was at fault. She may imagine that the parent killed himself because of something she did or did not do. She may feel that she displeased the parent in a way that made him so angry that he killed himself—or she may feel that she was not good enough to give the parent a reason to live. Children with parents who are mentally ill and who are aware of the parent's illness may also feel that they did not help the parent enough to prevent the suicide. And unfortunately there may sometimes be evidence for these ideas; the parent who suicided may have actually been angry with the child prior to the suicide, and/or the surviving parent or other relatives may blame the child.

The child whose parent committed suicide may wonder whether the parent loved her. She may reason that if the parent did love her then he would not have abandoned her—and therefore he must not have loved her. This is an extremely troubling thought and one which can lead to feelings of being permanently unloveable or unworthy of love. The child who feels this way may be prone to attempts to distance herself from her memories of the lost parent and she may also be vulnerable to reexperiencing anger and guilt when memories do surface (Wood et al., 2012). Moreover, future efforts at attachment may be fraught with fears of abandonment.

Children of parents who commit suicide are particularly likely to be misinformed about the circumstances of the death or enjoined to silence due to the family's shame and embarrassment. The family may want to keep the fact of the suicide a secret from the general public due to their fear of social stigma.

Also, as Bowlby (1980) noted, children of parents who commit suicide may be viewed and treated as though they inherited the mental illness from which the parent suffered and thus it may be felt—either by the family or by the children themselves—that they are doomed to follow a similar fate.

Moreover, the child whose parent died by suicide will likely experience a host of mixed feelings regarding the lost parent. Ambivalence may be particularly high given the tendency for children to feel that a parent who committed suicide deliberately deserted them. Other conditions may also predispose the child to ambivalence toward the parent. The situation in the home may have been characterized by inadequate care of the children due to the parent's preexisting depression or disturbance; there may have been marital strife, psychological or physical abuse, and/or there may have been previous suicidal gestures or attempts—all of which may have led the child to feel some combination of fear, dislike, hatred, or anger alongside her feelings of love for the parent even before the suicide.

For all of the reasons cited above, the child who has experienced the suicide of a parent is particularly at risk—for experiencing difficulties in the grieving process, for developing psychopathology, for future difficulties in interpersonal relationships, and for making a suicide attempt herself at some time in the future. As Cerel and Roberts (2005) found in their study, those children who had experienced a suicide death by a family member were 2.5 times more likely than control participants to report suicidal ideation, 6.5 times more likely to have a history of their own suicide attempt in the past year, and 3.1 times more likely to report inflicting serious injuries on others. These findings can be understood in part by the bereaved child's identification with the parent who committed suicide and by her internalization of some of the negative characteristics and behaviors of the parent.

In his analysis of an adult patient, Bisagni (2012) helped his patient to reconstruct his memories of his father's suicide when he was nine:

> Who knows why but all of a sudden I heard the sound of the river. The water flowing and dad telling me to mind the current: "Careful Fabrizio, be careful. Hold on tightly to the paddle. Slowly Fabrizio. OK, that's it. Don't be afraid. Don't be afraid. Don't be afraid." Why does dad always tell me not to be afraid? What was there to be afraid of? Boys don't get afraid, almost never. What is there to be afraid of? ... It was practically by chance that I went

into the small room behind his office with these words in my head. In an instant the blue of my eyes became filled with the shape of dad who was hanging from the ceiling. A rope around his neck, a rope that left a blue mark on that crooked neck. I would never have guessed a neck could have bent like that, making your eyes swollen and almost open, bloodshot. ... And his skin, why wasn't it tanned the way it had been this morning? It looked white. No ... yellow. No ... white. I thought I knew the colors. Dad had taught me the colors when I was little. But I'd never seen these. I thought I knew all the colors. ... I don't remember how I made my way home. I can't remember if I ran, or if my feet were dragging slowly and heavily. The way they do in dreams sometimes, when you want to run but your feet won't move and they feel as if they're as heavy as stones, and you're really afraid because someone who means harm is following you. Yes ... that's it! When you're afraid ... sometimes it happens that you're afraid in dreams, so dad was right. Who knows, maybe what is happening now, dad hanging from a rope with a crooked neck ... maybe it's a dream too ... I can only remember that lots of tears were falling from my eyes and I couldn't close them. The only thing I remember is that it took ages to get home. Silence. I had no thoughts or words. (p. 26)

Communication with the bereaved child about the death

The way in which the child is told about the death of a parent is of great importance in determining the adaptation which she is to achieve. The development of particular fantasies may be contributed to by the wording used to describe death in general, and the parent's death in particular. While this will be discussed at greater length in a subsequent chapter, suffice to say for the present discussion that the young child who is told that the parent has "gone to sleep," "gone to God," or "gone to heaven" is more prone to confusion regarding the death than the child who is given a more concrete explanation. Vague explanations such as those mentioned suggest a continued existence of the parent and the child may hope that reuniting with the parent is possible. These explanations may also lead to the conclusion that heaven is a desirable place to go and, in some children, the hope of a reunion in heaven can lead to wishes for death. Furthermore, the idea that someone who has died has "gone to sleep" can be extremely frightening to a child who is expected to go to sleep each night, and anxiety around sleep and sleep difficulties may ensue.

The child who is given a clearer, more matter-of-fact, or biological explanation of the death will be in a better position to come to a reality-based understanding of what has happened. The younger the child, the more necessary the provision of concrete details regarding death. Allowance for any questions or concerns she has regarding her parent's death is also crucial. The timing of the explanation is important. Frequently, children are not told for days or weeks about the death due to the surviving parent's feeling that telling the children will be too difficult both for her and for the children. The appropriate management of these issues will be discussed in the following chapters.

The funeral

Another factor which may affect the child's adaptation to loss is the extent to which the child is allowed to participate in the family grieving process. As will be discussed later, there is great concurrence in the literature regarding the importance of the child's attendance at the funeral or memorial service. It is the feeling of most authors on the subject and clinicians who treat bereaved children that with preparation and an adult available to explain the proceedings to the child and/or to take the child out if she wants to leave, participation in these events can be of great use. When children attend a funeral, a wake, a shiva, or other memorial event they can see that they are not alone in their sadness and grief; they become a part of the ritual of saying goodbye; they can become more aware of the spiritual aspects of death and mourning and they can feel part of a community of mourners.

Decathexis/detachment from the lost loved one

The bulk of the psychoanalytic literature on childhood bereavement might agree with much of what has been stated so far, that is, that young children can experience the feelings associated with loss when defensive functioning does not interfere with such experience. What has been discussed but not dealt with fully so far, however, is the point of view of Deutsch (1937), Wolfenstein (1966), and others that young children can *not* accomplish the sine qua non of mourning, decathexis. These theorists believed that children prior to adolescence cannot perform the intrapsychic tasks necessary for successful separation from the lost loved one in order to allow them to be available for the establishment of new, satisfying, and stable relationships.

Whether or not young children can detach themselves from lost loved ones through the painful and prolonged process of remembering and reality testing was debated for years, as shown in the review of the literature provided above. Much was written to demonstrate the difficulties experienced by adults who were bereaved as children. Psychopathology, difficulty maintaining relationships, and experiencing various feeling states were linked with early loss. However, in describing mourning, Freud himself stated that mourning processes in all people are opposed from within. He said, "It is a matter of general observation that people never willingly abandon a libidinal position, not even, indeed, when a substitute is already beckoning to them" (1917e, p. 154). Just so in children. Defenses are utilized to deny and avoid the loss and sometimes to preserve the idea that the loved one has not died. It is for precisely this reason that, as previously stated, the ego of an available adult is necessary to aid the child's reality testing and to remind her that the loved one is truly gone as well as to support her expressions of grief.

With such help, children *can* grieve. The process of acknowledging the loss can occur as can the work to reconstruct the loved one within through the internalization of aspects of that lost loved one.

But the questions remain, to what extent is decathexis from the lost loved one necessary in order to reattach to new loved ones, and *is* decathexis truly the sine qua non of a successful mourning process?

Many researchers in the mid- and late twentieth century took a more optimistic view than the early psychoanalytic writers. Robert Furman was one of the earliest of these. The case of a six-year-old boy who Furman (1964b) saw in analysis provided the source for his divergence from mainstream opinion on this matter. He wrote:

> To my surprise this neurotic little boy was able to accept the
> painful reality of the loss of his mother and was able to respond

affectively to the loss. In addition, he proceeded in a recurrent sorrowful remembering and missing of his mother in what seemed like every situation in which he ordinarily would have been aware of her presence. This process I felt differed in no essential way from the mourning of adults. (p. 52)

The degree to which children must decathect (disconnect) from the lost loved one in order for mourning to be accomplished will be discussed at greater length below.

New theoretical constructions of mourning

Not only have more recent researchers, such as Robert Furman (1964b), Erna Furman (1974), and Bowlby (1980), shown that children from the age of four to five *can* mourn with support, but those studying grief and mourning in the twenty-first century have suggested that decathexis is *not* necessarily the goal of mourning. In recent years the theory has changed radically and what constitutes healthy mourning has been redefined.

Over and over it has been demonstrated that in healthy mourning mourners of all ages maintain some kind of relationship or connection rather than completely detaching themselves from the lost loved one. Moreover, in recent years, transformation of the mourner through internalization of aspects of the lost loved one has been heavily emphasized as one of the goals of the mourning process. Additionally, the importance of relational and interpersonal support for the bereaved child has begun to be considered crucial for the accomplishment of mourning.

Does anyone truly detach from a lost loved one?

It was formerly held that it was necessary to detach (decathect) from a lost loved one for mourning to be complete and for attachment to new loved ones to occur. However, recent developments in research and theory now demonstrate that many people, regardless of age, do not entirely detach. They hold on to the idea that a loved one who has died still exists in one form or another—whether in heaven, as a spirit which makes occasional visits, as an ephemeral companion who can be talked to when needed, or as an internalized aggregate of characteristics, values, and interests of the lost loved one. As mentioned previously, widows studied by several different researchers reported talking to their dead husbands, and/or never fully believed that their husbands were gone. Children studied have been shown to hold on to parental possessions, values, dictates, and actual (internalized) voices.

At the same time as they maintain connection with lost spouses, many widows and widowers do remarry and many children who have lost a parent do accept a stepparent or grandparent as a substitute parent quite fully. So which is it? Do people who have suffered the grievous loss of an intimate partner or parent need to disconnect from the lost loved one in order to reconnect to a new intimate other or if they hold on to the lost loved one do they therefore have difficulty reconnecting?

The task of mourning is to free the ego for uninhibited functioning. While it is clear that children can be helped toward relatively uninhibited functioning, further work must be done to explore to what extent the connection to the lost loved one can still be maintained and at the same time allow for ongoing development, functioning, and reconnection.

Recent studies show that in children, the use of identification and internalization and/or the maintenance of feelings and memories are not in conflict with continued successful development. In fact, in his later work, Bowlby (1980) concluded that a continuing sense of the deceased individual's presence in the bereaved child or adult's inner world can be found in many healthy individuals. He felt that observations about pathological mourning made by early writers including Deutsch, Fleming and Altshul, Jacobsen, Wolfenstein, and others (referred to earlier) were inappropriately generalized and incorrectly applied to theory regarding healthy grief and mourning (Baker, 2001). And, as stated previously, even Sigmund Freud said that he was unsure as to whether anyone ever totally gave up their connection/cathexis to lost loved ones.

Baker (2001) said that it is necessary to reevaluate the role of decathexis in mourning and to consider redefining the successful outcome of mourning. Perhaps a successful outcome of mourning can be described more accurately as involving the transformation of the connection to the beloved person who has died into a sustaining internal presence which operates as an ongoing component in the individual's inner world.

Most bereaved children embark on the work of mourning and many, especially those who are well supported in their mourning, will successfully mourn a lost loved one to the extent that they are then able to reconnect to new loved ones. For these children, no arrest in development will be incurred (R. Furman, 1968) and difficulty in accepting substitute parenting will not be severe. These children will find a way to maintain their connection to the lost parent while also being capable of attaching to new loved ones to receive the love and care they need.

Recathexis/reconnection

The ability to replace the lost loved one with someone new is, as Pollock (1961) stated, not part of the mourning process per se, but an indicator of its degree of resolution. In children, the ability to attach to a new nurturing adult following the loss of a parent is critical in terms of the ongoing development of the child.

As Pollock said, object replacement depends upon the instinctual needs of the mourner, the degree of energy liberation or replenishment resulting from the mourning process, and the maturity of the superego. In children, the instinctual needs for the nurturance and investment of a parent are high. The degree of energy available for the reestablishment of a relationship, however, may depend on the course of the grief process.

In humans, the response to a child who has lost a parent is fairly universal. We experience the desire to pay special attention to the child and to protect her from the pain of loss. This natural outpouring of additional attention is crucial for the child. However, this outpouring of support is often temporary and, as life resumes its normal rhythm, the child remains in need of both consistent, ongoing support and parenting and an internal solution to the mourning process. To receive what she needs and to accomplish the internal tasks necessary it is important for the child to be able to make use of new relationships.

It was once thought that if only the child could "complete the tasks of mourning" she could then be available to connect to a new loved one. However, as stated above, since the 1980s this theoretical construct has been challenged. It has become outmoded to suggest that there is "completion" to the mourning process. More contemporary theorists believe that the individual who has suffered grievous loss must go through a lengthy process over time. She must find ways to redefine herself in the context of the loss, reconnect with this new self, and transform the "self–other" relationship which she previously had with the living loved one into an internal self–other relationship with an internalized object. This is what Gaines (1997) called "creating continuity" between the old self who had the loved one and the new self who does not. The child—or adult—is transformed by the loss and by her internal reconstruction. She preserves aspects of the lost loved one within her own personality through internalization as well as within herself in a continuing self-object relationship with the lost loved one.

One way to measure the extent to which a child has accomplished the creation of continuity is to look at her reaction when a substitute care-taker is offered. If the caretaker is appropriately warm and loving, and able to adhere to the customary routines and rituals of the family, the child who is progressing well will gradually come to accept the care offered and begin to develop feelings for the new caretaker. Of course this may be preceded by a period of anger and sadness. A new caretaker will be a reminder that the parent is gone and painful feelings will often ensue for a period of several weeks or months. If, after six months to a year, the child continues to demonstrate disturbance in her ability to connect to a new caretaker, shows signs of extreme anger or clinginess, or if the child seems to be incapable of a stable, ongoing reattachment, this must be seen as evidence of difficulty and indicates the need for professional intervention.

Other signs of a disordered mourning process include a child's inability to experience the feelings associated with her loss. In such cases the child may not be able to effectively defend herself from being over-whelmed by her loss, she may not be able to sustain a nourishing sense of the presence of the lost parent, or she may not be able to internalize aspects of the lost parent sufficient to maintain a stabilizing continued object relationship with that parent. In these cases, pathological variants of the mourning process are present. A variety of disturbances can be identified and these will be described below.

Pathological mourning in children

Deutsch (1937), Bowlby (1961, 1980), and others discussed pathological mourning. Their descriptions may be used to highlight the symptoms and signs to look for in evaluating the bereaved child.

Deutsch described pathological mourning as being characterized by:

- An omission of reactive responses to death
- Replacement of the usual responses with persisting ambivalence regarding the lost loved one
- Severe anxiety.

Bowlby described pathological mourning as characterized by:

- An unconscious effort to recover the lost object
- Unconscious longing for the lost object
- Pathological self-reproach and self blame.

For healthy mourning to take place, Bowlby stated that it is necessary for the bereaved child to experience and express anger at the lost loved one. He said that when yearning and reproach are not openly expressed these feelings may persist. Circumstances (whether internal or external to the child) which inhibit the expression of the feelings of anger, sadness, yearning, and reproach create the situation in which pathological mourning can occur.

In pathological mourning the conditions which are present according to Bowlby are:

1. Repressed yearning with persistent unconscious desire to recover the lost object
2. Repressed reproaches against the lost object with persistent unconscious anger and conscious reproaches directed toward various objects including the self
3. Caretaking for others as a means of receiving care through the mechanism of projective identification
4. Prolonged denial that the object is permanently lost.

Pathological self-reproach can be the consequence if the child has no one against whom she can permit herself to be angry. She therefore turns her anger against herself. This anger turned inward is likely to result in depression, self-harm, and/or feelings of being responsible for the parent's death. Indeed, self-reproach was Freud's pathognomonic sign for melancholia or chronic depression.

When the child can permit herself to feel reproach against others, this may take the form of anger at the surviving parent or other relatives, anger at the doctors who were caring for the parent who died, anger at God, or, when in treatment, anger at the therapist or analyst. Others may be blamed for causing the death of the parent or for doing too little to prevent it. Bowlby understood this continuation of anger through the lens of attachment theory. As was discussed earlier in the literature review, Bowlby viewed crying and anger as behaviors designed to bring the love object into proximity and to discourage her from leaving again. By continuing to feel angry at the lost parent, the bereaved child is demonstrating her unconscious belief that she can convince the lost parent to return.

The bereaved child may start to take care of others in a new or more intense way as a substitute for real mourning. She may try to take care of siblings, the surviving parent, other children, or pets rather than express her own vulnerability. Without activation of a healthy mourning process, children may then engage in compulsive caregiving throughout their lives. This activity may take on an adaptive form—for example, in the pursuit of a career in medicine, psychology, social work, etc., and/or it may occur to a point of personal depletion. Caregiving performed due to the unconscious wish to receive care for oneself through projective identification often results in the persistent feelings of never truly being loved or taken care of.

As for persistent denial, this may be seen as in derivative form. The child may have recurring dreams, fantasies, or play activities which can be understood as relating to the lost parent; she may memorialize large numbers of objects belonging to the lost parent; she may have frequent periods during which she talks to the parent or to a picture of the parent, and/or she may have a great deal of magical thinking about the parent's continued protection or observation of her. These signs are not necessarily pathological, however, unless they take up extreme amounts of the child's time or energy or seem to replace other forms of grief and mourning.

In each of these variants of the mourning process, Bowlby observed that the bereaved individual acknowledged the reality of the loss on a conscious level. He stated that the pathology lies in the repression of some or all of the customary responses expected in mourning and the unconscious maintenance of yearning and longing for the parent.

A variety of factors may contribute to the development of pathological mourning in children. Environmental factors, that is, matters external to the child, are one kind of possible interference to the normal mourning process. For example, the child may live in a home where her fears and concerns are unrecognized or not discussed. Another factor which is potentially damaging to the progression of healthy mourning is further loss. When a family moves, thus separating the child from her familiar environment, friends, school, well-known caretakers, etc. the amount of loss may be overwhelming to the child. Similarly, if other family members are lost at the same time as the parent (due to a natural disaster, house fire, or any tragedy with multiple fatalities), or if the child's care is disrupted by the loss of a familiar babysitter or nanny at the same time or shortly after the death of the parent, the normal mourning process may be interfered with due, again, to the double dose of loss.

Other contributing factors to the development of pathological mourning include processes internal to the child's psyche. Overidentification with the dead parent, for example, can predispose the child to pathological mourning. In such cases, the child may fear that she will die too. Identification with the deceased parent is a natural mechanism for maintaining a part of the lost parent; however, the child requires help from the surviving adults to separate her fate from that of the dead parent (E. Furman, 1974). When identification with the parent's last illness and/or the fear of sharing her fate is not experienced on a conscious level, mourning may be considered to be taking a pathological course. In such cases reunion fantasies may also occur. These arise out of a desire to share in death with the parent in order to reunite with the parent. Evidence of suicidality in bereaved children, particularly those who are unhappy with their current home environments, must be looked for and, if found, taken extremely seriously.

Other common manifestations of difficulty in the mourning process which serve as symbolic requests for help by the bereaved child include persisting blame and guilt, aggressivity, antisocial acts such as delinquency in adolescence, over-independence, and somatic complaints (particularly those which mimic symptoms of the lost parent's last illness).

Incomplete mourning

Mourning which has begun but has not continued has been called "incomplete mourning." One sign of this is ongoing denial of the loss, as described by Altschul (1968). He stated that the child may attempt to maintain the self-image that had been attained at the time of the loss and therefore resist the internal changes necessitated by the loss of the parent. Arrest at the level of development achieved by the ego at the time of the loss may occur. In this case intervention is necessary to allow for the continuation of mourning, continuation of development, and the prevention of later psychopathology such as depression or anxiety.

Chethick (1970) suggested further criteria for identifying incomplete mourning:

1. Exaggerated and continued aspects of normal grief such as depression, poor appetite, denial
2. Defense against further loss by resisting involvement in close relationships
3. Inappropriate identification with the dead parent
4. A too rapid attempt to replace the dead parent
5. Memorialization of the dead parent.

Case example

Caroline was nineteen when her mother was diagnosed with an inoperable brain tumor. In order to receive this diagnosis her mother had to endure numerous difficult diagnostic tests including an angiogram in which dye was injected and scans were taken of the brain to locate the tumor. Caroline's mother was treated for six months to no avail and she died at home with Caroline and her father at her bedside. Caroline was initially very sad but after a month left for her second year at college where she socialized with her friends and did well academically for the first semester. Over Christmas vacation, however, Caroline began to experience severe headaches and insisted that she needed to see a neurologist. She was sure that she too had a brain tumor and described symptoms similar to those her mother had experienced. Caroline succeeded in getting the neurologist to order tests including an angiogram—and her belief that she had a tumor did not remit until the results of the tests and scans came back negative. Rather than mourning for her mother Caroline had substituted becoming her mother. She developed the same symptoms as her mother had experienced in her last illness.

Following Caroline's negative test results, her father, a sensitive and psychologically minded man, insisted that she begin psychotherapy. In the course of this therapy Caroline entered a second period of mourning for her mother during which she experienced the sadness and pain which had been interrupted during her first effort at grief.

Maturational grief

Johnson and Rosenblatt (1981) distinguished between incomplete grief and maturational grief. They stated that following the initial loss of a parent, the child may reexperience grief at a variety of points in the maturational process. They said that this represents the child's need to reintegrate the loss on successively higher levels and also stated that this does not necessarily indicate the presence of incomplete mourning. They remarked that this differentiation is important for the purpose of deciding whether psychotherapy is necessary. While incomplete grief may need in-depth therapeutic intervention, grief experienced as a result of maturation typically needs only supportive reassurance that such grief is normal and that it occurs frequently for those who have lost a significant person. The child or teen experiencing maturational grief may or may not be conscious of the fact that she is missing her lost loved one. Maturational grief is commonly seen, for example, when bereaved children experience a birthday or graduation. Although the death of the parent may have occurred years in the past, the child feels sad on the day of the event. If consciously experienced, the child recognizes anew that the parent is not there to celebrate and may feel sad, even though the actual event is a happy one. When not consciously experienced, the child may need help from a supportive adult to realize that she is sad because her beloved parent is not present on her big day.

Case example

Katherine was thirteen when her father died of a massive heart attack. She was intensely sad for months following his death but recovered gradually and resumed life as an outgoing, academically talented teen. When it came time to graduate from high school she looked forward to her graduation and to all the festivities surrounding it. On the actual day of graduation, however, she found that she was not hungry for breakfast and she felt down in the dumps. When her mother asked what was going on, Katherine replied that she was thinking about all the pictures that would be taken at graduation and the fact that her father would not be in any of them. High school graduation was one of many milestones that her father did not live to see and as each one occurred, Katherine mourned her father's death again.

Chronic mourning

Chronic mourning is a state of prolonged mourning which lasts beyond the first year after the death. This involves profound feelings of sadness, dejection, loss of self-esteem, and possibly depression. Chronic mourning is characterized by unusually intense and prolonged emotional reactions, in many cases with persistent anger and/or anxiety. This pathological reaction is not the same as the simple persistence of thoughts and feelings about the lost loved one, which is common (Baker, 2001).

Case example

Marie was ten when her father died. She and he had been particularly close. He was a teacher of martial arts and had taught her several forms of martial arts to a point of proficiency for someone of her age. She had just started to compete at the time of her father's death. After he died, Marie refused to do her school work, instead spending every day after school and all day on the weekends at the dojo. There she was observed to cry intermittently while attending classes and practicing. Her desire to practice and compete was more intense than ever and seemed extreme. When Marie's grades dropped, both her mother and the adults at the dojo became increasingly worried about her. A year after her father's death, very little seemed to have changed in Marie's internal state or behavior.

Chronic mourning is characterized by an unusually prolonged and intense emotional reaction to loss. When a child or teen continues to feel very sad, angry, or guilty for over a year, she can be said to be in a state of chronic mourning.

After the first six to eight months of mourning it is natural for a young child to feel sad at times, to think about her lost parent, and to review memories of the parent now and then. It is especially natural to feel very sad on particularly important days (as stated above)—because the parent is not there to celebrate with the child. It is also normal to resist changes being made to the familiar routines or to the environment in which the child lived with the deceased parent. However, ongoing depression, anger, or intense feelings of guilt over the parent's death must be attended to if they persist beyond the first year after the death. Psychotherapeutic consultation is recommended in this situation.

Traumatic bereavement

Children who suffer traumatic bereavement are at far higher risk for developing pathological grief reactions as well as other pathological states such as post-traumatic stress disorder. But before discussing traumatic bereavement, trauma itself must be defined. The original definition of trauma has largely been forgotten. Currently the word is used to describe the effects of almost any difficult event. However, for trauma to have occurred, by definition, the ego and the defenses which protect the ego must have been overwhelmed. In other words, the individual must have either suffered a breakdown in normal defensive functioning due to the severity of her reaction to the event or the individual must have been too immature to have developed sufficient defensive functioning to protect her from affective overwhelm, and as a result, the ego must have been flooded by primitive anxiety.

Freud defined the term saying, "Trauma is the experience of overwhelming affect in response to an event" (1926d). Many years later, the definition has been updated but has changed little. Bessel van der Kolk (2014), a contemporary expert in the area, defines trauma as an event that overwhelms the central nervous system, altering the way we process and recall memories. He says that trauma is not the story of something that happened back then but, rather, the current imprint of that pain, horror, and fear living inside people now. Vivien Dent (2020), a contemporary psychoanalytic thinker, has added an important relational aspect to the experience of trauma in saying that for a child to be deeply traumatized, in addition to the traumatizing event there is usually also an absence of adequate soothing and containment following the event. Dent's comment highlights the importance of several factors which affect the experience of trauma and the recovery from it: the availability of attachment figures following the event, the child's capacity for taking in soothing and reassurance, and the child's attachment history and attachment style prior to the loss.

The experience of trauma is defined by several other factors as well: the magnitude of the threat experienced, the person's developmental level at the time of the event, the person's temperament, the person's history of previous trauma, and the meaning the event has for the person following the event (Coates, 2016).

Furthermore, there are physiological concomitants to trauma. Gilkerson (1998) said that at the highest levels of perceived threat the activation of the hypothalamic-pituitary-adrenal axis, the sympathetic nervous system, and the limbic brain move into a hyper aroused state and the individual's ability to effectively respond breaks down. The events that occur in this state will not be accessible to memory in the usual way and they will not be integrated into the individual's psyche and life narrative (Coates et al., 2003).

Traumatic bereavement occurs when a loss is suffered as a result of terrible circumstances such as suicide, murder, natural disaster, or the like. Children or teens can be traumatized by such a loss and the feelings associated with it. They can also be traumatized vicariously, through exposure to parents who have experienced an event as traumatizing and who are incapable of reflecting on the event sufficiently to process it for themselves.

The results of traumatization are severe. Without help, or without others with whom to share and process their feelings, these children may experience a change in their attitude toward life and a sense that things can never be the same again which may predispose them to a notion of limited future possibility (Coates et al., 2003).

For example, children who lost a parent on 9/11 in the attack on the World Trade Center or who lost a first responder parent, *if* they felt overwhelmed by the enormity of their loss and the circumstances surrounding it, can be said to have been traumatically bereaved. Children who lose a parent during wartime in their own countries or whose homes or schools are beset by violence, natural disasters, mass shootings, or the like and whose ability to respond adaptively is compromised can also be said to have been traumatically bereaved.

Case example

Lawrence was a senior in high school when his father committed suicide in a particularly brutal way. Lawrence's parents were estranged and his father had no close friends or relatives. Lawrence had been the father's sole confidant.

Following the father's death, his landlord called Lawrence's mother to say that someone had to clean up the scene of the suicide in the father's apartment. This job fell to Lawrence. Lawrence's mother was too involved with her own chaotic life to be of help. Lawrence was left alone to confront and deal with the horrific scene.

Subsequently Lawrence continued to live with his mother but he had to care for himself due to his mother's own difficulties. While his high school girlfriend applied to college, Lawrence failed to complete any of his applications. She reminded him over and over, hoping that they might go to the same state school together but Lawrence never followed through. He stayed at home, living with his mother, playing video games for most of the day and working at a part time job far below his level of ability.

Lawrence had been traumatically bereaved and without help or support for his grief and trauma, his forward development was stymied.

Absence of mourning

The absence of mourning occurs when a child or teen does not grieve for the lost parent for six months or more after the parent has died. While it is quite normal for children to be in a state of shock following the death of a parent, it is not common for children to show few signs of overt grief for this length of time. Some children are unable or unwilling to talk about what has happened and/or what they feel, and some children insist on going forward with planned activities despite the parent's death. Younger children, especially, are often observed to play and socialize as if nothing has happened. However, none of these reactions necessarily denotes an absence of mourning if they occur in the first days or weeks after the death and if they are accompanied by an acknowledgment that the parent has died and some signs of sadness.

Often it takes time for a child to understand and to accept that the parent has actually died and is never coming back. And frequently the child's grief reactions are expressed in symbolic form—through displacement (e.g. sadness or anger over other things) or through play activities.

However, if a child has not spoken at any length about her loss *or* if she has not displayed obvious emotions over her loss during and beyond the first six months after the death, there may be an absence of mourning and psychotherapeutic evaluation is indicated.

Case example

Danny was eleven when his father died. When he was thirteen his mother called to schedule an appointment. She was very worried about the fact that Danny had never cried about his father's death and had spoken very little about his father since his death. The therapist who evaluated Danny had the difficult task of determining whether Danny's lack of reaction to his father's death was a developmentally appropriate and expectable response or whether he was suffering from a pathological variant of the mourning process such as an absence of mourning.

In Danny's case, the therapist found that Danny did miss his father. He was able to tell the therapist about his sad feelings and about how hard it was to talk to anyone about them. He said that he had not talked very much about these feelings because he worried that talking to his mother would just make her sadder than she already was and he did not feel his friends would understand if he talked to them. He was also afraid of crying in front of his friends, something that he felt would be extremely embarrassing.

Danny was on the cusp of adolescence, an awkward time when children often feel especially self-conscious. It was difficult for Danny to know how to talk about his sadness and who to talk to about it. However, he was not experiencing an absence of mourning. The therapist found a group for Danny to join which was made up of tweens and teens who had lost a loved one. While quiet in the group, Danny did participate occasionally and he told his mother that it was good to know that he was not the only one who had had the experience of losing a parent.

Delayed mourning

Mourning can be considered delayed when it starts more than six months after the death of the parent.

Case example

Patricia was twelve when her father died in a motorcycle accident. She accepted his death in a fashion that was quite matter of fact. She continued to do very well in school, to help around the house, and to help her mother with her two younger brothers.

This continued for two years until Patricia was fourteen. One day her mother was called by the school to say that Patricia had failed a Latin test and was in the nurse's office crying uncontrollably. When her mother went to pick her up, Patricia could not explain what she was feeling to her mother. It was true that she did not like failing the test—this was, in fact, unheard of for her—but her reaction was obviously not just about the test.

When Patricia was taken to see a psychologist at the local community mental health center she looked sad and downtrodden. She told the therapist that she did not know what was wrong with her. On questioning, Patricia told the therapist that the family had recently moved from the house where they had lived when her father was still alive. She couldn't say much more so the therapist asked if she could draw a picture about her feelings. She drew a "rainbow heart." The picture was of a many-colored heart and featured a large crack down the middle. The therapist asked gently if perhaps Patricia was very sad because she and her family had moved away from the place where she was last able to be with her father and if perhaps the heart that was breaking was hers. She nodded yes. This drawing and Patricia's acknowledgment of its meaning allowed the therapist and her to start to understand her sadness and to talk about all the ways she had kept these feelings inside for so long in order to be a "good" girl and to continue her high level of achievement.

At times mourning can be delayed by a child either for a short time or for a very long time. It is often not obvious that this is occurring as the child may seem to be coping well and continuing on with her life. Often the adults around the child are pleased at how well the child is doing.

However, when a child does not mourn the loss of so significant a relationship as that with a parent, there is a toll to be paid. In the case example cited, Patricia functioned well, presumably in order to maintain her self-esteem and to be able to help her mother to cope with the sudden loss of her husband and all the duties this entailed. However, Patricia's good level of functioning was superficial. Deep feelings and the work of mourning were being kept at bay and were only able to emerge when Patricia's rather brittle ego was overtaxed by the sale of the home she associated with her father. The precipitating factor for the onset of feelings was failing her Latin test but of course her feelings went much beyond this event.

The dead mother complex

André Green described a variant on the mourning process caused by the lack of availability of the surviving parent due to her own mourning or preoccupation with other internal matters. He discussed the danger which is present for a child who was previously well attached to the surviving parent and then loses the emotional connection to that parent due to the parent turning inward and focusing on her own sadness and pain. In such cases, he said, the child strives to reconnect with the surviving parent and when she is not able to do so, identifies with the cold, dead interior of the parent in a way that can result in a lifelong sense of internal deadness and/or narcissistic preoccupation (Green, 1986).

Case example

Leo was three years old when his grandfather died. His mother was devastated by her father's loss and turned inward in her grief for months after the death. She was preoccupied by thoughts and memories of her father as well as feelings of intense sadness. While she was there physically for Leo and his sister, doing all the tasks of running a household, she was not there emotionally in the way that she had been previously. She was distant, not her usual affectionate, fun-loving self. Leo strove to reconnect with his mother, helping her in all the ways he could think of, making few demands on her and trying to be "good." His mother recovered for the most part within the year but unfortunately for Leo, she also became pregnant and gave birth to a new baby at this time and was therefore busy and emotionally involved with the newborn. Leo was a bright and capable child but to survive he developed a way of removing himself from close contact with others in order to protect himself, instead concentrating intensely on his own interests. This way of coping became a part of Leo's character and affected his relationships and his ability to be close to others from there on. As an adult he was quite narcissistically focused, interested in his own ideas and accomplishments to the exclusion of those of the people around him.

Conclusion

In summary, mourning in childhood can be conceptualized as being on a progressive developmental continuum. While the toddler may be able to experience some of the feelings associated with loss such as sadness, longing, and anger, the three-year-old is more able to experience both these affects and some of the mental work of mourning. By four the child is able to experience the affects associated with loss and to accomplish the intrapsychic work of mourning, given appropriate environmental support and guidance. At this age, defensive functioning may include the use of denial, repression, regression, identification, and introjection. The success of the progression of mourning will be dependent upon the degree to which defensive maneuvers are utilized to ward off feelings and on the degree and quality of external support available to aid the child in her mourning process. Preexisting internal factors such as the constitutional strength of the child, the existing ego capacities of the child, the child's temperament and degree of vulnerability or resilience will also affect the ability of the child to mourn. External factors such as the preexisting relationship with the parents, the stability of the home, the manner in which the loss occurred, the way in which and the time at which the child was told of the death, the emotional presence of the surviving parent and/or other supportive adults, and the continued stability of the home and routine will also have significant implications on the progression of the mourning process.

CHAPTER 4

How children understand death

Tia was two and a half when her father died. A bright, verbal child, Tia asked over and over where daddy was. No matter how often her mother told her that daddy had died she kept asking if she could go to see daddy.

* * *

Tom was five when his father died. He came into treatment due to what his mother thought was depression. In his play therapy Tom repeatedly ran a small car up the wall. He would stretch his body to see how high he could get it. When his therapist asked where the car was going, Tom said, "To heaven, to see Daddy."

* * *

Alyssa was eleven when her grandmother died at age eighty. She was sad and missed her grandmother but she was also very curious about why her grandmother had died. She asked over and over again about the specifics of her grandmother's last illness, what the doctors had and had not done, and whose fault it was that her grandmother had died.

Theoretical underpinnings

The child's cognitive understanding of death will affect her ability to comprehend and to mourn the loss of a loved one. And it has long been held that as development progresses, the understanding of death becomes more and more sophisticated and reality based. The following is a summary of psychological thought regarding the young child's understanding of death through the 1960s. The work of Jean Piaget on the development of cognitive processes, as well as the observations of a variety of researchers, are helpful in further understanding the development of theory regarding the child's understanding of death.

Most theorists believed that very young children can not understand that death is permanent. It is not until around age seven that it was thought that children can understand that once someone has died, they cannot return. At this age it was thought that children do not understand that death can happen due to natural forces.

Piaget described the young child prior to the age of two as being in the "sensorimotor period." He believed that during this time, the infant and toddler are egocentric on both a physical and a mental level; up until approximately eighteen months of age the child believes that things cease to exist when she cannot see them. He said that at this time there cannot be said to be any concept of death. The infant and young toddler will notice if a familiar caretaker is not present, they will yearn for her and search for her, and they may be sad if her absence is prolonged, but the child of this age cannot conceptualize a permanent loss, as in the example of Tia, above.

It was thought that sometime between eighteen and twenty-four months of age the infant gives up her egocentrism on a physical level and comes to realize that even when she cannot see a person or object they *do* continue to exist. This new understanding was called "object permanence" by Piaget. At this age the child is also becoming less passive; she has learned that she can effect some change on her environment and she has a primitive understanding of cause and effect. During this time, she is moving from what Piaget called "physical operations" to "mental operations."

By age two, Piaget felt that the child enters a new phase which he called the "preoperational period." At this point Piaget saw the young child as being capable not only of external action but of interior action; that is, of representational thought. At this age, however, the child remains largely egocentric on the mental and emotional level, feeling that everyone thinks just as she does and that all things in her environment relate to her needs. Similarly, she feels that she controls many of the events in the environment and, as a result, she may feel responsible for the events which occur in her life which may not actually be within her control. At this age what is real for the child is viewed as being objectively real. There is little separation between internal and external reality. Moreover, the child cannot put herself in the position of others.

Many researchers (S. Anthony, 1972; Gesell & Ilg, 1946) have stated that up until the age of three children live in the present and have little understanding of time. As such, concepts involving time and finality do not make sense to them. For this reason, and because the permanence of death is not understood, the idea that they may be able to reunite with people who have died, as in the case example of Tom, above, is common.

Piaget (1960) found in his studies on the concept of life that from two until approximately six, the child attributes both life and will to most inanimate objects. Pretend play flourishes during this time with stuffed animals, toy figures, and even rocks and trees having thoughts and feelings. Life is sometimes viewed as being synonymous with any kind of activity or movement.

In his study on children's ideas about death, Koocher (1973) found that children under six explain death in ways which are closely related to their own experience. Ideas and associations to death will be both highly personalized and very concrete. Children in the preoperational period may use fantasy reasoning or magical thinking to explain and understand death. In the case of Jacky, a three year old whose father died by suicide, it was clear that because of his own developmental stage in combination with the confused explanation given him by his grandparents that his father was "up there" (i.e. pointing toward the sky, meaning in heaven), he came to believe that his father lived on the roof of the house or on the moon.

If a parent dies during this stage, the child's reaction to the loss is complicated by her own personalized understanding of death. At this time, she may interpret the death as an absence which she herself caused.

As a result of her sense of magical omnipotence, she may interpret the absence of the parent as a failure of her ability to keep the parent present.

In the case of the preoperational child, the word absence is used rather than death as she does not understand the concept of death including its permanence. In one of the only direct studies done on the subject, Nagy (1948) found that prior to age five death is seen as being reversible and as being a temporary separation, like sleep or a departure. Therefore, someone who is dead may be fantasized as living on—in the cemetery, in heaven, on the moon as in the case of Jacky, or elsewhere. At this age, children believe that something which is dead may become alive again. They do not understand the concept of irreversibility. In children's cartoons and video games this theme is constantly played out with complete credulity on the part of the young audience.

Due to the young child's egocentrism and feelings of omniscience, Rochlin (1967) suggested that she cannot tolerate the limitations imposed by death. Instead, the young child will often deny or negate death by reversing the explanation that has been given to her. Rather than being the end of life, young children (and others) believe that people live on after death. While it may be explained to the child that the dead cease to move and do not carry on such functions as seeing or hearing, young children may instead believe the reverse—that is, that the dead are all-seeing, hear everything one says, and are omnipresent. Instead of giving up the usual attributes of life, "powers that were previously limited are extended without boundaries" (Rochlin, 1967, p. 53). Rochlin explained that "The facts of death, like the facts of life, are to the child heavily embossed with every conscious and unconscious emotion at his disposal" (p. 63) and result in defensive functioning against the overwhelming feelings aroused by the frightening notion of death.

The preoperational period lasts until approximately six to seven years of age and is followed by the stage which Piaget called "concrete operations." It is not until this time that Piaget viewed the child as being able to think logically and to be able to take the perspective of others into account. This has been referred to as the process of "decentering" (Piaget, 1960).

Other researchers have used Piaget's framework as a springboard for looking specifically at the child's conception of death. Palumbo (1981), for example, utilized a cognitive-developmental schema for examining children's understanding of death. From Piaget's stages of intellectual development, Palumbo isolated six cognitive preconditions for the understanding of death.

In order to understand death, Palumbo stated that the child must be able to:

1. Distinguish animate from inanimate
2. Understand transformations, that is, that something that was once animate can become inanimate
3. Understand the principle of irreversibility, that is, that once dead a person or animal cannot become alive again
4. Understand time and the idea that all living beings have a finite life span
5. Understand the concept of infinity and, in contrast, that life is finite
6. Understand causality.

Until far along into mid-childhood, the understanding of causality and the idea that death can occur as the result of natural causes is also not developed. Nagy (1948) stated that while by age nine children have a relatively mature concept of death, they still do not conceptualize themselves as being able to die. They see death as the result of an active cause, that is, they see death as resulting from having been killed. Death is thought of as resulting from strife, from defiance of authority, from retaliation for some wrong-doing, or as the result of hostility directed by one person (or animal) against another. As Koocher (1973) said, at this stage death is seen as being inflicted—whether intentionally or unintentionally.

Piaget believed that it is not until approximately nine years of age that the child begins to understand death in the same way as adults. However, while Piaget stated that the young child's cognitive development does not allow for an adult-like understanding of death, others postulate that experience with death, the stage of psychosexual development achieved, defensive operations, and other factors contribute to determining the child's ability to understand death (E. Furman, 1974).

Some analytically oriented writers (Plank & Plank, 1978) have differed from the thinking of Piaget and others, suggesting that the child can come to an understanding of death following resolution of the

Oedipus conflict. They stated, "As the need to grapple with his death wishes is lessened, the child can use the cooler climate of latency years to look at death more objectively" (p. 615).

Others, such as Gregory Rochlin (1967), have suggested that defensive operations prevent full exposure to the reality of death. He stated,

> Long before the child has discovered death he has acquired some experience with frustration, the failure of fulfillment of many of his wants and some practice at compromise with his demands. Confronted now with this fresh assault on his security, he refines a system of defenses which relieve the burden of the dread of abandonment. This elaborate web of self-protective emotional devices is not only directed toward the grim realities but also against the conflicts which they arouse within himself. (p. 52)

The child's ideas about death are thought by some to be closely linked to her particular stage of development and the psychosexual concerns and instinctual impulses typical of the stage. Rochlin (1967) provided excellent case examples illustrating the ideas of very young children about death. He described a four year old whose grandmother died after having suffered a broken hip. This little girl became very cautious following her grandmother's death, fearing that she would break one of her own bones and die as a result.

Modern theory

Other researchers such as Robert Furman (1964a, 1964b), Erna Furman (1974), Bowlby (1980), Palumbo (1981), and others, however, have taken a radical departure from the previously presented material in their belief that the child's experience with death affects not only the nature of her fantasies, but her level of understanding and her ability to accept the death of a parent, as well.

Erna Furman (1974) stated, "We found repeatedly that a child's ability to understand the death of a parent was helped considerably if he already had a realistic concept of death in its concrete manifestations" (p. 13). She discussed the child's contacts with dead insects and animals as being important for her understanding and mastery of the concept of death. As she said, "Many children have been spared experience with the death of people, both loved ones and strangers. None, however, had escaped encounters with dead birds, squirrels or other animals. These incidents had aroused their curiosity and, at times, their sadism or pity" (p. 13). The initial understanding of death seemed easier to deal with when it was not associated with the loss of a loved person. Easiest for the young child seemed to be the explanation and support for questions regarding death in the context of animals with the understanding later expanded to include people who had died but upon whom the child did not depend.

Furman's opinion regarding the effect of direct experience with death upon children's understanding of death is supported by the work of Bluebond-Langner (1978) with terminally ill children. In examining these children, who ranged from three to nine years of age and knew of their condition, she found that it was clear that they did know that they were dying before death was imminent. She stated:

> The role of experience in developing awareness explains why age and intellectual ability were not related to the speed or complete-ness with which the children passed through the stages [of the acquisition of factual information about death and the likelihood of their own deaths]. Some three and four year olds of average intelligence knew more about their prognosis than some very intelligent nine year olds who were still in their first remission. (p. 169)

The age at which children acquire an understanding of death is not as clear, then, as might have been initially assumed from examination of the findings of Piaget and other earlier theorists and researchers. It seems that experience and other variables may affect the age at which the child reaches a more sophisticated understanding of death.

Bowlby (1980) stated that children's ideas about death are strongly influenced by cultural traditions and criticized Nagy (1948) and other researchers for having failed to recognize this. His contention regarding the effect of culture on children's views of death is supported through-out the literature. It is often stated that adults in North America (and in other developed societies) shield their children from experience with death. Death, just as sex and money are, is a taboo subject which many parents prefer that their children learn about elsewhere or wait to learn about when they are "older." Children are even further shielded from death, due to the fact that many if not most people now die apart from their families, in hospitals or nursing homes. In other societies where death is more visible, where cultural traditions and rituals around death are elaborate and participatory and where attitudes about death differ from ours, children's experience and understanding of death will differ significantly.

Within our own society the findings of Bluebond-Langner (1978) support the notion that most children are protected from knowledge about death, even their own deaths. In her work with dying children, she found that although these children often had knowledge about their own conditions and the inevitability of their death, they did not discuss this. She stated, "The children and those they interacted with were part of a social order that could only be preserved through the practice of mutual pretense" (p. 198).

Erna Furman (1974) suggested that the explanations given to children regarding death and the support provided for the discussion of this matter can affect the way in which the child understands death regardless of her age. She felt that by the age of two, with the aid of adults to help the child understand and integrate her knowledge of death, the child can begin to develop a concrete understanding of death. This position differs radically from that of most of the researchers cited previously and raises an interesting controversy. For example, Selma Fraiberg (1951), in her article, "Enlightenment and Confusion," suggested that regardless of the explanation given to young children about sexuality, they will develop fantasies according to their age and stage of development. Similarly, Piaget found in his research on "The American Question" that it was not possible to speed up cognitive development with detailed explanations of processes typical of the following stage of development. One must wonder, therefore, if indeed it is possible, as Erna Furman (1974) suggested, to circumvent the young child's inability to understand certain concepts (long considered to be acquired developmentally) such as the irreversibility of death or the development of fantasies out of her own stage related concerns.

Robert Furman agreed with his wife but went further. He believed that if a child is given a reality based explanation of death early enough, that is, by age two to three, she will accept this explanation and adopt it. He stated, "If the very young child is taught about death he will accept this education with equanimity, as part of all the information he is busy acquiring about the world around him" (1968, p. 72). Furman thus suggested a possibility that bears further investigation. That is, if a two or three year old is given factual information and support for asking questions about death, she will accept the idea of death as it is presented to her. Will this knowledge modify the development of later fantasies? He believed that it would and that a child can start acquiring a reality comprehension of death from two on. He stated, "When the explanation first comes to him later (at four, five or six), his fantasy life is much livelier and contains many aggressive thoughts that are difficult for him to master" (1968, p. 72).

The Furmans suggested, then, that there is an interaction between experience and developmental stage. They presented the idea that the younger the child, the more extensive the child's experience with non-traumatic death, and the more available the explanations about death, the earlier and the better the child may come to understand death. As Erna Furman stated regarding children she had observed, "Normally developed children above the age of two years could achieve a basic understanding of 'dead' if they had been helped to utilize their daily experiences with this goal in mind" (1974, p. 15). Anna Freud and Dorothy Burlingham, in their experience with children in wartime England, supported this idea: "It can be safely said that all the children who were over two years at the time of the London Blitz realized that the house will fall down when bombed and that people are often killed or get hurt in falling houses" (1943, p. 15f.).

Conclusion

It is obvious that there is a great deal of disparity of opinion in the literature regarding the child's ability to understand death, just as there is regarding the child's ability to mourn. While some researchers posit a specific developmental sequence to the ability to understand death based on cognitive ability or psychosexual development, others have been eager to demonstrate that even the youngest of children can understand death with the help of adult support.

It appears that an integration of these two extremes is necessary. Children's understanding of death may be facilitated by the opportunity for modulated direct experience with death from very early on. Clear factual explanations are also necessary and helpful. At the same time, fantasies regarding death inevitably develop related to the child's stage of development and defensive functioning and may prevail even when faced with adult support and explanation.

Moreover, it cannot be overlooked that cultural attitudes and other experiential factors affect the child's understanding of death. For those children whose parents provide an early education about death and who experience a modulated amount of direct experience with death, an earlier, more realistic understanding may develop. However, at every stage prior to the one at which there is an independent understanding of death, the child must rely on the adult's superior reality testing and ability to separate out fantasy from actual reality in order to maintain a reality based understanding of death.

Part II

Clinical consideration

CHAPTER 5

Treating childhood bereavement

Introduction

Providing psychotherapy or psychoanalysis to a bereaved child is a task requiring deep reservoirs of sensitivity and compassion. Those of us who do this work are inevitably affected by our young patients' feelings. Their devastation can become our own, given the internal reverberations regarding loss which inevitably occur within the therapist when treating bereaved children.

The impact of the child's situation, feelings, and material may at times be facilitative of our understanding and empathic attunement with the child. At other times our own feelings in response to the child may become compromising. The degree of pain or empathy stirred up within us will depend on our own experience with loss and our own defensive makeup. Too great an identification with the child's pain may stall our cognitive processing abilities or may compromise our judgment in regard to appropriate reactions, boundaries, and technique. As Susan Coates noted during her time with children at Ground Zero, working with traumatized and bereaved children can create a situation both within the child and within the therapist of unusual conditions of arousal, vigilance, dissociation, and aliveness.

Making the task of treatment even more difficult, the therapist must not only feel with the child and understand the child's feelings but she must also take into consideration the surviving spouse, siblings, grandparents, and other family members. The child is bereaved but so are the child's family, making it more difficult for them to meet the child's needs for care and understanding.

As John Bowlby (1961) stated, "It is now widely recognized that loss of the mother figure in the period between around six months and three or four or more years is an event of high pathogenic potential" (p. 10). While many studies have been performed to illustrate this point, too little has been written regarding the actual treatment of bereaved children. A few very sensitive clinicians, most notably those in the Cleveland group and those who were at Ground Zero following 9/11, have described successful work with young bereaved children and their families through individual case reports.

Why does treatment help?

In *Macbeth*, Shakespeare wrote, "Give sorrow words; the grief that does not speak knits up the o're wrought heart and bids it break."

More recently another poet and writer, Natasha Tretheway, echoed these same sentiments. Regarding her mother's murder when she was nineteen, she said, "If I had not been able tell the story I ran the risk of being overtaken [by grief]. I had to put my grief in the mouth of language, because it's the only thing that will grieve with me" (Layman, 2020).

In psychotherapy and psychoanalysis the bereaved patient—whether child or adult—is helped to express her feelings about loss and all the upheavals it brings. Whether these feelings are initially expressed using verbal language, the body, or symbolically through play, they are brought to the fore and into the realm of the relational dyad between therapist and patient where they can be understood together. Bringing the experience of and feelings regarding loss into shared consciousness allows meaning to be made of them. As Shakespeare said long ago and as Tretheway said recently, it is unexpressed grief which threatens to overwhelm an individual. The therapist or analyst helps the bereaved child first by facilitating the expression of feelings, then by naming these feelings, and finally by recognizing that these feelings can be talked about, understood, tolerated, and survived.

The therapist's job is to name the child's feelings when the child cannot name them herself, to accept these feelings as important, and then to clarify their meanings with the child. This process allows the child to think more freely about her own sadness, anger, and loss and to struggle actively with the new meanings she and the therapist discover together.

Evaluating the bereaved child

In "Mourning and Melancholia," Freud (1917e) pointed out that in the case of adults, grief and mourning are expectable reactions to loss and do not, in general, require therapeutic intervention. However, given the special circumstances which children encounter in the loss of a parent, it must be questioned whether this statement applies to them.

When there is both adequate ego development and optimal external circumstances, starting at four to five years of age the child can begin to mourn the loss of even an important person in her life. However, given that children often live in less than optimal circumstances and/or have less than adequate internal and external resources for coping with overwhelming experiences, and given that in certain cases pathological variants of the mourning process will develop, outside intervention to help children mourn is often necessary.

While support for children experiencing such a devastating event as the loss of the parent might at one time (or in some societies) have come from extended family, clergy, or other resources, in the United States and other developed nations such a task now often falls to mental health practitioners. It is important, therefore, to discuss how such practitioners may go about evaluating the need for treatment in bereaved children.

The criterion for assessing the need for treatment may, at least in part, be determined by the clinician's theoretical orientation and position on the ability of children to mourn. For those who believe that children cannot mourn, indications for intervention would merely include the patient's status as a child prior to late adolescence who has experienced bereavement.

However, in so far as the position taken in this work is that many children can successfully mourn, starting at age four to five, more specific criteria must be delineated in order to assess the degree of difficulty which the individual child is experiencing or may potentially experience in her attempt to navigate the mourning process.

The bereaved child who presents for evaluation may not exhibit any overt symptomatology. Instead, the child is brought in by the surviving parent because of the parent's worry over how the child is metabolizing her loss. The parent may worry about any of a number of possibilities:

- The adult may fear that the trauma of loss may have imposed too difficult a task of adaptation upon the child
- The adult may see treatment as a preventative measure to head off future difficulties for the child
- The adult may view treatment as a way to alleviate her guilt over her unavailability to the child as a result of her own grief
- The adult may view treatment as a way to alleviate her guilt due to her anger at the child for serving as a reminder of the lost partner or for any real or imagined sense of the child's complicity in the parent's death.

The absence of symptomatology, particularly immediately following the death, may occur as a result of the child's experiencing either the shock or the denial phase of mourning or because the child is embarking on a normal mourning process involving feelings of sadness, yearning, and some self-reproach. The child may have no pathological regression or other symptoms of psychological illness. In this case, it is appropriate to look to the child's history and current life circumstances to provide relevant information regarding the child's adjustment.

A three-pronged evaluation is suggested in the case of any bereaved child:

- First, the child must be evaluated in terms of her current level of functioning as compared to her functioning previous to the loss
- Second, the environment in which the child lives must be examined for evidence of support or the lack thereof

- Third, the surviving parent must be evaluated as to her own need for support and or treatment and her own ability to nurture the child at present.

Additionally, the information necessary for the evaluation of any child must be collected. This includes the developmental, social, medical, and school histories of the child, brief histories of each parent's developmental, school, medical, family, and psychiatric histories, a relational history of the parents' relationship, and a brief history of the extended family.

In addition there are questions which are particularly relevant for the evaluation of the bereaved child. The following should be asked of the surviving or surrogate parent at the time of the initial interview:

1. What was the nature of the home situation prior to the death of the parent?
2. What was the specific nature of the child's relationship to the lost parent?
3. What was the nature of the child's relationship to the surviving parent prior to the loss?
4. What was the child's previous experience with loss including separations and divorce, the death of other family members or friends, the loss or death of pets, etc.?
5. What was the child's previous understanding of death? Had she been curious about the subject?
6. When was the child told about the death of the parent?
7. What, specifically, was the child told? What were the exact words used?
8. How did the child react to the news?
9. Who took care of the child at the time of and just following the death?
10. Did the child attend the funeral or memorial services?
11. Who was with the child at the service?
12. How has the child acted since the death? What has the child asked about the death?
13. Have there been any regressions? Nightmares? Illnesses? Accidents? Toileting problems, eating or sleeping issues?
14. How has the child's school performance been since the death?

15. How have the child's peer relationships been since the death?
16. How has the child responded to subsequent separations from other loved ones?

Premorbid functioning

In the evaluation of the bereaved child, it is important to get a sense of the child's pre-morbid functioning. This is crucial as a basis for comparison in assessing the nature of the child's functioning following bereavement and necessary in order to determine whether arrest, regression, or inhibition has occurred. For example, in the case of a young child who was well adjusted prior to bereavement, who enjoyed popularity with peers, good school performance, and a relatively happy home life, it is not enough that development in general should seem to be progressing following the loss if, for example, there is a marked change in social function compared to what it was prior to the loss. If the child still socializes with other children, for example, this is fine, but the important question to ask is whether contact with peers has decreased or if there seems to be an inhibition in the formation of *new* friendships. This comparison of pre-morbid to post-morbid functioning will make it more clear whether the child has withdrawn significantly—even though compared to peers she may look quite adequate.

The initial interview

The initial interview will include the surviving parent and anyone else who the parent wants to include in the session. Information can be gathered in the context of a relaxed, open-ended interview without the child present. For the richness of information necessary to evaluate the child to emerge, the parent, grandparent, or caretaker must feel free to elaborate, to reminisce, and to experience and express his or her own feelings. If the child is in the room for this initial session, the adult may feel inhibited in expressing the full range of his or her own feelings. It will inevitably be the case that the provision of information regarding the spouse's death will be painful to the adult; however, the opportunity to discuss the loss may actually be helpful in terms of providing an outlet for these feelings. This initial session can also be seen as a way of helping the parent to begin to channel her energies into helping her child.

The second and third portions of the initial evaluation can be conducted simultaneously with the first. This includes an assessment of the child's support system and the status of the surviving parent. In the event that the surviving parent presents, the initial interviews provide an excellent opportunity to take a look at that parent's overall functioning and level of distress. The fashion in which the parent presents herself and the course of her mourning should be closely noted by the clinician as important information (in so far as the parent is a critical aspect of the child's current milieu and support system).

Recommendations

Following the initial interviews with the parent or other adult, a decision must be made: Does the child need treatment, does the surviving parent need treatment, or can the situation be helped most by the provision of parental guidance or treatment by way of the parent without the child coming in?

If the child seems to be in sufficient distress, several play sessions may be recommended. These will serve to provide the opportunity for further observation and evaluation. In these sessions the clinician will pay attention to:

1. The child's overall appearance of wellness vs. distress
2. The child's ability to separate from the surviving parent
3. The child's ability to form a trusting relationship with a new adult (the therapist)
4. The child's willingness or ability to acknowledge the loss of the parent and to discuss it or show feelings about it through art work or play.

Once the necessary information has been gathered during the evaluation, there are a number of ways in which to select out those bereaved children who are in need of treatment. This task is made easier by utilizing specific guidelines or criteria. It is suggested that any evidence of significant regression or inhibition, pathological, delayed, inhibited, or incomplete mourning or developmental arrest or interference be considered necessary and sufficient criteria for determining the need for treatment.

Alternatively, if it is determined prior to seeing the child that the child is not in acute distress and the surviving parent is in need of treatment, then treatment for the parent may be recommended first and may, in and of itself, be helpful to the bereaved child. Similarly, if the surviving parent seems capable of accepting and utilizing parental guidance, this may be recommended and prove sufficient in helping the child. In this case, the child may not need to come in at all—even for the evaluative play sessions.

If either the parent begins treatment or the parent comes in for parental guidance, the clinician can continue to listen to see if the child herself needs to be seen in treatment at any point.

Specific factors requiring intervention for children who have suffered the loss of a parent

Kliman (1968) provided a list of specific factors indicating the need for intervention for children who have lost a parent. He stated that any one of the following makes preventative intervention with the bereaved child desirable:

1. Suicide as a cause of the parent's death
2. Very poor relationship between child and dead parent
3. Very poor relationship between child and surviving parent
4. Dead parent was mentally ill and living with the family the year prior to death
5. Remaining parent is mentally ill
6. Maternal bereavement of a girl less than eight years old or any two of the following:
7. Age of less than four at bereavement
8. Child at one time having had a neurotic or psychotic illness
9. Paternal death during a boy's adolescence
10. Maternal death during the adolescence of a girl especially from childbirth, breast cancer, or cancer of the reproductive organs
11. Severe economic hardship or precipitous geographic move following the death

12. No readily available substitute love object of same sex and appropriate age (as the deceased parent) is available to help care for the child
13. Remaining parent shows signs of pathological mourning
14. Remaining parent has increased physical intimacy with the child to an extent that seems inappropriate to the developmental needs of the child or is more related to the needs of the parent than the child
15. Child over eight years sheds no tears in the first month after the death
16. Child over four does not talk about the dead parent or the fact of the parent's death
17. Child over five refuses to participate in the funeral or religious observation
18. Child had an unusually cheerful mood during the first week after the parent's death
19. Death was abrupt and unexpected
20. Terminal illness lasted more than six months
21. Terminal illness was unusually disfiguring or involved mental deterioration or physical mutilation
22. Family did not explain the illness to the child or deliberately concealed the illness from the child
23. Family delayed informing the child of death when others knew for more than one day.

In suggesting these criteria for treatment, Kliman pointed up many of the potentially problematic circumstances under which a child may suffer bereavement. While these indications stem directly from Kliman's anterospective work with bereaved families, it seems that he stopped short of extrapolating from his data. For example, it would seem that children of either sex might require intervention in the event of a carcinoma of any of the sexual organs of either parent. While it has been shown in Kliman's work that girls often fear growing up and becoming adult women and/or mothers when their mothers have died from breast, uterine, or ovarian cancers, it can be suggested that boys might fear entering into relationships with women, especially sexual relationships, following the loss of their mothers to a disease affecting the organs which are associated with sex and reproduction. Similarly, while the death of the father during the boy's adolescence may be especially problematic, the father also plays an extremely important role for the adolescent girl. Therefore, it might be suggested that the death of the father during adolescence would also point to the need for evaluation for girls. Or, going further, that the death of either parent during the difficult period of adolescence might warrant evaluation.

Case example: Jacky

Evaluation

Jacky was almost three and a half when I saw him for evaluation, eight months after his father's suicide. He presented as an appealing three-year-old boy with brown hair, brown eyes, and a stocky physique. His ready-for-action demeanor alternated with coy shyness in a fashion more reminiscent of a toddler than a three-year-old. He was brought into the clinic by his maternal grandmother. She was concerned about what she called a speech impediment, as well as excessive drooling, multiple phobias, and sleep and separation difficulties.

Jacky's mother and grandmother were seen together for the first evaluative session to provide information regarding Jacky's developmental history and to discuss their ideas regarding his current difficulties. Mrs. B., Jacky's grandmother, presented as an attractive, outspoken, and well-dressed seventy-year-old woman. Her daughter was a very tall, attractive thirty-year-old woman who came casually dressed in blue jeans and high-heeled boots. Developmental history was taken and an account of the parents' marriage was elicited.

The couple were married when they were each twenty-five years old. At that time, the father worked as a carpenter for a large construction company and the mother worked in an insurance office. After a year of marriage, Jacky's mother became pregnant. Although they had not planned on having a child "so soon" she reported that they were "not unhappy" about the pregnancy.

Jacky was born following an uncomplicated pregnancy. Labor was twenty hours long and the dad aided in the delivery. Jacky remained in the hospital for three weeks after his mother went home due to minor complications. She brought breast milk in bottles to the hospital each day and after discharge he was breastfed for two years and gained weight normally. Regarding early developmental history, the mother was able to report that Jacky was a cuddly but energetic baby who walked at approximately one year and was toilet trained by age two and a half. He spoke his first words shortly after his first birthday and was able to speak in short sentences by age two. He had no significant illnesses except for recurring ear infections. Jacky went "everywhere" with his parents, Mrs. B. explained; he had no set schedule for eating or sleeping from the time that he was born until he moved to his grandparents' home following the father's death.

When Jacky was two years old, his father appeared to lose interest in his work and in the various hobbies which had previously entertained him. He stopped going out with his friends and let his gym membership lapse. Various family members suggested to him that he might be depressed but he refused to discuss the matter. He slept poorly at night and napped frequently when he came home from work and on the weekends. He no longer took pleasure in playing with Jacky and spoke to his wife only in monosyllables. He refused to seek help even when his wife begged him to do so.

On the night of his death, his wife felt worried about him. Although exhausted, she stayed up most of the night trying to talk with him. When she fell asleep he went to the basement of their home and hanged himself.

Jacky's mother was not sure as to Jacky's whereabouts at the time of the discovery of the suicide. She thought that perhaps Jacky was watching cartoons on his tablet as he often did first thing in the morning. She stated that Jacky knew nothing about what was going on. However, at another time, she said that Jacky might have been at the top of the stairs when she went down to the basement to look for her husband.

After she found her husband's body Jacky's mother ran up the stairs to the first floor of the house and called her parents. She then called the police and both arrived at the same time. Jacky saw the police come in but was quickly taken from the house by his grandfather who took him for a ride in the car. Later that day, Jacky was told by his mother and grandparents that his father "had gone to live with God." Later, he was repeatedly told that his father was "up there."

Jacky and his mother immediately moved to her parents' home. All of the furniture from their apartment and most of Jacky's toys were put in storage. Shortly after the suicide, there was a police investigation regarding the death at the request of his family. The death was ruled a suicide with no outside help or complicity from anyone.

At his grandparents' house, Jacky was terrified of the basement and of his bed. Mrs. B. felt that Jacky's father might have taken him to the dark basement despite Jacky's fear of the dark and also that he might have hit him or spoken roughly to him while he was in his bed. Jacky's mother did not share these suspicions, although she did say that she had sometimes been afraid that her husband might have neglected Jacky's needs when she left them alone together during the last months of her husband's life.

One month after his father's death, Jacky became ill with the flu and experienced deterioration in his functioning. He would not go with his mother when she went to do the laundry in the basement and at the same time he did not want his mother to leave him. He clung to his mother when she tried to go to the basement and whenever she attempted to go out.

Evaluative sessions

For the second evaluative session, Jacky's mother was to come in alone to provide more developmental history and to give me a chance to talk with her about her feelings regarding her husband's death and her current life situation. She was late coming home from work, so instead Mr. and Mrs. B. came. They discussed the disruption in their lives which Jacky's father's suicide and their daughter's and Jacky's moving in with them had caused. Having two more people live in the small home they had just purchased for their retirement was a burden to them. They also discussed their concern about Jacky's mother, saying that they felt she was depressed but that they didn't know whether to talk to her about this or not. Mrs. B. said that Jacky's mother had cried for hours in the weeks following her husband's death and that even now she didn't seem interested in dating. Although she acknowledged that it was rather soon for her daughter to be doing this, she also stated that nothing would improve for anyone until she remarried. She mentioned a young man in the neighborhood who loved Jacky and who had come to her, expressing interest in her daughter. Mrs. B. thought that he would be "ideal" for her daughter. The grandparents also reported that Jacky's mother, who had taken a new job as an administrative assistant after her husband's suicide, was keeping long hours at work. Moreover, they felt her drinking was excessive and represented an escape from her feelings.

Mr. B. demonstrated significant insight into Jacky's behavior during this interview. He offered his opinion that Jacky might be afraid of the basement because his father had been found there and that he might have developed an idea that this part of the house had something to do with his father's death.

The third appointment was kept by Jacky's mother. While guarded at first, she eventually began to talk about her current living situation, and her own early history. She said that she had been diagnosed as "learning disabled" and that she had seen a psychiatrist as a child. She described nightmares that she had had when she was younger and reported that she had frequently been beaten for what her father considered to be "bad" behavior and poor grades. She also offered the opinion that Jacky was a "normal little kid" with no more problems than he had ever had. During this session, Jacky's mother admitted to considerable anger at her husband and his family and she discussed her own feelings of guilt over her husband's death. She felt she should have done more for him, that she should have been able to convince him to seek mental health treatment, and that she should have known that he was planning to kill himself. Worst of all for her, she wondered if he would still be alive if she had not fallen asleep that last night.

The information which she provided indicated to me that Jacky's mother might benefit from some psychotherapy for herself. Her anger at her husband and his family and her self-reproach were significant. The recommendation for psychotherapy was made to her but she rejected the idea, saying that she wanted treatment only for Jacky.

How to conduct the initial session with the child

As with any child, the initial sessions are extremely important for establishing the therapeutic relationship and for helping the child to understand what kind of person the therapist is. The first few sessions must be conducive to the child's feeling sufficiently relaxed to talk and play freely, and thereby to demonstrate her concerns. If the child indicates that she feels shy, if she hides from the therapist or demonstrates anxiety about separating from the adult who brought her for the evaluation, the therapist may invite the adult into the playroom with the child. If this involves having the parent or grandparent sit on the couch or on the floor nearby to where the child is playing, then it is best to encourage this. The nature of the child's anxiety about separating from the parent may be addressed at this point by simply stating how hard it is for her to leave daddy/mommy/grandma/grandpa and by the clinician's accepting this for the moment. The information regarding the relative ease or difficulty in separation will be taken as important data regarding the child's overall reaction to the loss as well as her current level of functioning.

The child's ability or willingness to discuss her feelings about the loss are also a valuable source of information. In one case cited by Kliman (1968), a young boy who had been reported by the mother to have not shed one tear over the father's death discussed his feelings at length and cried during the initial evaluative session. When asked about this, the child replied that his mother had not been able to listen to his worries, undoubtedly due to her preoccupation with her own feelings, and therefore he had not tried to talk with her about them.

The child's play will provide perhaps the most valuable source of information regarding the child's feelings.

The initial sessions with Jacky

The fourth appointment with the B. family was Jacky's first appointment with me. Jacky hid shyly behind his mother when I went to introduce myself to him in the waiting room. He was reluctant to come with me without his mother and began to cry as soon as I suggested this. As a result, I invited Jacky to bring his mother with us. On the way to my office, while Jacky continued to be shy, he was amenable to a little discussion with me about what kinds of toys might be available for him to play with in my office.

Once at my office door, when I suggested that mommy wait outside the office for us, Jacky again began to cry. Clearly he was too anxious to separate from his mother so I invited her to sit in my office with us for the first half of the session. During this time, Jacky chose to play with the doll house. He sat near to me on the floor, gradually establishing more eye contact and interacting more with me by asking or answering questions. When he did so, Jacky would look at me with an intense, incorporative gaze which evoked strong feelings in me.

To start, Jacky played with two male dolls both of whom he referred to as "Daddy." When he threw one behind the doll house, I inquired what had happened to the daddy. He replied, "He went up there!" When I asked where that was, he said, "To the moon!" thus revealing his idea of where his own father had gone.

For the second half of the session, Jacky permitted his mother to sit outside the office with the door left open. When it was time to clean up, Jacky wanted nothing to do with this activity, instead spilling even more toys onto the floor. I commented that he really did not want to stop playing with me. However, when it was time to go, he gleefully ran out to his mother, jumped in her arms, and left hugging her tightly.

At the time of the second session with Jacky, he again hid shyly from me in the waiting room and demanded that his mother come down with him to my office. When we got to the door of the office, he enjoyed the game of speculating what might be inside. This time he allowed his mother to sit outside the office from the start, although he did want the door left open so that he could see her whenever he wanted to. At the beginning of the session, Jacky went straight to the doll house and again played with the daddy doll. This time he said that the daddy was on the roof of the house and put him there while the other figures went about their activities inside the house. Then he quickly changed the play, choosing gorilla and Popeye dolls from the toy cabinet. He had them fight, calling the Popeye "Superman." When I commented on how angry they must be to be fighting so fiercely, he dropped them and started to punch the air himself. When I asked him why he was fighting, he replied, "I'm mad—I'm mad at God!" When I suggested that he was mad at God for taking his father away, he said nothing but looked satisfied.

For the third session, Jacky was brought by his grandmother. He did not allow her to sit outside, insisting instead that she stay in the session with us. I mentioned how much Jacky liked to be with grandmom and mommy and how he did not want them to leave him. His grandmother then described how upset he became when his mother had to go to work or leave the house for any reason. I said (to both Jacky and his grandmother), "Jacky must be very worried that when mommy leaves the house she won't come back."

Recommendations for treatment

Following the initial sessions with the surviving parent (or caretaker) and those with the child, another meeting will be scheduled with the adults in order for the therapist to make recommendations.

There are a variety of possibilities in regard to what form the treatment might take:

- The therapist may feel that neither the child nor the family require treatment at this time and will recommend that the family check back in several months to update the therapist about the child's progress
- The therapist may feel she is not sure that the child requires treatment and will recommend an extended evaluation of three to ten play therapy sessions
- The therapist may feel that the child does not require direct treatment but recommend parental guidance once weekly or once every other week
- The therapist may decide that in addition to any one of the possibilities mentioned, the parent themselves requires help and may recommend treatment for the parent
- The therapist may feel that the child requires treatment and recommend once weekly treatment
- The therapist may recommend a more intensive treatment for the child of anywhere from two to five meetings a week (three to five meetings generally indicating a psychoanalysis if the therapist is a psychoanalyst)
- The therapist may also recommend other resources to the family including psychological testing, family therapy, grief groups for children or adults, or a family grief support center.

In the case of Jacky, following the evaluation sessions with Jacky's grandparents and mother, Jacky participated in three play therapy sessions and then feedback was provided to the mother and grandparents. During the feedback session, I presented the results of the evaluation to the B. family. Given that Jacky's mother had rejected the idea of treatment for herself, these recommendations only concerned Jacky. Specific indicators for the need for psychotherapy (as enumerated by Kliman) were present in this case. These included:

1. Jacky's father's death having occurred as a result of suicide
2. The father having suffered from mental illness prior to his death
3. Jacky's age of less than four.

I recommended twice weekly psychotherapy for Jacky. I explained to the family that Jacky's newly acquired separation difficulties, nightmares, and phobias represented evidence of a developmental interference caused by the death of his father. Moreover, I recommended a speech evaluation in order to determine whether Jacky's difficulty with enunciation and drooling were occurring as a result of a regression or were due to an actual speech or articulation disorder. I also helped the family to understand Jacky's current feelings. I elaborated on his sadness and anger and I described his confusion over the whereabouts of his father. This had been made obvious in Jacky's play and describing this play to the family helped them to understand better how to talk to Jacky about his father's death and about death in general.

The family admitted that they had seen evidence of Jacky's confusion about death. They said that Jacky often talked about his father as being "in the big house," meaning the apartment where the family had lived prior to the father's death. They accepted my recommendations, although with some reservations on Jacky's mother's part. She was not convinced of the need for twice weekly psychotherapy, but agreed to give it a try.

Beginning treatment

Once a child has been evaluated and the determination has been made that treatment is necessary due to an actual or potential disturbance in the mourning process, the decision must be made as to what type of treatment will be most helpful. There are many levels at which the clinician may intervene depending both on her assessment of what is necessary for the child and her evaluation of what may be possible for the family to accept. Parental guidance, treatment of the child by way of the parent, psychotherapy for the surviving parent, family therapy or individual psychotherapy, or psychoanalysis for the child are all possible modalities for aiding the bereaved child and family.

Work with the parent

Robert Furman (1968) stated that when the child's reaction to loss is basically adaptive, all efforts of the clinician should be directed toward removal of any external threats. That is, when the child's reaction to loss occurs in the expectable fashion, without signs of pathological grief or developmental interference, intervention should focus on ensuring that the child's needs will be met throughout the period of mourning so that mourning can progress naturally. This often translates into helping the surviving parent and/or other family members so that they can support the bereaved child.

As Barnes (1964) stated, the bereaved child needs adult assistance in allowing a period of mourning. The child also needs help in expressing her thoughts and feelings about her loss. When the bereaved child experiences the normal pain of mourning and transitory effects of the mourning process, the only intervention necessary may be to help the surviving parent to maintain a stable environment for the child in which to experience her feelings.

In this case it is this parent who is most important in determining the outcome of the mourning process for the child. The parent must be able to communicate her own feelings to the child as well as to listen for the child's feelings. However, there are some families in which feelings are not well tolerated and it is felt that demonstrations of love and attachment are best grown out of. In these families, the surviving parent can be helped to understand that it is actually extremely important for the child to be able to express her feelings including her love for the lost parent.

In many cases, even in families where emotional expression is welcome, the child's feelings may be discouraged due to the surviving parent's own painful feelings regarding the loss. The surviving parent may find it hard to tolerate her child's sadness. In this instance, the parent can be encouraged to use the therapist who is conducting the parental guidance as a container for her feelings of pain and to allow the child to demonstrate her unhappiness, anger, confusion, and rage. If it is found that the parent continues to have difficulty tolerating the child's expression of grief or if the parent has trouble maintaining a stable environment for the child, psychotherapy for the parent and/or an extended evaluation of the family situation may be recommended.

Psychotherapy for the parent

Of course it will sometimes be found that the surviving parent is experiencing extreme difficulty adapting to the loss of the spouse. In a study of fourteen bereaved families, Rafael (1977) found that all but one surviving parent experienced a pathological grief reaction. In such cases, the parent can be referred to her own psychotherapy. For example, Clark (1972) presented the case of a twenty-five-year-old, previously well-functioning woman who sought treatment for her two-and-a-half-year-old daughter following the sudden death of her husband. The little girl had begun to suffer from sleep disturbances and a general decrease in affective responsivity, especially in regard to her mother. Following an evaluation in which it was found that the mother felt overworked, cut off from adults her own age, and unable to express her grief, a short-term treatment was initiated for the mother. When the mother was educated as to the needs of her daughter and helped to mourn the loss of her husband, the daughter's difficulties cleared and the mother was more available both to her own daughter and for the initiation of new relationships.

In studies of parents who lost spouses on 9/11, Coates et al. (2003) found that parents often sought treatment for their children and not for themselves even though they were experiencing significant difficulty overcoming the trauma of 9/11 and loss of the spouse.

Parental guidance

In other cases it may be the child who most needs help. For those children who require some added support and guidance in their mourning process, but who do not seem to require psychotherapy, parental guidance may be the treatment of choice. In this case, the parent must be emotionally available and sufficiently energetic in order to enable the treatment to be effective. And this can be helpful to the parent as well—in aiding the child, the parent assumes an important role for herself during a time in which she might otherwise feel quite helpless.

One of the first interventions in parental guidance will be to help the parent to understand that her child neither experiences loss nor understands death in general in the same way as the parent. The adult can be educated as to the limitations of the child's ability to understand death cognitively at her particular developmental level. The parent can then be helped to explain death to the child. Particularly in the time just following the loss, it is of great help for the child to feel that this is a subject which can be discussed. Depending on the child's developmental age, the explanation will differ. For the very young child, the adult will have to stay on a very concrete level. The explanation that all biological processes have stopped, that the deceased parent cannot breathe or eat or talk or walk or ever come back is necessary. The method of burial or cremation will also be important to discuss. Moreover, it may be helpful to say to the child that if the parent could return she would do so, but that people who have died cannot come back, even if they would have wanted to.

The way in which death is explained to the child is important in determining the fantasies that develop. As Arthur and Kemme (1964) stated, the child that is told that "Mommy is in heaven" may believe that the mother continues to exist somewhere (just as Jacky did). Especially in young children, the cognitive inability to understand that death is irreversible is supported by this type of explanation. One six-and-a-half-year-old girl, upon being told that daddy was in heaven, repeatedly asked, "What do they wear in heaven? What do they do there?" and "What do they eat in heaven?" (Becker & Margolin, 1967, p. 755). The parent is often perplexed by such questions and does not know how to answer. Often fear of getting into such dilemmas or fear about the child's ability to handle the information causes the parent to delay informing the child about the death or discussing the death once the child knows about it.

It is important that the clinician help the parent to match the explanation of death with the parent's own belief system (Chethik, 1970). Becker and Margolin (1967) present the case in which a parent did otherwise: "Despite the fact that Mr. D. did not believe in heaven and immortality himself, he told his daughter Judy that 'Mother is an angel and angels watch over you' since he thought this fantasy would be comforting to her" (p. 755). The questions which evolved from this explanation were then difficult for Mr. D. to answer sincerely, based as they were on a belief system which he did not share. For the non-religious parent, as for parents in general, the biological explanation of death is often most helpful to the young child's accepting the reality of death.

The parent can also be helped to view the loss from the child's emotional perspective, that is, from the internal milieu of the child. For example, while a parent may view the loss of the spouse as overwhelming, with time she may attain perspective and understand that she can go on with life and perhaps even marry again. The parent must be helped to understand that for the child, the loss of a parent, especially early in life, is a loss like no other. There will never be another mother or father.

In explaining the experience of loss, an adult whose mother died when he was three years old said to me that it felt as though, in adult terms, his wife had died, all of his children had died, his house had burned down, he had lost his job, and he had lost all of his friends and his means of communicating. He said that the loss of his mother at that age had sent him into a state of complete confusion and anxiety. This is the sort of explanation that the parent of a young child may need to hear in order to fully understand their child's experience of loss.

When parents do not understand their child's experience of loss, the child may experience increased distress. As Coates et al. said, "Where parents were unable to take in and keep in mind what their children were experiencing, children seemed to develop more stress related symptoms, to struggle more with states of shut down and confusion, and perhaps transiently to feel unable to know what was real" (2003, p. 46).

Contrary to popular belief, some specific details about the illness or the accident which caused the parent's death can be provided for children of all ages. The clinician working with the parent can help her in deciding what to say. The child may be told, for example, that daddy was very sick, that the doctors tried to help daddy, but sometimes someone is so sick or hurt badly enough that even doctors cannot always help. For the older child, more details may be given about death in general and about the illness or means of death in specific terms. Adams-Greenly and Moynihan (1983) gave the example of two boys, five and ten years old, whose father was diagnosed with leukemia following a profuse nosebleed that occurred suddenly at home. The five year old was told that the father had a serious problem, that his blood was not strong enough, and that he would have to see the doctor often to get special medicines to make his blood stronger. The ten year old, on the other hand, was helped by a more sophisticated explanation about leukemia, thereby aiding him in gaining an intellectual understanding of his father's illness.

In Susan Coates's work with survivors of 9/11 she noted that in cases where the surviving adults were unable to tell the children under their care that a parent had died, even very young children often knew the truth. An aunt who told her two-year-old nephew that his mother had gone to a meeting and would be back soon was told by the little boy, "Mommy went up in the clouds with the smoke. Mommy burned. I saw it." In this case, the adults, who were still in shock themselves, could neither take in what the children already knew nor communicate honestly with the children.

The surviving parent can be helped to understand the importance of telling the child the truth, for telling the child about the death themselves, for doing so immediately, and for making the child feel that it is alright to discuss feelings about the death. For children who are brought in during the terminal illness of a parent, preparatory work can be done with the well parent and also with the sick parent if he or she is able. The child can be told what is happening and what is likely to happen and can be guided as to the best ways to express her feelings to her ill parent.

In families where the death has occurred due to a violent or potentially traumatizing event, further recommendations may be given to the parent. Coates et al. (2003) worked with children immediately following 9/11 and outlined steps necessary for the therapist to take in helping a parent whose spouse has died under traumatic circumstances. These steps can be taken by the therapist in the course of parental guidance, during treatment by way of the parent (a particular form of treatment for children where the parent is taught to treat their own child, described in more detail below) or in the sessions prior to the beginning of individual therapy for the child. Many are relevant to parents of children who have experienced any sort of loss:

1. Normalize the parent's reaction. Coates et al. helped the parents to understand that they were not going crazy and that their fears,

anxieties, and flashbacks were normal reactions to a severely traumatizing event.

2. Support the relationship between parent and child by helping the
   parent to understand the child's feelings and by facilitating parent-
   child communication. Coates et al. tried to help parents recognize
   what their children understood and did not understand about what
   had happened. They let parents know how important it was to be
   accessible and to answer all of their children's questions directly and
   honestly without providing more information than the child needed.
3. Help the parent make sense of their children's perplexing expressions and behavior. Coates et al. helped parents to understand their
   children's drawings, dramatic play, dreams, nightmares, and fantasies.
   This helped to reengage the parent's own reflective functioning.
4. Help the parent to understand the child's experience. Coates et al.
   found that some parents became angry or disturbed by their children's
   increased clinginess, anger, or tantrums. Parents were afraid that
   these reactions were signs of lasting damage or future pathology.
   Parents needed help seeing these as expectable and temporary responses. Children, in turn, became more frightened when the parent
   responded with anger or anxiety and their already heightened separation anxiety was further fueled.
5. Help parents to protect children from adult conversations about the
   event.
6. Encourage the family to return to normal routines as soon as possible.

The child's primary concern just following the death will often be about
who will care for her. It is crucial to explain that although mommy
or daddy has died, the child will be taken care of and the surviving
relative(s) will see to it that all of the missing parent's jobs will be done.
When the child inquires about replacing the parent, the surviving parent
may reassure the child that no one will ever replace the mother/father
and that while the parent may someday remarry or while the child may
love other people, mommy/daddy will always be special and unique to
the child.

For the parent who presents for therapy prior to the death or just
subsequent to it, it is important to discuss the child's attendance at the
funeral or memorial service. Many writers (Bowlby, 1980; Fulton, 1967;
Plank & Plank, 1978, and others) stress that the presence of the child at

the funeral allows her to truly recognize that the death has occurred. And she can see that she is one of many who share the sorrow of the loss. Moreover, she may receive attention and support from relatives or friends who might not otherwise be so demonstrative. Furthermore, the child who fears that she was in some way responsible for the parent's death may receive comfort from the favorable responses that she receives from others at the funeral. It is important, however, for the parent to discuss attendance at the funeral with the child. The parent may describe the proceedings to the child and allow her to make her own decision about attendance. Some feel that even children under five can make such a choice.

Glicken (1978) suggested explaining the funeral in this way:

> A funeral is a way of saying good-bye to those we love. Very often we do not have an opportunity to say good-bye or to tell someone of our love before death. [The funeral] is a way for many people who share love and grief ... to come together. Many people find funerals a good way to say good-bye but some people find them much too sad. Some people like to say good-bye in a different way. (p. 78)

If a child is to attend the funeral, it is important to suggest to the parent that the casket remain closed. It is also helpful to mention the importance of not forcing the child to greet people in a long reception line. Moreover, it is a very good idea during the service for the child to be with a supportive adult with whom she can interact and who will be willing to leave with the child if she should need time to go outside and play or if she should ask to go home.

Visits to the cemetery in the months and years following the loss can also be useful. Such a trip works against avoidance and denial on the part of both parent and child and allows a time and place for the expression of painful feelings and the sharing of memories. Many children will not be ready to take such a trip immediately following the loss (and they may not want to go to the graveside after the funeral) but at some point in their development they may actually ask to visit the parent's grave and may want to make a tradition of doing so. Watching the movie *Coco* can help some young children understand that there are a variety of traditions possible for mourning and remembering our loved ones who have died.

Similarly, as Becker and Margolin (1967) stated, formal religious or cultural observances of the anniversary of the death can help parents and their children share feelings about the death which might otherwise be difficult to bring up. For example, in Judaism, a year after the death there is often a ceremony for the unveiling of the tombstone. In the case of two children aged eleven and fourteen whose mother died after six months of illness, the father suspected that the children would not want to attend. He spoke with them about it, explaining who would be there and what would happen and he learned that he had been right. Instead of attending the unveiling they each spent the day with friends. The father willingly accepted this, preferring himself to keep the ceremony small and brief, but he did show the children a photograph of the stone he had chosen, asked their opinions about it, and talked to them about what inscription to have engraved on the stone. He also talked with the children after the ceremony and they showed interest and engaged with him around what the experience had been like for him.

The clinician who works with the parent may explore the family's plans for such observance and even suggest, in the absence of tradition in their religious affiliation, that the family create their own observance. On the first anniversary of the death or prior to this, the family might set up a table in the house full of pictures of the lost parent; they might make or paint frames to put pictures of the parent in to keep in their rooms, they might bake a special dessert or make a special meal to remember the parent. These sorts of observances can occur randomly or they can be planned on the birthday of the lost parent, or on Mother's or Father's Day or the like.

The remaining parent may have to be helped to understand that the child has the need to actively remember the parent who has died. Pictures and other reminders should not be hidden away. Memories may be discussed when appropriate. The parent can also be helped to understand that the child may need someone of the same sex as the lost parent to whom she can respond and relate. The important role of the short-term parent substitute is her ability to sympathize with the child's feelings of longing for the real parent, to assist her in tolerating and expressing these feelings, and to provide a role model for the child (E. Furman, 1974).

As time progresses following the loss, the surviving parent will need to be helped to understand the child's behavior vis-à-vis the loss and her mourning process. Often, without insight into the meaning of the child's behavior, the parent will identify the child's behavior as "bad" without connecting it to the loss. In the case of Jacky, presented in Chapter 4, when this three-year-old boy was taken to a barber, he cried and refused to sit still. The mother reported to the therapist that Jacky was "just being bad" and that she had slapped him to punish him for his behavior. When questioned as to previous haircuts, the mother reported that the father had always taken Jacky to the barber.

The mother was helped to understand that the child's first haircut following the loss of his father was a logical time for him to remember his father and to feel sad and confused as to this change in his life. His "bad" behavior was not actually bad; it was just an indication of his feelings about his great loss. As Barnes (1964) stated, parents also need help in recognizing the defensive adaptations such as denial, reversal of affect, displacement, and transformation of passive into active. To encourage the investigation and understanding of such manifestations, Barnes encouraged all caretakers to keep detailed reports of the child's daily activities and to bring these in to their parental guidance sessions with her.

As work progressed with the caregivers, Barnes reported being able to give simple explanations of the behaviors the parent observed. At times she was able to counsel parents to verbalize the child's feelings when emotional reactions were too painful for the child to tolerate or unrecognizable to the child because of the defensive overlay. In this way, she helped parents to reflect on their child's behavior, and indirectly she helped the child learn how to reflect on her own feelings.

To illustrate, Robert Furman (1964b) reported the case of a six-year-old boy who had previously been a good student. Following his mother's death, he stopped doing his homework or bringing home his test papers. In trying to understand this behavior, the child's older brother was of help to the father. He said that because there was no mother to show the papers to, his brother was sad and felt he had no reason to do his homework. The younger boy agreed that this was indeed the case and, as a result, both he and his father were better able to understand that sadness and missing mommy were at the root of his behavior.

It is also often necessary for the surviving parent to have help in coping with their own feelings of loss. They can be encouraged to express their feelings in words and in emotions even in the child's presence. As Bowlby (1980) noted, it is important for parents to be able to talk to children about the death and to share their feelings as many children take the parent's behavior as their own model for mourning. When the parent is afraid of feelings, the children will hide their own. Children need the opportunity to witness the feelings of others, to openly ask questions, and to express and experience their own feelings. If they feel that the surviving parent is too overwhelmed by his own grief, the child will attempt to protect her parent by not overburdening him with her own feelings. In some cases, it may not actually be the child's ego which is too weak to experience the feelings or the work of mourning, but it is the surviving parent who cannot tolerate, accept, or model the emotions associated with acute grief.

In keeping with this, in Rafael's (1977) study of fourteen bereaved families, she found that a significant number of parents did not see their children as being affected by the death. During the research interview, the parents seemed unable to perceive and respond to clear indications of their children's loss related distress. Rafael explained this by saying that in the fourteen families studied, all but one of the parents had pathological grief reactions of their own.

One explanation for this is that issues from the parent's past may interfere in their mourning process. As Becker and Margolin (1967) pointed out, a parent's own unresolved mourning issues often make aiding their children more difficult. Adams-Greenly and Moynihan (1983) stated that parents with unresolved early loss or separation experiences were hampered in helping their own children.

Treating the child by way of the parent

Treatment of children by way of the parent is a technique which has been used throughout the history of psychotherapy. While Sigmund Freud used this method in helping a father deal with his phobic six-year-old son, the famous Little Hans, more often this method is used with mothers for the purpose of preventative care or in the treatment of developmental difficulties in children under five (Fries, 1946; E. Furman, 1957; Jacobs, 1949; Ruben, 1947).

In the case of the bereaved child under five years of age or with an older child who seems to be experiencing minor problems of adjustment, or who refuses to come in for her own treatment, the clinician may consider treatment via the surviving parent. As was reviewed in the section on parental guidance, it can be of great help to both parent and child if the parent is aided in understanding the origin of the child's difficulties and their appropriate management.

Treatment by way of the parent involves helping the parent to understand the child's behaviors and internal experience as well as helping the parent to encourage the child to talk about and understand her own feelings about her loss. This sort of discussion is, in and of itself, salubrious for the bereaved child. Participants in the study performed by Koblenz (2016) said that they wished that their lost parent was discussed more in the home and they said knowing more about the parent who had died was crucial for their own identity development.

In treatment by way of the parent, the parent comes to the therapist each week to discuss the child's current behavior, play, and feelings. The therapist can help the parent first to understand what the child is expressing through her behavior and play and then by teaching the parent how to help her child to elaborate on her feelings and how to begin to master them.

The parent can be educated as to the methods of play therapy in its simplest form. With children under ten, parents can play on the floor with the child. They can allow the child to lead the play and they can learn how to pick out themes involving loss, disappearance, absence, etc. The parent can be taught how to elaborate on such play and how to talk about the play so that the child can understand more about the feelings that the play expresses. In this way, the parent becomes the therapist by proxy.

Parents can also receive suggestions about play activities which may help the child to actively engage in the mourning process. Creative activities can be suggested such as drawing, painting, work with clay or Model Magic, making photo albums or picture frames or even a photo wall in the house. The therapist can help the parent to understand and discuss the child's reactions to such activities. When appropriate, the parent can also be helped to encourage the child to choose some mementos, items that belonged to the parent, and can support the child's use of these in remembering the parent.

Concurrent treatment of parent and child

In some cases where both the parent and the child have suffered loss, the relationship between the child and the surviving parent helps to protect against traumatization and in other cases traumatization works to put both parents and children out of touch with each other (Coates et al., 2003). As Coates and her colleagues observed with families who lost a loved one on 9/11, the children's mutual or concurrent trauma with the surviving parent affected both relatedness and attachment to their caregivers.

This observation is extremely important given the bereaved child's need for a non-traumatized, emotionally available surviving parent. As Anna Freud noted in her wartime studies, children who were subjected to the Blitz in London were protected from fear and anxiety if their mothers did not show these emotions. She said,

> War acquires relatively little significance for children so long as it only threatens their lives, disturbs their material comfort, or cuts their food rations. It becomes enormously significant the moment it breaks up family life and uproots the first emotional attachments of the child within the family group. (Coates et al., 2003)

For children who suffer their own trauma (for example, a shooting at their school), the parent will be an island of safety and reassurance. For the child whose parent has also suffered the trauma—as in traumatic bereavement—that source of safety may be absent.

In cases in which both parent and child are traumatized, they may be treated together, in the same room at the same time. This is particularly useful if the child is under five years of age, due to the special nature of the young child's tie to the parent. With older children, another option is to suggest individual treatment for each person with the possibility of some conjoint sessions when indicated. Children and parents who have been traumatized by the same event may have lost touch with one another's feelings due to their preoccupation with their own pain and devastation. In such cases conjoint treatment can be used to help them to come back into relationship with one another and to understand each other in a deep way. However, if a parent is too severely traumatized and is expressing profoundly disturbing feelings of anguish, fear, or grief, exposure to these feelings may be overwhelming for the child and best dealt with in an individual treatment for the parent, at least initially.

Family treatment of early childhood bereavement

Some clinicians and theorists (Gelcer, 1983; Crosby & Jose, 1983; Rosenthal, 1980) see mourning as a "family affair" (Gelcer, 1983, p. 501) and treat it as such. Gelcer felt that the work of mourning is best thought of as a shared family experience. She suggested that although a death in the family may affect each member differently, depending on his or her relationship with the deceased, the death affects all family relationships with equal power. She stated that the individual who is experiencing pathological mourning and is attempting to deny the death and avoid grief has a negative effect on the entire family. As a result, she stated, the family's growth is arrested. While it may be the individual child who presents to the clinic for treatment, she felt that family treatment may still be the treatment of choice in some instances.

Rosenthal also redefined a child's pathological mourning as the family's problem and provided criteria for taking a family into treatment when one bereaved member has presented for treatment:

1. Individual, group, or residential therapy has been tried with the identified child patient and/or other family members but was not productive
2. Adequate functioning existed prior to the loss with regression of the identified patient and/or siblings to the developmental level at the time of the loss and/or concomitant regression in the surviving parent with resulting obliteration of the normal generational gap

3. Absence of parental communication to the child/children regarding the loss giving rise to acting out behavior by the identified patient and/or other family members
4. Resolution of grief has been aborted through massive use of defenses blocking conscious awareness of grief
5. The family's experience with other treatments produced skepticism
6. Unusual cohesiveness of the family with resistance to any pending separations.

Crosby and Jose (1983) stated that death introduces multiple changes in the family which demand immediate attention. They said that individuals and families react to these demands in ways which either promote or impede recovery. Crosby and Jose promoted a model of constructive grief work which depends upon the network's ability to be permissive of feelings. They stated that within the family, energy should be directed at talking about the actual loss it experienced collectively with expression of real feelings without scapegoating, blaming, placating, or excessive caretaking of any family member. They believed that particularly in families where the loss cannot be experienced directly with the full expression of feelings, family treatment may be indicated.

To illustrate the use of family therapy in the event of early childhood bereavement, Rosenthal presented the case of a six-year-old girl who was brought to treatment because she had become withdrawn, refused to go to school, complained that she hated her mother, and had threatened suicide, all approximately six months after her father's suicide. The family consisted of the mother, the identified patient, and two siblings, age three and one years old. The mother was seen by the clinician as being preoccupied with her own grief and the child was seen as suffering from pathological grief. The family was seen for a short course of family treatment during which the events around the father's death were clarified.

The therapist helped the mother to explain to the children what had happened to the father and to explain that his suicide was no one's fault. The therapist also encouraged the mother to talk about the father's problems in simple terms stating that he had not wanted to live and that although she had asked him to get help for himself, he had refused.

In this way, the mother was able to communicate to the children that she felt that neither she nor they were responsible for the father's death. In the course of treatment, the six-year-old began to talk about how she felt that her mother was very sad and she explained that she had a theory that this was because the younger sister bothered the mother and made too many demands on her. Again, the mother, with the help of the therapist, was able to clarify that it was her own grief over her husband's death that made her sad and not any of the demands which the children made on her. Additionally, in the course of treatment, the mother was helped to set new limits with the children and to establish a new routine with them including spending special time with each child.

In this case, both the mother and the children were helped by the family treatment. The mother learned how to be more expressive of reality circumstances with her children and she began to understand and address her six-year-old's real concerns. The six-year-old was relieved of her feeling that her sisters (and she) were burdens on her mother, and as a result she improved dramatically in regard to her presenting symptoms.

Gelcer (1983) provided examples of family treatment in which the children were adolescents who were bereaved as young children. In the cases reported, no awareness existed on the part of the family regarding the connection between the current symptomatology and the early loss. Gelcer hypothesized that unresolved mourning in a family causes the ghost of the un-mourned parent to become a part of the family system. She said that until the dead family member is psychologically buried and mourned, the role of the ghost colors all relationships in the family, and plays havoc with each family member and with the group's accomplishments of their normal life cycle tasks. She stated that this is particularly problematical when the surviving parent has remarried as it impedes the development of the parental relationship between the new parent and the children, and it hinders the marital relationship between the bereaved parent and the new spouse.

It can be seen that family treatment may be helpful in a variety of circumstances. This modality can be particularly useful when the parent needs help both in modeling emotional expression and in learning how to discuss the loss with the children. Family treatment will also be helpful when the frequent contact required by individual psychotherapy or psychoanalysis may not be possible due to the limitations of time and/or financial resources.

Group treatment

Children often find solace in meeting with other children who have also lost a parent—especially shortly after the loss has occurred. One of the common themes among parentally bereaved children is the sense of being alone or of being different from their peers. Meeting with other children who have lost a parent can help alleviate these feelings and can be very supportive to children and to their family members. Group activities may include a gamut of possibilities including talking together, doing artwork together, or participating in activities together.

In her study of bereaved children Koblenz (2016) mentioned a boy who wanted to be a part of such a group but did not know of one. In the absence of one being available, he started a group of his own with three friends who had also lost a parent which they called "The Dead Parents Club."

Communities which have a center for grieving children or a center for grieving families are indeed lucky as these are rare. Such centers can provide a much-needed sense of community and nurture for families who have lost a loved one. One caveat, however, is that it is important to allow children whose parents have died by suicide to have a separate group as this experience is quite different from that of losing a parent through illness or accident. Moreover, stories of a parent's suicide may be disturbing to children whose parents died in other ways. And stories told by the children whose parents died by virtue of illness or accident may not seem relevant to children whose parent has committed suicide.

Individual treatment

As Lopez and Kliman (1979) stated, "Young children given adequate help are capable of profound mourning" (p. 230). In the absence of an adequately supportive network, in the presence of a regression, developmental arrest, or other indication of pathological grief, this help may take the form of individual psychotherapy. In particular, the analytic approach to psychotherapy or a full child analysis allows the unique opportunity for the clinician to understand the child's internal perception of her loss and for the child to have an intensive experience of understanding and working through her own feelings as well as having a meaningful relationship with an adult whose job it is to understand her. However, some parents will prefer to enlist the help of a behavioral therapist for some cognitive behavioral therapy for their child.

The individual therapy of the bereaved child can be conducted in the same fashion as the individual therapy or psychoanalysis of any child. In the case of children who come for treatment following loss, the treatment will be used, at least in part, to facilitate mourning. As was mentioned in the case of Diane (Lopez & Kliman, 1979) the child's play will often be replete with themes of loss and restitution.

Robert Furman (1964b) mentioned having considered discontinuing analysis of his patient, Billy, at the time of Billy's mother's death due to the extreme trauma imposed by this life event. Furman believed that the child's ego might be unable to manage the demands of an analysis at this time; however, Furman decided instead to continue the analysis. In so doing, Furman found that not only was Billy able to proceed with the analysis in the face of a real-life trauma, but the analysis was actually critical to helping Billy to accomplish his own mourning process.

In order to understand which aspects of the grief process a child needs help with, it is useful to look at Bowlby's stages of grief, described previously. These stages included numbing, yearning and searching, disorganization, despair, and reorganization. It is in the numbing or denial phase or the yearning and searching phase that the child may begin to experience difficulty. For lack of intrapsychic capacity, lack of appropriate support, or lack of appropriate modeling, the child may have difficulty relinquishing the conscious or unconscious belief that the parent continues to exist. She may, therefore, become stuck in the denial and/or the yearning and searching for the parent rather than proceeding with all the feelings associated with acknowledgment of the loss. In the absence of recognition of the permanence of the loss, the work of mourning, in which each memory of the lost parent is reviewed and compared to the reality of the parent's absence, will not proceed.

For example, in the case of Diane, presented by Lopez and Kliman (1979), they stated that nineteen-month-old Diane was told the facts of the mother's suicide repeatedly. While she verbally acknowledged them, for weeks after the mother's suicide she also repeatedly asked about her mother's whereabouts and when she would return.

In treatment, the child can be helped by:

1. Gently identifying the defenses which interfere with the acknowledgement of the loss
2. Gently confronting these defenses
3. In a sensitive fashion, bringing to conscious awareness the reality of the loss and the unconscious fantasy of the ongoing existence of the parent
4. Facilitating the expression of anger and reproach at the lost parent or through the transference rather than at the self or an inappropriate third party
5. Interpreting the meaning of the attempts to escape from mourning
6. Helping to review the child's memories of the lost parent and comparing this with the reality of his or her absence.

Lopez and Kliman (1979) beautifully illustrated the psychoanalysis of a young child in their case report of Diane, mentioned above, who was four years old at the time of her analysis. They stated that Diane experienced a process in the course of her analysis that differed in no significant way from what Freud (1917e) called the work of mourning. In order to help her to proceed with the mourning process, however, the analyst had to help her to master the fantasies and ideas which emerged during the analysis which dated from the time of the loss of her mother. In describing this process, they elucidated the need to bring to awareness the reality of the loss and the unconscious fantasy of the ongoing existence of the parent.

In the first four weeks of treatment, Diane did not acknowledge her mother's death at all. Only when a game of losing toys was interpreted by the analyst as being like losing the painful feelings that we don't want to feel did Diane provide any material at all demonstrating her concern about her mother's death. For the following ten weeks of treatment, themes of searching for the mother were played out, thus bringing into the analysis her unconscious fantasy of her mother's continued existence. Lopez and Kliman described the analyst's efforts during this time as gentle repudiation of Diane's denial of the loss of her mother and the denial of her painful feelings about the loss. To Diane's barely veiled negation of her belief in ghosts (i.e. the ongoing presence of the mother) the analyst stated that perhaps at times she did believe in such ghosts. To her wishes of reunion with her mother, the analyst conveyed his understanding that she wanted very much to be with her mother again. It was through this clarification and interpretation of her feelings and the empathic stance of the analyst that Diane was able, by the end of the analysis, to come to the conscious and unconscious acceptance of the fact that her mother no longer existed and then to make a significant attachment to her new stepmother.

The facilitation of anger and reproach felt toward the object is illustrated by Robert Furman (1964b) and Gauthier (1966) as sometimes occurring through the transference. They found that the anger of the child was often directed at the analyst. While Gauthier was called "moose," "dumb," "stupid," "crazy" (p. 487) by his ten-year-old patient, Furman was called "you stinky" (p. 381) among other things by his six-year-old patient. In this fashion, the analyst provided an object upon whom the child could turn his aggression. Bowlby stated, "Nothing is easier for a child than to mistakenly blame someone including himself for having caused or contributed to a parent death" (1980, p. 352).

Other feelings of anger or aggression toward the parent which are displaced onto the analyst may arise from the child's anger at having been left by the parent. As Gauthier (1966) suggested, one of the tasks of child analysis in the case of early bereavement is for the child to work through her ambivalent feelings about the lost parent. It is important that this be done so that the parental introject does not contain too many unacceptable attributes which made the child angry at the parent and, following the introjection, angry at herself. It is common to direct aggressive feelings toward the self as a result of the feeling that the abandonment was brought on by the child's own misbehavior or innate badness. To prevent the onset of a depression caused by the turning of these feelings against the self, as Gauthier suggested, treatment or other means which allows the expression of these feelings is necessary.

The transference also serves other functions in the treatment of the bereaved child. It may provide the child with the opportunity to organize "the memories and situations of expectancy which demonstrate the libido's attachment to the lost object" (Freud, 1917e) by providing the child with an object on whom she can focus (Lopez & Kliman, 1979). The child may either take flight from establishing a relationship with the clinician or she may develop an intense relationship. In either case, the clinician can be of help in discussing the intensity of the child's feelings with the child and help the child to understand the meaning of these.

The meaning of pathological escapes from mourning must also be interpreted, and this is beautifully described by Robert Furman (1964b). Regarding the analysis of six-year-old Billy, he said, "All through the period described in this report I felt that a process was unfolding on its own within Billy and that he was asking my help in keeping his defenses from interfering with this process and with his conscious contact with it" (p. 395).

As Furman stated, he, as the analyst, "basically confined his work to the interpretation of the defenses Billy's neurosis offered him to ward off his pain" (p. 395). He stated that following the death of his mother, Billy experienced many angry, anxious, and out of control feelings. Upon further work, however, these were revealed to be caused by what Furman termed "mommy missing feelings" (1964b, p. 394). He said that his young patient experienced these in every situation that one would expect a six-year-old first grader to do so—in getting dressed, in going to school for the first day, in coming home for lunch, etc. He stated that each instance had to take its turn in a process which could not be accelerated.

Furman talked to Billy about the meaning of his angry, anxious, and out of control feelings and helped him to label them. In so doing, Furman allowed Billy to understand his upsets around these daily routines and aided him to consciously experience these sad "mommy missing feelings." Billy was thus enabled to work through one more aspect of his mourning—his as of yet uncompleted longing for his mother.

This, then, is perhaps the most important work of individual treatment in the case of childhood bereavement: to allow the child a place in which it is safe to experience her feelings and an ally who will be able to help her to do so. As Lopez and Kliman stated in the case of Diane, "It was the context provided by the analytic relationship as a whole that made mourning possible for Diane. The therapeutic alliance (Greenson, 1965), the analyst's remaining alive and loyal to her; the relationship extending over a period of time; the consistent, organized, verbal mode of communication all contributed to providing Diane with the piece-meal process of working through" (p. 266).

The therapist or analyst may also serve the function of taking on the role of an auxiliary ego, especially in the treatment of very young children or children who experienced loss at a very young age and who did not or do not have the ego capacities (mentioned by E. Furman, 1974) to proceed with mourning. For the child whose loss came before she had a sufficiently stable and differentiated self and object representation, the analyst will have to help her to separate herself from the lost object, specifically to separate her fate from that of the lost parent. This is also the case in individuals of all ages who heavily identify with the lost parent.

In the child whose understanding of death is colored by cognitive immaturity or instinctual interpretation, reality clarification and explanation is necessary. That is, the secondary process thinking of the analyst or therapist is needed to bolster the primary process-influenced thinking of the young child, in regard to death in general and relating to her understanding of her own loss. For example, a child who thinks that she caused the parent to leave her when she was two years old because she was messy and dirty and still used a diaper can be helped to understand that the parent died due to illness (or other cause) having nothing to do with her.

The individual treatment of a bereaved child may also serve another function. In the intense contact between the child and the analytically oriented therapist or the child analyst, the child is provided with the opportunity to develop a significant relationship with an understanding and uniquely interested adult. While it is not appropriate for the therapist or analyst to become a substitute parent, it must be acknowledged that the relationship with the therapist may fill a temporary void in the child's life for a sympathetic ally in the absence of the lost parent. While the relationship between the analyst or therapist and the child is designed to help the child to understand her feelings and to work through the unconscious fantasies previously discussed, this relationship also can be considered to constitute a considerable support to the child and a relational milieu for mourning. Unlike the healthy adult who can function quite well independently, the healthy child has a need for the continuing love, investment, and care of the parents or other important adults.

With the loss of one of the parents this need continues and must find an outlet. There are difficulties inherent in the therapeutic situation for both the child and the analyst or therapist due to the real neediness of the child. The potential problems for the therapist or analyst will be discussed in the following section devoted to counterreaction and countertransference in the treatment of the bereaved child.

It must be further stated in regard to the treatment of bereaved children that the atmosphere of the treatment must be one in which there is a commitment to the proposition that children can mourn. It is to this attitude in their supervision and among their colleagues that Lopez and Kliman (1979) attributed their success with Diane.

Treatment: Jacky

Jacky was brought in for the first treatment session (which was his fourth session with me) by his mother even though he appeared to be getting a cold. Jacky allowed his mother to sit outside the office and went immediately to the doll house. After about twenty minutes of play, he got up to see his mother. When he went out to his mother's chair, he found that she was not there and became quite upset. I commented on how frightening it was to not be able to find someone that you thought would be there and I assured Jacky that we would be able to find his mother. Jacky continued to whimper until we found his mother at the water fountain. From that point on until the end of treatment, Jacky did not allow his mother to sit outside of the office again. Sensitized to unexpected departures of his loved ones as he was by the sudden death of his father, Jacky could not tolerate even the remotest possibility of another such occurrence.

During the next several sessions, Jacky became increasingly free in his play. He messed up the office, pulled toy after toy out of the toy cabinet, and spilled the blocks and checkers out of all their containers onto the floor. He tried to throw blocks at his grandmother, to paint me and the rug in my office, to smash Play-Doh into the rug and to throw the Play-Doh at me. While I set few limits on these activities, his grandmother was very intolerant of them. Even after a session with her during which I explained the necessity for his being able to express himself freely in the office, she continued, although in muted fashion, to cast disapproving glances at him when he engaged in these activities. She explained that at home he threw blocks at his uncle and seemed very angry while doing so, but that she prohibited this activity. Moreover, she was very unhappy about Jacky's not wanting to help to clean up the office at the end of the scssion, saying that at home she insisted that he clean up.

It was clear that Jacky was angry. He wanted to be messy; he wanted to throw blocks at people. He had been dealt a rough deal in life and he wanted to express his anger and frustration at not having his father. It was also clear that his grandmother was intolerant of his anger and skeptical of my interpretations regarding its meaning.

At the same time, Jacky started to become reluctant to leave the sessions. He had become very fond of the Popeye doll and often asked to take it home. He cried pitifully the first time that I told him that Popeye would have to stay in the office and that he would be there for Jacky along with me and all of the toys when Jacky came back. I suggested that Jacky put Popeye away in a special place and say goodbye to him. I also suggested that he take home some of the pictures he had made instead. He agreed to do this and these activities became the ritual for ending during many subsequent sessions.

During this period when it came time to leave, Mrs. B. would usually get up abruptly, help Jacky on with his coat, then walk out without him. If Jacky was reluctant to leave, she often said, "Well, I'll see you next week, Jacky" or "If you don't want to come home with me, I'll find another little boy who does." These statements would send Jacky scurrying after her. I often watched them depart with Mrs. B. walking quickly ahead and Jacky running behind her. This pattern necessitated my explaining to Mrs. B. during an individual session with her that Jacky's separation fears were such that he required her to assure him of her desire to have him with her rather than threaten him with her departure. She was receptive to this and thereafter was more patient and reassuring to Jacky.

At the time of the ninth session, Jacky had one of his many colds and a bad cough. He pretended to be asleep in the waiting room but popped awake in time to accompany his grandmother and me to the office. In the office he threw all the toys out of the toy chest and got in himself. He played peek-a-boo, opening and shutting the door to the cabinet, then getting out to turn on and off the lights, to "Now I see you, now I don't."

Following many repetitions of this game he helped to clean up the office for the first time ever. After cleaning up he resisted the idea of the session ending saying, "Me no want to go!" to which I replied that it was very hard for him to leave me and the office and the toys especially when we were playing such important games and doing such important work.

Although clearly under the weather, Jacky used this session well. Over and over he worked on his confusion around the disappearance of his father. Hiding in the toy box and all the games of peek-a-boo and "Now I see you, now I don't" contained this theme. He made himself invisible to me and then he turned off the lights to make us each invisible to the other. His ability to pop out of the toy box at will and to turn on the lights after he had turned them off were ways of mastering disappearance. Rather than being the passive victim of his father's disappearance he became the one who disappeared. Moreover, he put me, the therapist, in his place in so far as I was the one who had to look for him, wonder where he was, and wait for the lights to go back on to see him. Jacky turned passive into active in this play, a common way that young children attempt to master difficult experiences.

The next session was cancelled due to Jacky's illness. During the following session, Jacky drew on the blackboard and asked that his drawing not be erased. During this session, his mother complained bitterly about her job and her life at home with her parents. Clearly, Jacky was still working on his confusion about disappearances while his mother was more caught up with her own immediate concerns. Jacky did not want his drawing to disappear while he was gone, perhaps wanting to make sure I kept him in mind even as his mother seemed to have other things on her mind.

At the time of the twelfth session, Jacky seemed very happy to come to the office. He played with the doll house then crawled under my desk and hid. He banged on the desk with his feet, laughing gleefully when I complained about the big noise. After several minutes of this, Jacky peeked out and asked, "Is my daddy on the roof?" His question took me by surprise, realizing as I did that he must have been wishing that I could tell him the whereabouts of the daddy he had been missing for so long. When I did respond, I said that I understood how confused he was about where daddy disappeared to and how much he wished that I could tell him that his daddy was nearby. He retreated back under the desk for a moment and then came out to play some more. He played with the gorilla and Popeye dolls, asked for an angel doll to play with, and stated that he had an angel at home over a mirror on the wall.

Jacky's grandparents' explanation to him that his daddy had gone "up there" had been elaborated on by this time by a further explanation that daddy was "with the angels." Jacky was clearly interested in the roof and angels, trying to work out where daddy was and what and where angels were.

The next several sessions were cancelled due to illness and holidays. On one occasion during this time when Mrs. B. called to cancel, Jacky asked to talk with me over the telephone. On another occasion when he did come with his mother, he was quite sick. His mother tried to encourage him to play. However, Jacky seemed only to want to stay next to mommy on the couch. She threatened Jacky with a variety of punishments until I suggested that perhaps when Jacky wasn't feeling well it was even more important than usual for him to be able to be with mommy because mommy was so important to him. With this, Jacky's mother picked him up and held him for the rest of the session while she talked about her own concerns regarding work and her plans for the future.

A significant event in the grandmother's understanding of Jacky's feelings about his father's whereabouts occurred in a subsequent session in which the grandmother came in. When she first saw me that evening, she announced that a beautiful full moon was out. She described how it had followed them all the way to the office. Jacky looked startled and said, "Daddy!" When his grandmother asked, "What about daddy?" Jacky said, "Daddy on the moon!" When Mrs. B. asked what he was doing on the moon, Jacky pulled over a small chair, sat up very straight in it, and said, "Like this." Not only did Mrs. B. have a chance to witness Jacky's fantasy about his father, but in this interaction I was able to see the development of Mrs. B.'s curiosity regarding Jacky's thought processes and her ability to sensitively question him about them.

Jacky was sick during the next session. He hid his face in his mother's lap for the entire forty-five minutes. When I asked the mother what was wrong, she said that Jacky was just being bad. Upon further questioning, however, she explained that they had spent all day walking around in the mall, that she had just given Jacky penicillin for his cold, and had given him a little too much as she hadn't had the right spoon with which to measure. She also said that Jacky hadn't had much dinner because the pizza that they were supposed to eat in the car before the session had been too hot. I suggested to her that maybe Jacky was just hungry and not feeling well tonight and that when he felt this way what he really wanted and needed was extra love and care.

Jacky's mother was young and he was her first child. She was not an experienced mother and, furthermore, she had just lost her husband and had to raise Jacky on her own. Obviously she was suffering—managing a work schedule, living with her parents, raising a small child, and mourning the loss of her husband all at once. Jacky still did not have a reliable schedule nor did he have the support he needed from his mother for his physiological and psychological well-being and for the support of his mourning process.

The next several sessions alternated with cancellations. When Jacky's grandmother did bring him she said that her daughter was no longer willing to bring Jacky and that she didn't see what good treatment was doing. I wondered if perhaps Jacky's mother had taken offense at my comment regarding Jacky's need for more care when he was sick.

Mrs. B. stated that she did not know how much longer she would be able to bring Jacky without help from her daughter. Jacky, on the other hand, was very engaged in the treatment at this time, playing messy games such as painting and making glue pictures. During this session, he wrote on the blackboard and said that no one else should be allowed to do so and that no other boys should knock on my door. In this way he demonstrated the importance that both the treatment and his relationship with me held for him.

Following the session in which he told me this, Jacky's grandmother arrived telling me that Jacky had had a terrible nightmare. When she went into his room to comfort him she found him on the floor, huddled next to his bed. Once in my office, Jacky took out the Candyland game. As we played, I asked him about his dream. He said that a green monster had been chasing him—and as he told me, we began to "play" the dream.

He took the green Candyland figure and began to chase my figure. We ran our figures all about the board until I said, "Who is going to save me?" Jacky replied, "No one!" When I asked him who saved him in the dream, his grandmother interjected, "I did." Jacky, on the other hand, again said, "No one!" When I asked him who he wished could have saved him, he said "Peter Pan—no—Popeye!" When I asked him where they were when he needed them, he said, "On the moon."

Jacky, a three-year-old, had interpreted his own dream. He wished that his father were still alive to save him from monsters *and* to comfort him following scary dreams. And he felt so alone, helpless, and vulnerable without his father. He equated his father with the fantasy figures, Peter Pan and Popeye, both of whom had special powers—Peter Pan was able to fly and Popeye was inordinately strong. In this way he vividly portrayed his father in the way that many three year olds see their parents—as strong and powerful. And when he said that both Popeye and Peter Pan were on the moon, he referred back to his fantasy that his father was now on the moon. This was a poignant moment indeed, indicating how Jacky felt without a strong daddy in his life.

During this session, Mrs. B. also mentioned that Jacky and his mother had gone on a "date" together with the neighborhood man she had told me about at the beginning of treatment. She was very happy about this and commented again about how patient this young man was in waiting for her daughter and about how good he was with Jacky.

For the next session, the grandmother came alone to discuss Jacky's progress. She said that she thought that Jacky was doing fine now—he was no longer drooling, he was not afraid of the basement or his bed, his speech was better, his separation difficulties had lessened, he was doing well at nursery school, and he was sleeping through the night each night. She said that he would be starting speech therapy twice a week at school to improve his articulation and that, as a result of all of this, she felt that he did not need to come for treatment any longer. Although I attempted to explain the difference between symptomatic improvement and improvement in Jacky's feelings about and understanding of his father's death, Mrs. B. continued to insist that he did not need to come anymore. As a result of her decision, we agreed on a termination period and I suggested that she call me if any problems arose in the future.

During the next several weeks, Jacky played happily in my office seemingly oblivious to my comments about ending treatment. At the end of the last session, I again explained how I would not be seeing him anymore and I suggested that he might like to have something to remember our time together. I gave him the Popeye that he had wanted to take home with him (and which had evidently represented a strong person and a daddy) throughout the treatment and he was ecstatic. He walked out of my office backwards repeatedly saying, "Bye-bye Popeye!" to me. In this way, Jacky showed me that he was now alright with saying goodbye; he had a transitional object to me and to our work; he had made some important progress in that work and he linked the powerful Popeye/daddy with me, the therapist who had been clear with him about his father's death and his sad, angry, and lonely missing feelings.

Discussion

The treatment of this paternally bereaved three-year-old boy demonstrates both the common dynamics and difficulties in the treatment of young bereaved children.

Within the time that Jacky was in treatment, he manifested fear of further separation from his mother, the surviving parent. Both the clinginess which he was reported to engage in at home when it was time for his mother to leave the house and his extreme reaction at not finding his mother in the chair outside my office during session five demonstrated this. He also showed extreme confusion as to the whereabouts of his deceased father and the meaning of death in general. In his belief that his father was "on the moon" or "on the roof" Jacky demonstrated his concrete interpretation of the explanation given to him by his mother and grandparents regarding his father's being "up there."

Jacky also evidenced the anger which he felt toward his father at abandoning him in his spilling of toys, messing of the office, banging on the desk, and in the displacement of anger onto me, his uncles, and his grandmother in his throwing toys at us. His anger at God was also expressed directly when he punched the air and stated in no uncertain terms that he was angry at God.

Perhaps most striking in Jacky's short treatment were his many attempts to turn passive into active. In his attempts to master his loss, Jacky played peek-a-boo. He controlled the door to the cabinet in which he hid and the light switch which he turned on and off so that he could see me and not see me at will. He also reversed roles with me in his identification with the aggressor (the daddy who left him). He made me the one who had to endure his disappearances, who had to look for him and wonder where he was, and he got to be the active one who disappeared and left me, the passive victim, behind.

Transference manifestations were made obvious by Jacky's desire to have "no other boys knock on my door." He wanted my exclusive attention in much the same way that a child of his age normally wants the exclusive attention of the mother and father. He wanted me to keep his productions on the blackboard from week to week, desiring evidence that they (and he) were so important to me that I would not erase/forget them/him.

This treatment was also fraught with a variety of difficulties: the needs of the child conflicted with the needs of the family; the needs of the family conflicted with the requirements of the treatment; and the counter-transferential feelings of the therapist may have sometimes interfered with the sensitive handling of the family's resistances to the treatment.

Because of the mother's need to avoid overt acknowledgment of her loss and to retreat into work and social activities (that is, to avoid her own mourning process), it was difficult for her to see the need for Jacky to mourn or to be helped to mourn. Because Jacky's mother preferred to see Jacky as being a "normal little kid," it was difficult to bring her into the treatment as an ally and to involve her in the investigation of Jacky's thoughts and feelings. In this respect, the grandmother was a better ally, but one whose own concerns and conflicts interfered in the full appreciation of Jacky's feelings.

The events following the death of Jacky's father were designed to fit the needs of Jacky's mother for child care. The immediate move to the grandparents' home represented the mother's desire to remove herself from reminders of her husband in their shared apartment and to immerse herself in work and social activities. It was undoubtedly difficult for her to continue to care for Jacky as she had since the time of Jacky's birth, due to the painful reminder such activity provided of her husband's absence. For Jacky, however, while he gained a stable and supportive home situation in the move to his grandparents', he lost his familiar home, his toys and, for the most part, the attention of his mother.

The outings in which the mother did involve herself with Jacky— going to the mall, and so on—were oriented toward her need for activity rather than Jacky's need to be with her. She scheduled these activities in a way that conflicted with the need to maintain a schedule suitable for a three-year-old. When it was suggested by the therapist that loving care more in keeping with an ill three-year-old's needs was necessary, the mother became less supportive of the treatment.

Moreover, the grandparent's belief that a substitute father for Jacky in the form of a husband for their daughter would solve all their problems worked against their involvement in the treatment. As the mother became more interested in dating, the treatment became less important to the grandparents and to the mother herself.

The family's desire to put the trauma of the suicide behind them was certainly understandable. Yet this worked counter to providing a setting in which the overt expression of grief over the loss could be encouraged. While Jacky's grandmother became more able to discuss his feelings and fantasies with him as treatment progressed, she continued to be reluctant to acknowledge that Jacky's father could not be replaced in his life. She felt that she filled in for the father quite well and that a new husband for her daughter could replace Jacky's actual father in Jacky's mind.

Attempts to educate the family as to how treatment would help Jacky were not entirely successful. The grandmother's conflicting feelings of resentment over the disruption of her life and, on the other hand, her feeling of responsibility to care for her daughter and grandson resulted in similarly conflicting feelings in her treatment of Jacky. While she did provide a consistent mothering function in Jacky's life, she also remained adamant about pursuing her own active social schedule. She was also quite rigid in her prohibitions against Jacky experiencing his angry feelings, both in and out of the treatment. She did not like his expressions of anger and could not tolerate his messiness when feeling angry. Her own ambivalent feelings were well demonstrated by the way in which she initially left Jacky's sessions with Jacky trailing behind. While I was able to work with her in understanding Jacky's feelings about separation and his need to be reassured about her continuing desire to have him with her, it was more difficult to help her to allow herself or Jacky a more expanded range of self-expression.

The termination of treatment at the time of symptomatic improvement occurred as a result of the family's need to view Jacky's situation in relation to their own needs. The termination was not clinically warranted at that time and was a disappointment to me due to my realization that Jacky had only just begun to establish an alliance with me through which we could work on his feelings about the loss of his father. Not only was this not obvious to the family, but the improvement in symptomatology seemed to them to be the desired result of the treatment—as is often the case in the treatment of children.

Had treatment continued, objectives might have included clarifying with Jacky the whereabouts of his father, helping him to understand the nature of death, discussing death on a level which could be understandable to him and which could be integrated with his own understanding of what had happened to his father. It would also have been helpful to work more with the family to help them to understand Jacky's feelings about the loss of his father and his understanding of death as well as helping them to establish an environment for him which could be more appropriate both in terms of allowing the emergence of the mourning process and providing appropriate routines for a three-year-old child. Optimally, work would also have included helping Jacky's mother with her feelings of loss and aiding her in bringing his sadness and guilt to the level of conscious experience and verbal expression.

It is a difficult job to meet all the needs of a family in which a death has occurred. Helping a young child with the mourning process means also helping the surviving parent with his or her mourning. Additionally the family must be helped to support the child in her ongoing development and overseeing the establishment of a stable and supportive environment. It is always difficult to know exactly how to proceed with a family who has experienced such a devastating trauma as each family's needs are complex and different. Moreover, each family member is experiencing unmanageable feelings of their own and each family member will need help of one sort or another.

In Jacky's case, short-term exploratory and supportive therapy provided him and his immediate family with assistance during a most difficult time. The treatment allowed Jacky a place to express his grief, his yearning, and his anger as well as providing him with a person who understood that expressing these feelings was of the utmost importance. I was able to help Jacky with his unmanageable feelings and to help Jacky's mother and grandmother to understand and to tolerate these feelings in Jacky—at least to some extent. As such, the treatment supported the beginning phases of Jacky's mourning. It helped the mother and the grandparents to be more aware of and more sensitive to Jacky's internal process as well as to his external needs for consistency, sensitivity, and nurture.

Treatment of children whose parent commits suicide

The treatment of children whose parent has committed suicide, as in Jacky's case, requires further discussion. For a child—or really for anyone close to a person who commits suicide—it is a loss like no other. When loved ones die due to illness or accidents the child or adult can fantasize that they were at fault—but there is reality to support the fact that they were not. Generally we do not cause illness in another (although there may be cases where contagious diseases like Covid-19 are passed from one to another) nor, except in very rare cases, do we cause accidents to happen. However, when a person commits suicide, they cause their own death—and the idea that a child (or adult) may have done something to cause the loved one to take their own life can be seriously entertained.

Even children as young as three years of age, like Jacky, can have some understanding that a person brought about their own death. And this is an extremely frightening idea—both for the child and for those who worry about what effect this event will have on the child. And it has been shown that children who have a parent who has attempted or committed suicide are more at risk than children who have not had this experience (see above: Burke et al., 2010; Wilcox et al., 2010).

In his beautiful and poignant article, Francesco Bisagni, quoted earlier, reconstructed a nine-year-old's experience with finding his father after his father's suicide by hanging. The child, Fabrizio, was clearly shocked and traumatized by the sight of his father's body hanging from the ceiling of the office. In order to manage, Fabrizio began to dissociate, and to derealize, removing himself from his own experience and from the undigestible reality of his father's suicide. He experienced an altered sensorium, losing all sense of time and motion as well as control of his own emotional state, crying uncontrollably, wanting only to reach a safe harbor, his mother.

Bisagni (2012) put it beautifully:

> For Fabrizio, the sudden sight of the father who had committed suicide and the moments that immediately followed, took the form of an invasion of perceptual fragments. Along with an

immensely powerful upset to the mental apparatus, there was disintegration of the symbolic, and alteration of space and time orientation. The sudden and momentary psychotic experience is expressed through the alteration of the contact barrier (Bion, 1962) and in the clearly defensive inability to distinguish between dreaming and reality. Has reality become one's worst nightmare? Is this reality just a nightmare? (p. 27)

Often, that is the question of the traumatized child, "Is this real?" When reality is too awful, there is a desire to imagine, whether consciously or unconsciously, that it is not so. And for the child who knows the awful reality is true, she may turn away from this knowledge through dissociation, as Fabrizio did.

Fabrizio's treatment with a sensitive therapist allowed him to reconstruct the experience of finding his father and of his recognition of his father's death. The therapist believed that there was "a potential for representation," that is, a potential for Fabrizio, who was very disorganized by the experience of finding his father, to reorganize and to put his experience into orderly form. This was a first step for Fabrizio to begin to understand what had happened to him. Fabrizio's analyst believed that the "three-dimensionality of the mental apparatus ... may survive, even in the most disturbed mental or non-mental states" and that the analyst's work can bring this (back) to life for the patient through the reconstruction of the experience in the treatment.

In addition to representing her experience, treatment also allows the child who has lost a parent through suicide to express and process all the feelings associated with her experience—especially the feelings of shock, protest, anger, rage, and sadness. And psychotherapeutic or psychoanalytic treatment can allow the child to carefully tease apart the implications of the parent's suicide including feelings of guilt and fault as well as blame of the parent who died, and blame of the surviving parent or other family members.

Fabrizio was older than Jacky at the time of his father's suicide and thus better able to comprehend the meaning of death and the implications of suicide. Jacky became frightened of things associated with his father's death—the basement, and so on—while Fabrizio became frightened by the very event, by his own feelings, and by death itself.

Starting by age four or five, children will understand certain elements of suicide and will have questions regarding why it occurred, what their role was in its occurrence, whether others will choose to do the same, and, as a result, whether further losses will follow. As the child grows older, the questions will become more sophisticated and the answers needed will be more nuanced. As part of the child's treatment, the therapist/analyst can help the surviving parent know how to answer the child's questions honestly without imposing too great a burden on the child. Information regarding mental illness will often be part of these discussions.

As Fabrizio's therapist said,

> Through his psychotherapy with me, Fabrizio was able to find a space where he could vent his anger towards his father who had committed suicide. He was able to be in contact with the despair and omnipotence that in suicide denies the help of the object, which characterises all acts of suicide as a hidden form of murder .... And it is not an option to circumvent the rage towards the person who—having committed suicide—denies the other the chance of a potential healing dialogue. (Bisagni, 2012, p. 30)

That conversation, I suggest, must take place between the therapist and the child—as represented in the transference–countertransference relationship and in actual, consciously spoken, and thus healing dialogue.

The therapist's reactions and countertransference

The often traumatic nature of the bereaved child's loss, the actual need of the child for a real object, and the intensity of either the child's feelings or her avoidance of feelings will evoke strong reactions in the therapist or analyst treating the child. To the extent that these feelings interfere with or aid the clinician in understanding and working with the child, they are important. Such feelings, whether conscious or unconscious, represent a previously under-discussed yet intensely difficult aspect of the treatment of bereaved children and one which bears further exploration.

Personal reactions (once known as counterreactions) are the therapist's or the analyst's consciously experienced feelings toward the patient; countertransference, on the other hand, is a complex phenomenon which has been defined as the reactivation of early emotional states and relationships under the influence of the transference (the transference being the patient's unconscious reaction to the therapist) (Kabcenell, 1974).

In understanding countertransference in the context of the treatment of children, however, a problem arises which is different from that which occurs in the treatment of adult patients. When the use of the term countertransference is defined as above, it is overly limiting. When we speak of the reactivation of early states and relationships, we omit the other important conscious and unconscious reactions that a therapist may have to a child patient. The child patient has a real need to use the relationship with the therapist in so many ways—as a support for her developing ego, as a role model for handling more sophisticated thought processes and ways of managing difficult feelings, and as a partner in reviewing painful feelings and experiences. Each of these needs in turn evokes a reciprocal response in the therapist. These may include the desire to save, soothe, nurture, and parent the child as well as the desire to compete with the actual parent in a game of "Who is the better parent?"

A more satisfactory definition of countertransference for use in discussing the particular problems of this phenomenon in the treatment of bereaved and traumatized children is thus needed. Marcus (1980) stated that countertransference has its origins in the unconscious or preconscious processes of the analyst/therapist, has specificity to the patient, to the transference or other components of the patient's material, and defensively interrupts or disrupts the analyzing function. Or, as Freud simply put it, "Countertransference is a result of the patient's influence on (the analyst's) unconscious feelings" (1910a, p. 144). The understanding of countertransference which can be gained from Freud's and Marcus's definitions will be utilized here.

The need of the parentally bereaved child for a relationship with a primary object is not limited to oedipal strivings or intrapsychic conflict, but is related to normal developmental needs which have been exacerbated by a real, often traumatic event and a resulting absence in her life. The feelings of the child are likely to be intense. The child may directly experience these feelings, she may attempt to ward off these feelings, or she may toggle between these two positions. In response to the child and in mirroring the child's feelings, the clinician may also experience intense feelings or the warding off of feelings.

Marcus (1980) stated, "When countertransference is aroused, its manifestations are quite variable and overdetermined" (p. 287). Among these are intense feelings of sadness, grief, and identification with the child as well as projective identification and a revival of omnipotent feelings in a desire to rescue the child. Inevitably, reactivation of the clinician's own early or later deprivations and losses will also occur. Additionally, the therapist may experience sibling or oedipal rivalry with the patient's parents in the desire to be a better parent to the child. In the case of the treatment of the bereaved child, one may also expand the list of countertransference manifestations to include a common desire: The therapist may find herself wishing to fulfill the role of the missing spouse to the surviving parent, acting for a time as a co-parent.

Obviously, there are cases which are more likely to evoke the extremes of personal reaction and countertransference than others. For example, when a bereaved child's loss is similar to a loss which the therapist has suffered, it is likely that the therapist will identify with the child and she may feel urgently pulled to help the child in an attempt to protect the child from having the same experience that she, the therapist, has had. And even in the case of a therapist who has not experienced a similar sort of loss, the clinician may find it difficult to avoid the overextension of empathy in treating a child just because the child's need is so great. The therapist may wonder at what point human reaction to such a child justifiably supersedes a professional stance. She may struggle with how much empathy to show and how much caretaking to do.

At the same time, it is extremely important for the therapist to be aware of her feelings and the impact they have on the treatment. For example, the extension of empathy born out of the therapist's need to comfort the child (and by extension, herself) will not be helpful when what the child needs in that moment is a therapist able to tolerate and hold her excruciating pain and sadness. Similarly, a therapist who becomes too involved with the surviving parent in an unconscious desire to co-parent or to show the surviving parent how to be a better parent (i.e. more like the therapist) will not be helpful when what the child needs at that time is a therapist who can be a steady companion devoted to accompanying her in her grief process rather than someone who attends more to her surviving parent.

As a vehicle for exploring the specific difficulties included in managing personal feelings and countertransference in the treatment of young bereaved children, vignettes from the case of Jacky will be used in combination with material from other cases.

Case example: Jacky

While Jacky had been cared for primarily by his grandmother since his father's death, the home situation was not a completely supportive one. Jacky's mother and grandmother disagreed on almost all aspects of his care. As a result, Jacky had no consistent schedule or discipline. He lived one day by his grandmother's strict rules and the next by his mother's permissive ones. It took no time at all for me, as the evaluating clinician, to see the difficulties involved in this situation for Jacky—and for my heart to go out to him. Moreover, his demeanor and play material were immensely evocative and painful to witness.

During the first therapeutic hour, I sat on the floor with Jacky while he played with the doll house. Following an initial reluctance to come down to the office and to interact, Jacky became progressively more engaged with me and more willing to play in my presence. During the latter half of the first session, Jacky seemed quite comfortable. He established intense eye contact with me while asking questions or answering them. His gaze was incorporative and hungry. When he looked at me in this fashion, it was difficult for me to maintain a feeling of being the professional in the room, so compelling was his expression and so compelling was his need; not only would Jacky have been an appealing child under any circumstances, but he seemed particularly so in light of the loss of his father at a time when a father was so necessary to him. The feelings evoked in me by Jacky's gaze were powerful and may be understood to represent my identification with Jacky's sadness and loss as well as his need for a nurturing parent. As Reich (1951) stated, countertransference represents a failure of trial identification; the analyst (or, in this case, the therapist) reacts to her patient's instinctual strivings with a direct response. The therapist may return love with love or hate with hate. Such direct responses, especially when they assume great intensity, represent the commonest and simplest form of countertransference.

In this case, not only was I responding to Jacky's instinctual strivings for love and nurturance (Ainsworth, 1969), but I was also responding to his exacerbated need for these following the loss of his father as well as to his need for a developmental object. Instead of going through what Reich (1951) described as a transient identification for the purposes of understanding, I remained identified with Jacky. In such circumstances the therapist's analyzing function can be hindered or entirely paralyzed, which may render her blind to aspects of the clinical situation requiring attention.

This vignette illustrates the situation in which the feeling of neediness in the bereaved child elicits strong feelings in the clinician as early as the first session. Depending on the clinician's own dynamics, these feelings may occur as either strongly positive or strongly negative ones. It did not take much work for me to uncover my desire to take on more of a role with this child than just as his therapist. I wanted to take care of this child, to rescue him from his terrible confusion and sadness, to actually be his missing parent, and short of that to advise his mother and grandmother in all sorts of ways including the best ways to take care of him when ill, to handle his schedule, and to supply him with the affection he so badly needed. However, because of the ease with which I could understand my feelings in this instance, I was able to limit my comments to those which were more boundaried and those which I felt they could hear in this early moment of my relationship with them. In general, following the initial upsurge of such feelings, it may be assumed that further work in the treatment will bring up even stronger feelings in the therapist. This was certainly the case in my work with Jacky.

Countertransference

In the course of treatment, feelings regarding the patient, her history, and her way of interacting are bound to bubble up within the therapist or analyst. Whether conscious or unconscious, these feelings are always a complex interweaving between the therapist's own psychic world, personal history and current life circumstance, and her reactions to the patient and the patient's material. It is informative to the therapist if she can be alert to signs of countertransference including any changes in her normal way of relating to patients (which might indicate unconscious reactions to the patient or her material) and to conscious manifestations of extremes of feeling where the patient is concerned.

Projective identifications such as those which I described above may occur in therapists who have unresolved grief issues of their own, who were bereaved as children or adolescents, or who have suffered other painful losses. I was one of these, having lost a parent during my early adolescence and I found myself, as stated, feeling intimately connected to Jacky and empathically attuned—although my so-called attunement may, as stated, have been at least partly a projection of my feelings about my own loss of a parent. Therapists who have their own childhood losses to draw upon are in a special position in regard to their potential ability to understand their young patients' feelings. However, they may also be vulnerable to imagining that their patients' feelings are like their own, thus prematurely foreclosing on the exploratory listening process which is meant to elucidate the child's actual feelings.

By adulthood most therapists have suffered loss of one sort or another, whether or not they suffered early loss, and as such may be sensitive to the reactivation of feelings when treating a bereaved patient. As A. Harris said of her feelings while treating a young widow, "The challenge for me was to hold my history and revived feelings of sudden, unexpected loss and attend to the specific and unique experience … that my patient was having" (2003, p. 160).

Moreover, the clinician who is at a vulnerable moment in her life (due to divorce, illness in the family, etc.) may attempt to care for the child (rather than providing treatment) as a way of caring for herself through the aforementioned process of projective identification. At the other extreme, the clinician may fail to empathize sufficiently with the bereaved patient in an attempt to avoid the reactivation of painful feelings of sadness and mourning. As a result she may unwittingly support the patient's own denial and resistance or she may ignore or minimize various needs and feelings of the patient.

What may also occur without adequate examination of the feelings of identification with the bereaved child is the development of an omnipotent desire to rescue the child and the feeling that this may actually be possible via the treatment. Such a reaction to bereaved or traumatized children is extremely common among the clinicians responsible for their care. Such feelings are bound to end in disappointment or feelings of impotence.

What is required for the therapist is vigilance to her feelings and a continuing examination of what constitutes her best professional role. As Robert Furman described in the case of Billy, a six-year-old whose mother was dying, "I was a bit chagrined to realize that the 'role' Billy wanted me to fill was that of his analyst. As I wondered why I had ever searched for a 'role,' I became aware of the anxiety engendered in being unable to do anything active to avert the tragedy that was unfolding" (1964b, p. 383).

This statement illustrates the sense of inadequacy which the therapist or analyst may initially feel in treating bereaved children due to the magnitude of their pain. The frustration at not being able to quickly or actively do something to "help" the child may engender other feelings as well, such as ambivalence toward the child or the child's treatment. This is another means by which a clinician may ward off the tremendous responsibility and emotionality of such a case. For example, when Jacky's mother or grandmother cancelled his sessions, I sometimes felt great disappointment and other times great relief. Feeling as incapable of altering either Jacky's experience with loss or his current home situation as I sometimes did, the case began to feel burdensome. I occasionally found myself glad not to have to try to continue this effort when the family cancelled the hour.

Anger, consciously felt or not, may also occur as a reaction to the already mentioned feelings of helplessness on the part of the therapist. The therapist may identify with the child's anger at having been abandoned and/or, in an interesting mirroring of the child's similar reaction, the clinician may find herself angry at the surviving parent or caretaker for any number of reasons. The clinician may feel that the child is not being adequately protected or supported or she may find herself in competition with the parent.

Fatigue may also set in. Such a reaction may result from the clinician's realistic appraisal of the arduous task ahead. It may also represent an identification with the child's hard work at mourning or it may result from attempting to "help" the child in a way which might not always appear to be immediately helpful. The need to encourage the child to experience great longing and sorrow for the lost parent is a difficult one and one which may be met by the child or by the family with resistance. Meeting this resistance with patience and equanimity is difficult work.

Following an initial desire to rescue the child and/or the family, a more realistic view of what can and cannot be done for the child and the family may feel like too little. Moreover, other countertransferential feelings may intrude as well. For example, the attraction of the female therapist to the widowed father of a young child or of the male therapist to the widowed mother may indicate the unconscious desire of the therapist or analyst to take on the role of the missing parent as both parent and spouse rather than as analyst/therapist.

The effect of over-empathy or its opposite or the alternating feelings of omnipotence and feelings of helplessness about the case may create blocks in the therapist's ability to understand the child and to manage the case. Reich stated that it is of significance that frequently the analyst is not consciously aware of her feelings in such cases, but becomes aware only of certain consequences such as anxiety, and other inappropriate and often over-strong emotions.

For example, during the second session with Jacky, it became obvious while playing in the doll house that Jacky had misconstrued his mother's and grandparents' explanation that his father was "up there" (in heaven) as meaning that his father was living on the roof of the house. He placed the father doll on the roof of the doll house while the other family members went about their business inside. Later in treatment, having established a positive relationship with me, during the twelfth session, Jacky hid under my desk, made lots of noise by banging on the desk with his feet, then peeked out and asked, "Is my daddy on the roof?" In reaction to this question, I was overwhelmed with anxiety. I quickly recognized that this anxiety was a defense against the great sadness I felt for this little boy who was so desperately looking for his father. I later realized that I may also have been warding off the feeling that he had exposed my real desire—to find or to be his missing parent for him. This anxiety temporarily immobilized my thought processes. While I was able to respond to Jacky when this moment passed, I was later aware that, paradoxically, the internal reaction of over-empathy had created difficulty in my actually expressing adequate empathy.

But at what point can the human reaction to the bereaved child (or her family) justifiably and temporarily supersede the professional (analytic) position? This question is a difficult one to answer, bordering as it does on a variety of professional, ethical, and philosophical issues.

One might first ask whether it is indeed helpful to the child for the therapist to go beyond the professional role to attempt to fulfill any of the child's needs for a real object. Depending upon one's orientation, what constitutes the professional role may differ. While some therapists might think it appropriate to direct a child's activities to encourage mastery, such as suggesting that the child make a book about her mother's death, another might prefer to follow the child in her expression and way of handling her own material, for instance, by identifying feelings in the play and the defenses against them. One therapist might go to a school play to support the child's participation in such an activity in the absence of a mother or father to do so—while others would consider this inappropriate. And newer manualized treatments, such as CBT, might recommend prepared protocols for treatment, thus avoiding many feelings or decisions on the therapist's part at all.

So, what to do? From the approach taken in this work, it is suggested that those activities which facilitate the accomplishment of the mourning process are those which are appropriate and therapeutic. Particularly in the case of the very young child this may include serving as an auxiliary ego at times, for instance, in terms of reality testing about the continued existence of the mother or father and, as an extension of this, in educating the child about death or in suggesting activities which might support remembering and mourning the lost parent. The role of the therapist as auxiliary ego may also extend to the care of other family members. As Adrienne Harris beautifully described regarding her work with the mother of two paternally bereaved children, "My role here is as protector and guide. At times I function as an arm draped over [the mother's] shoulder, a supportive voice in her head, helping her to make a space for herself, for the unique and delicate feelings that can arise, almost without warning, from the many expected and unexpected tasks of mourning" (2003, p. 155).

When a child's parent dies during the course of treatment and in the treatment of bereaved children in general, there may be certain reactions on the therapist's part which cause her to change technique. While this may not be strictly justifiable, it may not harm the treatment, and may actually support it in some cases. For example, in writing about the case of Billy, Robert Furman described his dilemma when Billy came for a session the day after his mother's death. Rather than meeting in the office, Dr. Furman and Billy walked around the block about ten times. This seemed the right activity for both of them and it allowed Billy some much-needed time and space to just quietly be with a trusted and beloved adult.

Moreover, Furman attended Billy's mother's funeral. He reported that he did so because "of [his] relationship with the mother" (p. 387). In defense of these activities, he stated, "I have no further explanation for these things … they just seemed the appropriate things to do at the time" (p. 388). He thus illustrated his very human and humane reactions to the reality of his young patient's situation. He acted on his feeling that the day after his mother's death Billy might not be available for the work of treatment as usual and that instead he as analyst could just be with Billy in an activity of Billy's choosing. In attending the funeral, it seems that his personal relationship with the mother and the family superseded his usual professional role and boundaries.

Other decisions may have to be made which represent temporary diversions from the usual technique. For example, Billy's father demanded that Furman accept his desire to put his dying wife's needs first. Furman therefore delayed discussing the wife's mastectomy with his patient as the mother could not tolerate her son asking her questions about it. Furman stated that in making his decisions regarding these matters, he was guided by the feeling that he had "to do everything to maintain my relationship with [Billy's father] in order to preserve Billy's analysis" (1964b, p. 382).

In summary, the therapist's or analyst's reactions, whether conscious or unconscious, play an important part in the treatment of bereaved children. While at one time it was believed that such emotional reactions on the part of the clinician represented obstacles that interfered with competent treatment, contemporary psychoanalytic and psychodynamic clinicians accept that the clinician's feelings are an instrumental part of treating the child and that both the awareness of these feelings and the examination of them will prove invaluable both in self-understanding for the therapist and in understanding the child and her experience.

Working through and decathexis—redux

Sigmund Freud suggested that normal mourning takes from one to two years. This idea has been widely accepted and for years has seemed accurate in regard to the bulk of the mourning process including the various tasks of mourning and the resolution of the strongest feelings of sadness and self-reproach. However, the process by which mourning occurs and the most desirable outcome of mourning has been hotly debated in more recent years—and particularly over the past two decades. Specifically at issue has been the question, as stated previously, of whether decathexis/detachment is the most desirable product of the working through process of mourning.

John Bowlby thought that normal mourning could include an ongoing sense of the presence of the lost loved one. He did not include detachment from the person who has died as a sine qua non of the healthy mourning process. And it has been shown in many research studies and clinical examples cited here that healthy children and adults alike often continue a connection to the lost loved one through either internalization of functions or characteristics of the deceased or through ongoing fantasy contact with them.

The work of Shuchter with widows and widowers (1986) pertains: He concluded from his research that the "task" of mourning is not the decathexis of the dead spouse (or lost loved one) but "the establishment of a form of continuing relationship that both satisfies the emotional need of the bereaved to maintain their ties and allows for grieving and living to proceed" (p. 319). Because this requires reworking many issues in the relationship, Shuchter suggested that the process will occur over a period of many years.

Furthermore, in their work, Marwit and Klass (1996) found that the lost loved ones of teen and adult subjects played crucial ongoing functions in their lives:

(a) As a role model with whom to identify
(b) As a source of situation-specific guidance in solving current life problems
(c) For clarification of values, especially values the deceased person believed in that could be either accepted or rejected by the bereaved

(d) As a remembrance or reminiscence that brought feelings of comfort or happiness to the individual.

J. William Worden (1996) suggested that a process takes place following the death of a parent in which the child must "construct" an image of the lost parent for themselves. In this way the child can develop an inner representation of the dead parent that allows her to maintain a relationship with the parent, a relationship that changes as the child matures. Worden (1996) stated that the child negotiates and renegotiates the meaning of the loss, and in time, relocates the dead person in her life and memorializes that person in a way that allows life to move on.

Hagman (2001) said that mourning involves "a crisis of meaning both on an intrapsychic level, through the transformation of psychological structure, and dialogically, through the maintenance of meaningful human connections in reality and fantasy" (p. 22).

To summarize, analytic thought and clinical practice have moved significantly forward since decathexis was identified by Sigmund Freud as the goal of mourning. In its totality, the working through process of mourning is now seen as taking far more than one to two years—in some cases lasting a lifetime—and it may not include a definitive detachment from the lost loved one. On the contrary, the internal relationship with the loved one may be preserved and used throughout life.

Working through loss, truly acknowledging that a dearly loved one is gone and will not return, is hard, painstaking work—and this acknowledgment is not always fully accomplished. It is a stepwise and ongoing process. Each time a memory of the lost loved one arises, each time an event occurs at which that person might have been expected to have been present, and each time an accomplishment, failure, illness, or accident happens in which the lost loved one might have been proud or pained or helpful, the recognition that this person is no longer present is brought to the fore. Feelings of shock, sadness, and loss are reexperienced over and over again.

As the years go by, these moments become less frequent. For both children and adults, the work of mourning becomes less arduous and less intense. Sometimes a birthday or an anniversary will occur and the lost parent will *not* be thought of. These too are poignant moments, but they represent the fact that the individual has moved forward in working through her mourning.

Contrary to what is often optimistically said about mourning, missing those loved ones who have died does not necessarily stop. Generally it becomes less painful and less frequent. The memories and the experiencing of the lost loved one often become more tolerable—and sometimes even quite sweet.

Adrienne Harris described an incident in which a young widow who lost her husband at the World Trade Center on 9/11 is told by a friend, "Your world did not end." Harris and the patient discussed this statement together and decided that it was both true and not true. The patient and her two young daughters *did* continue their lives, the children did grow and thrive with their mother's help, but, at the same time, an important part of their lives did end—the planned for and normally anticipated life of the family as a foursome *did* come to an abrupt halt. A new family emerged—it was one that would continue to make new memories together as a threesome while always, always, missing the life that didn't happen and the potential memory-making that was foreclosed upon by the death of their husband and father.

When mourning proceeds in an optimal fashion, the child (or adult) will eventually have sufficient energy freed up to attach again, to be able to love again, and to be able to have their developmental needs met by another loving figure, or by those already present. The degree to which the child divests emotional energy from the lost loved one, however, will vary, from almost complete divestment to partial divestment. Ongoing attachment of a partial nature to the lost parent may well continue even when the mourning process can be considered to have been healthy.

From mourning to meaning

The goal of mourning, then, is to accomplish sufficient detachment from the lost loved one to allow forward development to continue and to allow love and new relationships to flourish. It is also to make meaning of the loss—to understand the role that the lost loved one played in the life of the now bereaved, to understand the importance of their absence, and to value these new understandings.

It is time to normalize the idea that the mourning and the working through and the meaning-making of loss can last a lifetime for both children and adults—and additionally, that the acceptance and denial of the loss may continue to oscillate back and forth over the life of the bereaved. As a young adolescent said during a session six months after her father died, "I think about the things we did together and I feel sad because we won't do them again." And then she said, "But I know he's here. I know he's watching." This teenager knew her father was dead— and yet she also believed that he was with her. In the months following her father's death she recounted dreams in which her father appeared, she saw strange lights move through her room, and she witnessed "orbs" appearing in her mirror. She interpreted these phenomena as evidence of her father's presence in her life, which in turn gave her the strength to go forward.

A. Harris put it beautifully:

> There is a complex interweaving of melancholy and mourning, a continuing shift between acceptance and denial, an interweaving of fantasy and reality. Melancholic preoccupations, nostalgia, and ghostly sweet presences enrich psychic life. They are necessary and creative responses to the grueling work of mourning. (2003, p. 145)

And, as Margaret Little (1985) said, "Mourning is for life."

Conclusion

Because the child's ego is not yet fully developed, she is especially dependent on external love, nurture, help, and support and is particularly vulnerable when an important figure such as a parent is no longer available to provide for her due to death or other circumstances. Without an optimal milieu in which to express her feelings and to discuss her many concerns, the bereaved child is at risk for developmental interference or arrest and to experiencing one of the pathological variants of the mourning process.

The child who is unsupported in her mourning or who is beset by internal or external interferences to grief requires professional therapeutic help in completing the mourning process. And the very young child may require help in her mourning even under optimal circumstances. Without such help, the child may eventually suffer and experience difficulty making herself available for other relationships and activities in the world of the living. Furthermore, psychopathological processes may occur, leaving an indelible imprint on both current and later functioning.

We know that talking about thoughts and feelings early and often and participating in activities which operationalize the remembering process are necessary for the bereaved child of every age. We know that activity is preferable to passivity in the mourning process and can allow children to feel more in control of their sadness and grief. Psychotherapy and psychoanalysis are two places where talking about thoughts and feelings and making meaning of them is possible. Feelings of having been "done to" or having been the passive recipient of a terrible occurrence such as the death of a parent can be transformed into an active engagement with loss in the relationship with the therapist/analyst and in the psychotherapeutic process.

Furthermore, prompt support for the child's family is also necessary. While any bereaved individual, child or adult, requires a safe and stable environment in which to express grief, the support once immediately lent by the community is no longer readily available to most people. Nurturance and extra attention for bereaved children were at one time supplied by extended family and neighbors for the duration of their childhood or until a substitute parent was integrated into the family— but not so much anymore.

As a result of the changes which have occurred in family structure and society in most Western cultures, mental health professionals are now in an important position to actively support bereaved families and to facilitate the mourning process in the individual members and within the family. Early intervention work with the recently bereaved families is extremely important, but all too rare. More centers for grieving families are needed and more primary medical practitioners, pediatricians, teachers, psychiatrists, psychologists, and social workers need to be educated as to the special needs of bereaved children and families.

In regard to the study of childhood grief and mourning, the literature on the subject of effective interventions for bereaved children is phenomenally lacking. Further work in this area is critically important.

The families of bereaved children clearly require support from friends, community, medical personnel, and mental health practitioners in order to provide the environment necessary for their children to mourn and to thrive. As we know, the surviving parent is critical to the child's adjustment and thus we must find ways to help and support those parents. Based on their extremely large data base, Hoeg et al. (2018) found that whether or not children develop later problems often depends on the surviving parent and how well they can metabolize their own feelings of grief in order to be emotionally available to their children and to provide a stable home. John Bowlby referred to the process of reorganization following loss as attachment reorganization, a process which must be accomplished by both parent *and* child.

Moreover, as Ellis et al. (2013) point out in their beautiful narrative study, we as a society need to work together to provide more resources for bereaved or traumatized children and families. We need to find ways to provide what the extended family and community formerly provided in previous generations. Parents and children who have experienced bereavement need far more than psychotherapeutic support. While psychotherapy or psychoanalysis may help a child, a surviving parent, or the entire family to progress through a mourning process, support from extended family, school, community groups, etc. also helps a bereaved family to persevere through their experience of loss. These days online communities can provide opportunities for groups of people with shared experience to meet and find support. Social media can be used cautiously but creatively to provide safe spaces for children and their families to meet others like themselves. Organizations can provide resources online which can be accessed more quickly and easily than ever before.

It is hoped that this book will add to the existing body of knowledge in the area of childhood bereavement, will help clinicians in their work with grieving children, and will support the further exploration of this area.

References

Abraham, K. (1911). Notes on the psychoanalytical investigation and treatment of manic depressive insanity and allied conditions. In: *Selected Papers of Karl Abraham, M.D.* (pp. 137–156). London: Hogarth, 1927.

Abraham, K. (1924). A short study of the development of the libido, viewed in the light of mental disorders. In: *Selected Papers of Karl Abraham, M.D.* (pp. 393–407). London: Hogarth, 1927.

Adams-Greenly, M. A., & Moynihan, R. T. (1983). Helping the children of fatally ill parents. *American Journal of Orthopsychiatry, 53*(2): 219–229.

Ainsworth, M. D. S. (1969). Object relations, dependency, and attachment: a theoretical review of the infant-mother relationship. *Child Development, 40*(4): 969–1025.

Ainsworth, M. D. S., & Bell, S. M. (1970). Attachment, exploration, and separation: Illustrated by the behavior of one-year-olds in a strange situation. *Child Development, 41*(1): 49–67.

Altschul, S. (1968). Denial and ego arrest. *Journal of the American Psychoanalytic Association, 16*(2): 301–318.

Anand, K. J., & Hickey, P. R. (1992). Halothane-morphine compared with high dose sufentil for anesthesia and postoperative analgesia in neonatal cardiac surgery. *New England Journal of Medicine, 326*(1): 1–9.

Anthony, E. J. (1973). In: E. J. Anthony & C. Koupernik (Eds.), *The Child in His Family: The Iimpact of Disease and Death.* Yearbook of the International Association for Child Psychiatry. New York: John Wiley & Sons.

Anthony, S. (1972). *The Discovery of Death in Childhood and After.* New York: Basic Books.

Aragno, A. (2001). Transforming mourning: A new psychoanalytic perspective on the bereavement process. *Psychoanalysis and Contemporary Thought, 26*(4): 427–462.

Arsenian, J. M. (1943). Young children in an insecure situation. *Journal of Abnormal Social Psychology, 38*(2): 225–249.

Arthur, B., & Kemme, M. L. (1964). Bereavement in childhood. *Journal of Child Psychology and Psychiatry, 5*: 37–49.

Aubrey, J. (1955). *La Carence de soins maternals.* Paris: Presses Universitaires de France.

Baker, J. E. (2001). Mourning and the transformation of object relationships: Evidence for the persistence of internal attachments. *Psychoanalytic Psychology, 18*(1): 55–73.

Bakermans-Kranenburg, M. J., van IJzendoorn, M. H., & Juffer, F. (2003). Less is more: Meta-analyses of sensitivity and attachment interventions in early childhood. *Psychological Bulletin, 129*(2): 195–215.

Barnes, M. (1964). Reactions to the death of a mother. *Psychoanalytic Study of the Child, 19*(1): 334–357.

Beck, A. T., Sethi, B. B., & Tuthill, R. W. (1963). Childhood bereavement and adult depression. *Archives of General Psychiatry, 9*: 295–302.

Becker, D., & Margolin, F. (1967). How surviving parents handled their young children's adaptation to the crisis of loss. *American Journal of Orthopsychiatry, 37*(4): 753–757.

Bedell, J. (1973). The maternal orphan: Paternal perceptions of mother loss. Presented at symposium on bereavement by the Foundation in Thanatology, New York.

Bendiksen, R., & Fulton, R. (1975). Death and the child: An anterospective test of the childhood bereavement and later behavior disorder hypothesis. *OMEGA, 6*(1): 45–59.

Bion, W. R. (1962). *Learning from Experience.* London: Heinemann.

Bisagni, F. (2012). Shrapnel: Latency, mourning, and the suicide of a parent. *Journal of Child Psychotherapy, 38*(1): 22–31.

Black, E. (1997). What happens to bereaved children? *Proceedings of the Royal Society of Medicine, 69*(11): 842–844.

Blos, P. (1966). *On Adolescence: A Psychoanalytic Interpretation*. London: Simon & Schuster.

Bluebond-Langner, M. (1978). *The Private Worlds of Dying Children*. Princeton, NJ: Princeton University Press.

Blum, G. S., & Rosenzweig, S. (1944). The incidence of sibling and parental deaths in the anamnesis of female schizophrenia. *Journal of Genetic Psychology*, *31*: 3–13.

Bonnard, A. (1961). Truancy and pilfering associated with bereavement. In: S. Lorand & H. Schneer (Eds.), *Adolescents*. New York: Roeber.

Bowlby, J. (1953). Some pathological processes set in train by early mother–child separation. *Journal of Mental Science*, *99*(415): 265–272.

Bowlby, J. (1960). Grief and mourning in infancy and early childhood. *Psychoanalytic Study of the Child*, *15*(1): 9–52.

Bowlby, J. (1961). Processes of mourning. *International Journal of Psychoanalysis*, *42*: 317–340.

Bowlby, J. (1963). Pathological mourning and childhood mourning. *Journal of the American Psychoanalytic Association*, *11*(3): 500–541.

Bowlby, J. (1969). *Attachment. Attachment and Loss, Vol. 1*. New York: Basic Books.

Bowlby, J. (1973). *Separation: Anxiety and Anger. Attachment and Loss, Vol. 2*. London: Hogarth.

Bowlby, J. (1980). *Loss, Sadness and Depression. Attachment and Loss, Vol. 3*. New York: Basic Books.

Bowlby, J., Robertson, J., & Rosenbluth, D. (1952). A two year old goes to the hospital. *Psychoanalytic Study of the Child*, *7*(1): 82–94.

Brazelton, T. B., Koslowski, B., & Main, M. (1974). The origins of reciprocity: The early mother–infant interaction. In: M. Lewis & L. A. Rosenblum (Eds.), *The Effect of the Infant on Its Caregiver* (pp. 49–76). New York: Wiley-Interscience.

Brown, F. (1966). Childhood bereavement and subsequent psychiatric disorder. *British Journal of Psychiatry*, *112*(491): 1035–1041.

Burke, A. K., Galfalvy, H., Everett, B., Currier, D., Zelazny, J., Oquendo, M. A., Melhem, N. M., Kolko, D., Harkavy-Friedman, J. M., Birmaher, B., Stanley, B., Mann, J. J., & Brent, D. A. (2010). Effect of exposure to suicidal behavior on suicide attempt in a high-risk sample of offspring of depressed parents. *Journal of the American Academy of Child and Adolescent Psychiatry*, *49*: 114–121.

Burns, M., Griese, B., King, S., & Talmi, A. (2020). Childhood bereavement: Understanding prevalence and related adversity in the United States. *American Journal of Orthopsychiatry*, *90*(4): 391–405.

Cain, A. C., & Fast, I. (1966). Children's disturbed reactions to parent suicide. *American Journal of Orthopsychiatry, 36*(5): 741–752.

Calhoun, L. G., & Tedeschi, R. G. (2001). Posttraumatic growth: The positive lessons of loss. In: R. A. Neimeyer (Ed.), *Meaning Reconstruction & he Experience of Loss* (pp. 157–172). Washington, DC: American Psychological Association.

Centers for Disease Control and Prevention (2005). *Health, United States, with chartbook on trends in the health of Americans.* Hyattsville, MD: US Department of Health and Human Services, National Center for Health Statistics.

Cerel, J., Fristad, M. A., Verducci, J., Weller, R. A., & Weller, E. B. (2006). Childhood bereavement: Psychopathology in the 2 years postparental death. *Journal of the American Academy of Child and Adolescent Psychiatry, 45*(6): 681–690.

Cerel, J., Fristad, M. A., Weller, E. B., & Weller, R. A. (1999). Suicide-bereaved children and adolescents: A controlled longitudinal examination. *Journal of the American Academy of Child & Adolescent Psychiatry, 38*(6): 672–679.

Cerel, J., & Roberts, T. A. (2005). Suicidal behavior in the family and adolescent risk behavior. *Journal of Adolescent Health, 36*(4): 316–359.

Chethik, M. (1970). The impact of object loss on a six year old. *Journal of the American Academy of Child Psychiatry, 9*(4): 624–643.

Childhood Bereavement Estimation Model (CBEM) (2020). *Projected Estimates.* New York: New York Life Foundation, & Judi's House.

Clark, M. B. (1972). A therapeutic approach to treating a grieving two and a half year old. *Journal of the American Academy of Child and Adolescent Psychiatry, 11*: 705–711.

Clayton, P. J., Desmarais, L., & Winokur, A. (1968). A study of normal bereavement. *American Journal of Psychiatry, 125*(2): 168–178.

Clayton, P. J., Halikas J. A., & Maurice, W. L. (1972). The depression of widowhood. *British Journal of Psychiatry, 120*(554): 71–78.

Coates, S. W. (2016). Can babies remember trauma? Symbolic forms of representation in traumatized infants. *Journal of the American Psychoanalytic Association, 64*(4): 750–776.

Coates, S. W., Rosenthal, J. L., & Schechter, D. S. (Eds.) (2003). *September 11: Trauma and Human Bonds.* Hillsdale, NJ: Analytic Press.

Cohen, J. A., Mannarino, A. P., Greenberg, S. P., Padio, S., & Shipley, C. (2002). Childhood traumatic grief: Concepts and controversies. *Trauma, Violence, & Abuse, 3*(4): 307–327.

Cox, F. N., & Campbell, D. (1968). Young children in a new situation with and without their mothers. *Child Development, 39*(1): 123–131.

Crawford, T. N., Cohen, P., Chen, H., Anglin, D. M., & Ehrensaft, M. (2009). Early maternal separation and the trajectory of borderline personality symptoms. *Development and Psychopathology, 21*(3): 1013–1030.

Crosby, J. F., & Jose, N. L. (1983). Death: Family adjustment to loss. In: C. Fegley & N. McCubbin (Eds.), *Stress and the Family, Vol. 11 Coping with Catastrophe*. New York: Brunner/Mazel.

Dennehy, C. (1966). Childhood bereavement and psychiatric illness. *British Journal of Psychiatry, 112*(491): 1027–1034.

Dent, V. (2020). When the body keeps the score: Some implications of trauma theory and practice for psychoanalytic work. Presentation, Psychoanalytic Center of Philadelphia, September 25.

Deutsch, H. (1937). Absence of grief. *Psychoanalytic Quarterly, 6*(1): 12–22.

Dowdney, L. (2000). Childhood bereavement following parental death. *Journal of Child Psychology and Psychiatry, 41*(7): 819–830.

Dubois-Comtois, K., Moss, E., Cyr, C., & Pascuzzo, K. (2005). Behavior problems in middle childhood: The predictive role of maternal distress, child attachment and mother–child interactions. *Journal of Abnormal Child Psychology, 41*(8): 1311–1324.

Duckworth, A. (2016). *Grit: The Power of Passion and Perseverance*. New York: Charles Scribner's Sons.

Ellis, J. E. E., Dowrick, C., & Lloyd-Williams, M. (2013). The long-term impact of early parental death: Lessons from a narrative study. *Journal of the Royal Society of Medicine, 106*(2): 57–67.

Fenichel, O. (1945). *The Psychoanalytic Study of Neurosis*. New York: W. W. Norton.

Fleming, J., & Altschul, S. (1963). Activation of mourning and growth by psychoanalysis. *International Journal of Psychoanalysis, 44*: 419–431.

Fonagy, P., & Target, M. (1997). Attachment and reflective function: Their role in self-organization. *Development and Psychopathology, 9*(4): 679–700.

Fonagy, P., & Target, M. (2003). *Psychoanalytic Theories: Perspectives from Developmental Psychopathology*. London: Whurr.

Fraiberg, S. (1951). Enlightenment and confusion. *Psychoanalytic Study of the Child, 6*(1): 325–335.

Fraiberg, S. (1969). Libidinal object constancy and mental representation. *Psychoanalytic Study of the Child, 24*(1): 9–47.

Freud, A. (1952). The role of bodily illness in the mental life of children. *Psycho-analytic Study of the Child*, 7(1): 69–81.

Freud, A. (1960). Discussion of Dr. John Bowlby's paper, Grief and mourning in infancy and early childhood. *Psychoanalytic Study of the Child*, 15: 53–62.

Freud, A. (1965). *Normality and Pathology in Childhood*. New York: International Universities Press.

Freud, A., & Burlingham, D. (1943). *War and Children*. New York: International Universities Press.

Freud, S. (1895). Extracts from the Fliess Papers. Draft G.: Melancholia. *S. E.*, *1*. London: Hogarth.

Freud, S., & Breuer, J. (1895d). *Studies on Hysteria*. *S. E.*, *2*: 1–305. London: Hogarth.

Freud, S. (1897). Extracts from the Fliess Papers. Draft N. Notes III. *S. E.*, *1*. London: Hogarth.

Freud, S. (1900a). *The Interpretation of Dreams*. *S. E.*, *4–5*: 254. London: Hogarth.

Freud, S. (1910a). Five lectures on psycho-analysis. *S. E.*, *11*. London: Hogarth.

Freud, S. (1912–13). *Totem and Taboo*. *S. E.*, *13*: 1–162. London: Hogarth.

Freud, S. (1915b). Thoughts for the times on war and death. *S. E.*, *14*: 273–300. London: Hogarth.

Freud, S. (1917e). Mourning and melancholia. *S. E.*, *14*: 237–258. London: Hogarth.

Freud, S. (1923b). *The Ego and the Id*. New York: W. W. Norton, 1962.

Freud, S. (1926d). *Inhibitions, Symptoms and Anxiety*. *S. E.*, *20*. London: Hogarth.

Fries, M. E. (1946). The child's ego development and the training of adults in his environment. *Psychoanalytic Study of the Child*, 2: 81–112.

Fulton, R. (1967). On the dying of death. In: E. A. Grollman (Ed.), *Explaining Death to Children* (pp. 31–50). Boston, MA: Beacon.

Fulton, R., & Bendiksen, R. (Eds.) (1976). *Death and Identity*. Hoboken, NJ: John Wiley & Sons.

Furman, E. (1957). Treatment of under fives by way of parents. *Psychoanalytic Study of the Child*, 12: 250–262.

Furman, E. (1974). *A Child's Parent Dies*. New Haven, CT: Yale University Press.

Furman, R. A. (1964a). Death and the young child: some preliminary consider-ations. *Psychoanalytic Study of the Child*, 19(1): 321–333.

Furman, R. A. (1964b). Death of a six-year-old's mother during his analysis. *Psychoanalytic Study of the Child*, 19: 377–397.

Furman, R. A. (1968). Additional remarks on mourning and the young child. *Bulletin of the Philadelphia Association of Psychoanalysis, 18*(2): 124–138.

Furman, R. A. (1969). Sally. In: R. A. Furman & A. Keaton (Eds.), *The Therapeutic Nursery School* (pp. 124–138). New York: International Universities Press.

Furman, R. (1973). A child's capacity for mourning. In: E. J. Anthony & C. Koupernik (Eds.), *The Child in His Family: The Impact of Death and Disease*. Yearbook of the International Association for Child Psychiatry (pp. 225–231). New York: John Wiley & Sons.

Gaines, R. (1997). Detachment and continuity: The two tasks of mourning. *Contemporary Psychoanalysis, 33*(4): 549–571.

Gauthier, Y. (1966). The mourning reaction of a ten-year-old boy. *The Canadian Psychiatric Association Journal/La Revue de l'Association des psychiatres du Canada, 11*(Suppl.): 307–308.

Gelcer, E. (1983). Mourning is a family affair. *Family Process, 22*(4): 501–516.

Gilkerson, L. (1998). Brain care: Supporting healthy emotional development. *Child Care Information Exchange, 5*: 66–68, 167.

Glick, I. O, Weiss, R. S., & Parkes, C. M. (1974). *The First Year of Bereavement*. New York: John Wiley, Interscience.

Glicken, M. D. (1978). The child's view of death. *Journal of Marital and Family Therapy, 4*(2): 75–81.

Gorer, G. (1973). Death, grief and mourning in Britain. In: E. J. Anthony & C. Koupernik (Eds.), *The Child in His Family: The Impact of Disease and Death*. Yearbook of the International Association for Child Psychiatry. New York: John Wiley & Sons.

Granville-Grossman, K. L. (1966). Early bereavement and schizophrenia. *British Journal of Psychiatry, 112*(491): 1027–1034.

Green, A. (1986). The dead mother. In: *On Private Madness* (pp. 142–173). London: Hogarth.

Greenson, R. R. (1965). The working alliance and the transference neurosis. *Psychoanalytic Quarterly, 34*(2): 155–181.

Gregory, I. (1958). Studies of parental deprivation in psychiatric patients. *American Journal of Psychiatry, 115*(5): 432–442.

Gregory, I. (1965). Anterospective data following childhood loss of a parent. *Archives of General Psychiatry, 13*(2): 110–120.

Grossman, J. A., Clark, D. C., Gross, D., Halstead, L., & Pennington, J. (1995). Child bereavement after paternal suicide. *Journal of Child and Adolescent Psychiatric Nursing, 8*(2): 5–17.

Hagman, G. (2001). Beyond decathexis: Toward a new psychoanalytic under-standing and treatment of mourning. In: R. A. Neimeyer (Ed.), *Meaning Reconstruction & the Experience of Loss* (pp. 13–31). Washington, DC: American Psychological Association.

Haine, R. A., Wolchik, S. A., Sandler, I. N., Millsap, R., & Ayers, T. (2006). Positive parenting as a protective resource for parentally bereaved children. *Death Studies, 30*(1): 1–28.

Harlow, H. F., & Harlow, M. K. (1965). The affectional systems. In: A. Shriner, H. F. Harlow, & F. Stollnitz (Eds.), *Behavior of Non-Human Primates, Vol. 2.* New York: Academic Press.

Harris, A. (2003). Relational mourning. In: S. W. Coates, J. L. Rosenthal, & D. S. Schechter (Eds.), *September 11: Trauma and Human Bonds* (pp. 143–163). Hillsdale, NJ: Analytic Press.

Harris, M, (1995). *The Loss that Is Forever: The Lifelong Impact of the Early Death of a Mother or Father.* New York: Plume.

Hartman, H. (1952). The mutual influences in the development of ego and id. *Psychoanalytic Study of the Child, 7*(1): 9–30.

Heinicke, C. M., & Westheimer, I. (1965). *Brief Separations.* New York: International Universities Press.

Hilgard, J. R. (1963). Early parental deprivation in schizophrenia and alcoholism. *American Journal of Orthopsychiatry, 33*: 409–420.

Hilgard, J. R., & Newman, M. F. (1959). Anniversaries in mental illness. *Psychiatry, 22*(2): 113–121.

Hilgard, J. R., & Newman, M. F. (1961). Evidence for functional genesis in mental illness: Schizophrenia, depressive psychoses, and psychoneuroses. *Journal of Nervous and Mental Disorders, 132*(1): 3–16.

Hobson, C. J. (1964). Widows of Blackton. *New Society, 4*(24): 13–16.

Høeg, B. L., Johansen, C., Christensen, J., Frederiksen, K., Dalton, S. O., Dyregrov, A., Bøge, P., Dencker, A., & Bidstrup, P. E. (2018). Early parental loss and intimate relationships in adulthood: A nationwide study. *Developmental Psychology, 54*(5): 963–974.

Hofer, M. (2003). The emerging neurobiology of attachment and separation: How parents shape their infant's brain and behavior. In: S. W. Coates, J. L. Rosenthal, & D. S. Schechter (Eds.), *September 11: Trauma and Human Bonds* (p. 200). Hillsdale, NJ: Analytic Press.

Hopkinson, G., & Reed, G. F. (1966). Bereavement in childhood and depressive psychosis. *British Journal of Psychiatry, 112*(486): 459–463.

Howard, K., Martina, A., Berlin, L. J., & Brooks-Gunn, J. (2010). Early mother–child separation, parenting, and child well-being in Early Head Start families. National Center for Children and Families, Columbia University, New York City; Center for Child and Family Policy, Duke University, Durham, NC.

Howell, K., Barrett-Becker, E. P., Burnside, A. N., Wamser-Nanney, R., Layne, C. M., & Kaplow, J. B. (2016). Children facing parental cancer versus parental death: The buffering effects of positive parenting and emotional expression. *Journal of Child and Family Studies, 25*(1): 152–164.

Hung, N. C., & Rabin, L. A. (2009). Comprehending childhood bereavement by parental suicide: A critical review of research on outcomes, grief processes, and interventions. *Death Studies, 33*(9): 781–814.

Jacobs, J. R., Bovasso, G., & Gregory, B. (2009). Re-examining the long-term effects of experiencing parental death in childhood on adult psychopathology. *Journal of Nervous and Mental Disease, 197*(1): 24–27.

Jacobs, L. (1949). Methods used in the education of mothers: A contribution to the handling and treatment of developmental difficulties in children under five years of age. *Psychoanalytic Study of the Child, 3*(1): 409–422.

Jacobson, E. (1957). On normal and pathological moods: Their nature and functions. *Psychoanalytic Study of the Child, 12*(1): 73–113.

Jacobson, E. (1964). *The Self and the Object World.* New York: International Universities Press.

Jacobson, E. (1965). The return of the lost parent. In: M. Schur (Ed.), *Drives, Affects, Behavior, Vol. 2* (pp. 193–211). New York: International Universities Press.

Johnson, P., & Rosenblatt, P. (1981). Grief following childhood loss of a parent. *American Journal of Psychotherapy, 35*(3): 419–425.

Kabcenell, R. J. (1974). On countertransference. *Psychoanalytic Study of the Child, 29*: 27–33.

Kaufman, K. R., & Kaufman, N. D. (2005). Childhood mourning: prospective case analysis of multiple losses. *Death Studies, 29*(3): 237–249.

Kernberg, O. F. (1972). Early ego integration and object relations. *Annals of the New York Academy of Sciences, 193*: 233–247.

Kidman, R., Margolis, R., Smith-Greenaway, E., & Verdery, A. M. (2021). Estimates and projections of COVID-19 and parental death in the US. *JAMA Pediatrics.* Published online April 5.

Klaus, M., & Kennel, J. (1976). *Mother–infant Bonding.* St. Louis, MO: E. V. Mosby.

Klein, M. (1935). A contribution to the psychogenesis of manic depressive states. In: *Love, Guilt and Reparation and Other Papers*, 1921–1946. London: Hogarth.

Klein, M. (1940). Mourning and its relation to manic-depressive states. *International Journal of Psychoanalysis*, 21: 125 153.

Kliman, G. (1968). *Psychological Emergencies of Childhood*. New York: Grune & Stratton.

Koblenz, J. (2016). Growing from grief: Qualitative experience of parental loss. *OMEGA*, 73(3): 203–230.

Koocher, G. P. (1973). Childhood, death and cognitive development. *Developmental Psychology*, 9(3): 369–375.

Kranzler, E. M., Shaffer, D., Wasserman, G., & Davies, M. (1990). Early childhood bereavement. *Journal of the American Academy of Child and Adolescent Psychiatry*, 29(4): 513–520.

Krueger, D. W. (1983). Childhood parent loss: Developmental impact and adult psychopathology. *American Journal of Psychotherapy*, 37(4): 582–592.

Kwok, O., Haine, R. A., Sandler, I. N., Ayers, T. S., Wolchik, S. A., & Tein, J.-Y. (2005). Positive parenting as a mediator of the relations between parental psychological distress and mental health problems of parentally bereaved children. *Journal of Clinical Child and Adolescent Psychology*, 34(2): 260–271.

Layman, K. M. (2020, July 30). In Memorial Drive a poet evokes her childhood and confronts her mother's murder. *The New York Times*.

Lee, A., & Hankin, B. L. (2009). Insecure attachment, dysfunctional attitudes and low self esteem predicting prospective symptoms of depression and anxiety during adolescence. *Journal of Clinical Child and Adolescent Psychology*, 38(2): 219–231.

Lin, K. K., Sandler, I. N., Ayers, T. S., Wolchik, S. A., & Luecken, L. J. (2004). Resilience in parentally bereaved children and adolescents seeking preventive services. *Journal of Clinical Child and Adolescent Psychology*, 33(4): 673–683.

Lindemann, E. (1944). Symptomatology and management of acute grief. *American Journal of Psychiatry*, 101(2): 141–148.

Little, M. (1985). Working with Winnicott where psychotic anxieties predominate. *Free Association*, 5: 1–19.

Lopez, T., & Kliman, G. (1979). Memory, reconstruction and mourning in the analysis of a 4-year-old child. *Psychoanalytic Study of the Child*, 34(1): 235–271.

Luecken, L. J. (2008). Long-term consequences of parental death in childhood: physiological and psychological manifestations. In: M. S. Stroebe, R. O. Hansson, H. Schut, & W. Stroebe (Eds.), *Handbook of Bereavement Research and Practice: 21st Century Perspectives* (pp. 397–416). Washington, DC: American Psychological Association Press.

Macoby, E. E., & Feldman, S. S. (1972). Mother-attachment and stranger-reactions in the third year of life. *Monographs of the Society for Research in Child Development, 37*(1): 1–86.

Maddison, D. (1968). The relevance of conjugal bereavement to preventive psychiatry. *British Journal of Medical Psychology, 41*: 223–233.

Maddison, D., & Viola, A. (1968).The health of widows in the year following bereavement. *Journal of Psychosomatic Research, 12*(4): 297–306.

Maddison, D., Viola, A., & Walker, W. L. (1969). Further studies in bereavement. *Australian and New Zealand Journal of Psychiatry, 3*(2): 63–66.

Maddison, D., & Walker, W. L. (1967). Factors affecting the outcome of conjugal bereavement. *British Journal of Psychiatry, 113*(503): 1057–1067.

Mahler, M. S. (1961). On sadness and grief in infancy and childhood. *Psychoanalytic Study of the Child, 16*(1): 332–351.

Mahler, M. S., Pine, F., & Bergman, A. (1975). *The Psychological Birth of the Human Infant: Symbiosis and Individuation.* New York: Basic Books.

Marcus, I. M. (1980). Countertransference and the psychoanalytic process in children and adolescents. *Psychoanalytic Study of the Child, 35*(1): 285–298.

Marris, P. (1958). *Widows and Their Families.* London: Routledge & Kegan Paul.

Marris, P. (1974). *Loss and Change.* London: Routledge & Kegan Paul.

Marvin, R. S. (1972). Attachment, exploratory and communicative behavior in 2, 3 and 4 year old children. Unpublished doctoral dissertation. University of Chicago.

Marwit, S. J., & Klass, D. (1996). Grief and the role of the inner representation of the deceased. In: D. Klass, P. R. Silverman, & S. L. Nickman (Eds.), *Series in Death Education, Aging, and Health Care. Continuing Bonds: New Understandings of Grief* (pp. 297–309). Abingdon, UK: Taylor & Francis.

Masten, A. S., Cotuil, J. J., Herbers, J. E., & Reed, M. J. (2009). Resilience in development. In: S. J. Lopez & C. R. Snyder (Eds.), *Oxford Handbook of Positive Psychology.* Oxford: Oxford University Press.

Masur, C. (1984). Early childhood bereavement: Theoretical and clinical considerations. Unpublished doctoral dissertation. Drexel University, Philadelphia, PA.

McDonald, M. (1964). A study of the reactions of nursery school children to the death of a child's mother. *Psychoanalytic Study of the Child, 19*: 360–400.

Micia, Z. (1962). Psychological stress in children in the hospital. *International Nursing Review*, December 9: 23–31.

Nagera, H. (1970). Children's reaction to the death of important objects: a developmental approach. *Psychoanalytic Study of the Child, 25*: 360–400.

Nagy, M. (1978). The child's theories concerning death. *Journal of Genetic Psychology, 73*(1): 3–27.

Osterweis, M., Solomon, F., & Green, M. (1984). *Bereavement, Reactions, Consequences and Care*. Institute of Medicine (US) Committee for the Study of Health Consequences of the Stress of Bereavement. Washington, DC: National Academies Press.

Palumbo, J. (1981). Parent loss and childhood bereavement: some theoretical considerations. *Clinical Social Work Journal, 9*(1): 3–33.

Parkes, C. M. (1964). Effects of bereavement on physical and mental health—a study of the medical records of widows. *British Medical Journal, 2*(5404): 274–279.

Parkes, C. M. (1970). "Seeking" and "finding" a lost object: Evidence from recent studies of the reaction to bereavement. *Social Science and Medicine, 4*(2): 187–201.

Parkes, C. M. (1972). *Bereavement: Studies of Grief in Adult Life*. London: Tavistock.

Parkes, C. M. (1975). Unexpected and untimely bereavement: A statistical study of young Boston widows. In: B. Schoenberg, I. Gerber, A. Wiener, A. H. Kutscher, D. Peretz, & A. C. Carr (Eds.), *Bereavement: Its Psychosocial Aspects*. New York: Columbia University Press.

Pfeffer, C. R. (1981). Parental suicide: An organizing event in the development of latency age children. *Suicide and Life-Threatening Behavior, 11*(1): 43–50.

Pfeffer, C. R., Karus, D., Siegel, K., & Jiang, H. (2000). Child survivors of parental death from cancer or suicide: Depressive and behavioral outcomes. *Psycho-Oncology, 9*(1): 1–10.

Pfeffer, C. R., Martins, P., Mann, J., Sunkenberg, M., Ice, A., Damore, J. P. Jr., Gallo, C., Karpenos, I., & Jiang, H. (1997). Child survivors of suicide: Psychosocial characteristics. *Journal of the American Academy of Child & Adolescent Psychiatry, 36*(1), 65–74.

Piaget, J. (1937). *The Construction of Reality in the Child*. New York: Basic Books.

Piaget, J. (1960). *The Child's Conception of the World*. Paterson, NJ: Littlefield, Adams.

Pitts, F. N., Meyer, J., Brooks, M., & Winokur, G. (1965). Adult psychiatric illness assessed for childhood parental loss, and psychiatric illness in family members—a study of 748 patients and 250 controls. *American Journal of Psychiatry, 121*(12): i-x. doi: 10.1176/ajp.121.12.i.

Plank, E. N., & Plank, R. (1978) Children and death: As seen through art and autobiographies. *Psychoanalytic Study of the Child, 33*: 593–620.

Pollock, G. H. (1961). Mourning and adaptation. *International Journal of Psychoanalysis, 42*: 341–361.

Pollock, G. H. (1989). *The Mourning-Liberation Process.* Madison, CT: International Universities Press.

Prugh, D. G., Staub, E. M., Sands, H. H., Kirschbaum, R. M., & Lenihan, E. A. (1953). A study of the emotional reactions of children and families to hospitalization and illness. *American Journal of Orthopsychiatry, 23*(1): 70–106.

Pynoos, R. S., Gilman, K., & Shapiro, T. (1981). Children's response to parent suicide behavior. Unpublished.

Rafael, B. (1976). Preventive intervention with the crisis of conjugal bereavement. Unpublished thesis submitted for degree of MD, University of Sydney.

Rafael, B. (1977). Preventive intervention with the recently bereaved. *Archives of General Psychiatry, 34*(12): 1450–1454.

Rees, W. D., & Lutkins, S. G. (1967). Mortality of bereavement. *British Medical Journal, 4*(5570): 13–16.

Reich, A. (1951). On countertransference. *International Journal of Psychoanalysis, 32*(1): 25–31.

Rheingold, H. L. (1969). The effect of a strange environment on the behaviour of infants. In: B. M. Foss (Ed.), *Determinants of Infant Behaviour, Vol. 4.* London: Methuen.

Rinsley, D. B. (1976). An object relations view of borderline personality. Presented at the International Meeting on Borderline Disorders, The Menninger Foundation and the National Institue of Mental Health, Topeka, KS, March 19–21.

Robertson, J. (1953). A guide to the film, *A Two Year Old Goes to the Hospital.* London: Tavistock Child Research Unit.

Robertson, J., & Bowlby, J. (1952). Responses of young children to separation from their mother. II. Observations of the sequence of response of children aged 17 to 24 months during the course of separation. *Courr. Cent. Int. l'Enfance, 2*: 131–142.

Robertson, J., & Robertson, J. (1971). Young children in brief separation: A fresh look. *Psychoanalytic Study of the Child, 26*(1): 264–315.

Rochlin, G. (1967). How younger children view death and themselves. In: E. A. Grollman (Ed.), *Explaining Death to Children* (pp. 51–85). Boston, MA: Beacon.

Rosenthal, P. A. (1980). Short-term family therapy and pathological grief resolution with children and adolescents. *Family Process, 19*(2): 151–159.

Roy, C., & McLeod, D. (1981). *Theory Construction in Nursing: An Adaptation Model.* Englewood Cliffs, NJ: Prentice Hall.

Ruben, M. (1947). Home training of instincts and emotions. *Health Education Journal, 5*(3): 119–124.

Rutter, M. (1966). *Children of Sick Parents: An Environmental and Psychiatric Study.* New York: Oxford University Press.

Rutter, M. (1993). Resilience: Some conceptual considerations. *Journal of Adolescent Health, 14*(8): 626–631.

Schaffer, H. R., & Callender, W. M. (1959). Psychological effects of hospitalization in infancy. *Pediatrics, 24*: 528–539.

Schore, A. N. (1994). *Affect Regulation and the Origin of the Self: The Neurobiology of Emotional Development.* Hillsdale, N J: Lawrence Erlbaum.

Shap, K. V. (2020, July 24). Why did she leave me there? Modern Love, *New York Times.*

Shuchter, S. R. (1986). *Dimensions of Grief: Adjusting to the Death of a Spouse.* The Jossey-Bass social and behavioral science series. San Francisco, CA: Jossey-Bass.

Silverman, P. R., Nickman, S. L., & Worden, J. W. (1992). Detachment revisited: the child's reconstruction of a dead parent. *American Journal of Orthopsychiatry, 62*(4): 494–503.

Silverman, P. R., & Worden, J. W. (1992). Children's reactions in the early months after the death of a parent. *American Journal of Orthopsychiatry, 62*(1): 93–104.

Spitz, R. A. (1945). Hospitalism: An inquiry into the genesis of psychiatric conditions in early childhood. *Psychoanalytic Study of the Child, 2*: 113–117.

Spitz, R. A. (1965). *The First Year of Life.* New York: International Universities Press.

Spitz, R. A., & Wolf, K. M. (1946). Anaclitic depression: An inquiry into the genesis of psychiatric conditions in early childhood. *Psychoanalytic Study of the Child, 2*(1): 313–342.

Susillo, M. V. (2005). Beyond the grave—adolescent parental loss: Letting go and holding on. *Psychoanalytic Dialogues, 15*(4): 499–527.

Tedeschi, R. G., & Calhoun, L. G. (1995). *Trauma & Transformation: Growing in the Aftermath of Suffering.* Thousand Oaks, CA: Sage.

Terr, L. (1988). What happens to early memories of trauma? A study of twenty children under age five at the time of documented traumatic events. *Journal of the American Academy of Child and Adolescent Psychiatry, 27*(1): 96–104.

Tyrka, A. R., Wier, L., Price, L. H., Ross, N. S., & Carpenter, L. L. (2008). Childhood parental loss and adult psychopathology: Effects of loss characteristics and contextual factors. *International Journal of Psychiatry in Medicine, 38*(3): 328–344.

Van der Kolk, B. (2014). *The Body Keeps the Score: Brain, Mind, and Body in the Healing of Trauma.* New York: Penguin.

Vaughan, G. F. (1957). Children in hospital. *Lancet, 269*(6979): 1117–1120.

Wilcox, H. C., Kuramoto, S. J., Lichtenstein, P., Langstrom, N., Brent, D. A., & Runeson, B. (2010). Psychiatric morbidity, violent crime, and suicide among children and adolescents exposed to parental death. *Journal of the American Academy of Child and Adolescent Psychiatry, 49*(5): 514–523.

Wolfenstein, M. (1966). How is mourning possible? *Psychoanalytic Study of the Child, 21*(1): 93–123.

Wood, L., Byram, V., Gosling, S., & Stokes, J. (2012). Continuing bonds after suicide bereavement in childhood. *Death Studies, 36*(10): 873–898.

Worden, J. W. (1996). *Children and Grief: When a Parent Dies.* New York: Guilford.

Worden, J. W., & Silverman, P. R. (1996). Parental death and the adjustment of school-age children. *OMEGA: Journal of Death and Dying, 33*(2): 91–102.

Yudkin, S. (1967). Children and death. *Lancet, 289*(7480): 37–41.

Zetzel, E. R. (1965). The theory of therapy in relation to a developmental model of the psychicapparatus. *International Journal of Psychoanalysis, 46*: 39–52.

Zisook, S., & Shuchter, S. R. (1986). The first four years of widowhood. *Psychiatric Annals, 16*(5): 288–329.

Index

211